When the Yellow River Floods

When the Yellow River Floods

Water, Technology, and Nation-Building in Early Twentieth-Century Chinese Literature

Hui-Lin Hsu

Hong Kong University Press
The University of Hong Kong
Pok Fu Lam Road
Hong Kong
https://hkupress.hku.hk

© 2024 Hong Kong University Press

ISBN 978-988-8842-77-3 (*Hardback*)

All rights reserved. No portion of this publication may be reproduced or transmitted in any form or by any means, electronic or mechanical, including photocopying, recording, or any information storage or retrieval system, without prior permission in writing from the publisher.

British Library Cataloguing-in-Publication Data
A catalogue record for this book is available from the British Library.

Cover image: Arthur W. Hummel Sr. 1875. "Tongwaxiang zhi haikou xin Huanghe hedao di gong xingshi tu" 銅瓦廂至海口新黃河河道隄工形勢圖 [Map of the embankment project of the new lower reaches of the Yellow River] [between 1875 and 1876]. Colored map, 53 × 53 cm. The Map Collection of Library of Congress Geography and Map Division, the United States.

Digitally printed

Contents

List of Figures	vi
Acknowledgments	vii
A Note on the Text	x
Introduction	1
1. Hydraulics and Medicine: Remedying Body and Nation	26
2. Governance, Hydraulics, and the Vice of the Incorruptible	47
3. From Sediment to Sentiment: Transforming Flood Trauma into National Identity	68
4. Water, Landscape, and the Appearance of a New National Literature	89
5. Toward China's Rejuvenation: The Taigu School and Yellow River Regulation	112
Conclusion	140
Works Cited	145
Index	159

Figures

Figure 0.1: The 1855 course change of the Yellow River   3
Figure 0.2: The deployment of the oblique dikes   13

Acknowledgments

The completion of this book was made possible by the nourishing support of various individuals and organizations. I am profoundly indebted to my advisor at Columbia University, Wei Shang, whose wisdom and counsel significantly shaped my research. David Der-wei Wang merits special appreciation. His research on *The Travels of Lao Can* from the 1980s was a continual source of inspiration. His generosity, in particular, has left a lasting imprint on this work.

I would like to extend heartfelt thanks to Wai-yee Li for her unwavering encouragement, a beacon throughout my writing journey. Engaging conversations with Yu-yu Cheng, Siao-chen Hu, Chiung-yun Liu, I-hsien Wu, and Shou-jen Tseng were the wind in my sails, continually propelling my passion and resolve to delve deeper into *The Travels of Lao Can*.

A particular mention must go to my longtime friends and esteemed colleagues, Paize Keulemans and Christopher Rea. Paize's invaluable advice on writing strategy greatly contributed to sculpting the overall structure of this study. Chris's timely and comprehensive editing suggestions markedly improved the manuscript. Their professional expertise and our enduring friendship have been critical to completing this work.

My time at the National Taiwan University (NTU) brought me the opportunity to work with Chia cian Ko and Shaw-yu Pan, whose shared research interests proved instrumental in reinforcing my project intellectually during its formative stages. I am also grateful to Horng-jia Lin, my former colleague at NTU, whose expertise in oracle bone inscriptions deepened my understanding of the significance of Liu E's discovery in this specialized field.

Furthermore, I wish to convey my sincere thanks to my diligent and brilliant former students at NTU. Among them, Chung-wei Yang, Ting Yang, and Yi-an Hsieh consistently provided valuable insights that enhanced my interpretation of *The Travels of Lao Can*. Their keen intellect and dedication greatly propelled this work forward.

When I joined the Chinese University of Hong Kong (CUHK) in 2018, my colleagues generously offered their assistance and advice. Their generous sharing of experience and knowledge enriched my academic endeavors greatly. I want to thank Hsien-min Chu and Ruei-chen Yeh, my former students at NTU, whose warm words breathed new life into my efforts when I faced challenges adapting to new teaching methods and navigating research at CUHK. As long-standing friends, Hsueh-yi Lin and Mark Meulenbeld extended invaluable companionship that considerably eased my transition to life in Hong Kong. Their camaraderie and consistent backing were vital during the composition of this book.

During the challenging times of the pandemic, the informative online discussions with Dennis Cheng on Han dynasty classical studies and *Book of Changes* guided my work, particularly in the fifth chapter. From the environmental history perspective, Yu-cheng Shih offered me profound and conceptually significant ideas, prompting me to consider possible connections between Chinese literature and ecological history. Xiangjun Feng's research on *The Travels of Lao Can*'s reception during the Republican era and his generous sharing of resources aided in developing the arguments in my final chapter.

In the final stages of the project, assistance from Leanne Yan Lai, Wan-chun Chiu, Chi Hu, and Xinmeng Guo was indispensable. Leanne's meticulous handling of the bibliography and citations, Wan-chun's dedicated efforts in creating the map of the Yellow River's course shift, Chi Hu's facilitation of necessary image permissions, and Xinmeng's careful proofreading were vital for completing the book.

Numerous organizations also fostered my work. The National Science Council of Taiwan provided funding for research that helped define the book's initial structure. In 2017, the Harvard Yenching Institute (HYI) and Fulbright Foundation generously granted me financial support to access outstanding research resources and interact with Asia's foremost academics. In particular, HYI's contribution is fundamental, enabling my research on *The Travels of Lao Can* to transition from a collection of disparate articles into a unified ecocritical study. Additionally, I am thankful to the Harvard-Yenching Institute for providing a publication grant to Hong Kong University Press in support of the production of this book. The insights from Karen Thornber of Harvard University, who served as the discussant for my talk in the visiting scholars' series at HYI, enriched the development of this book profoundly.

I am also deeply grateful to the Tang Prize Foundation for granting me the Humanities Research Fellowship, instituted by the late Professor Ying-shih Yu. This fellowship considerably enhanced my progress and productivity during the pivotal stages of writing this manuscript. The Research Grants Council of Hong Kong kindly provided funding that enabled a thorough investigation of the novel's political discourse, an essential aspect of my work. This timely aid proved decisive for the completion of this research project.

Various publishers deserve my gratitude for permitting the inclusion of revised and expanded sections of my previously published works in this book. In addition, I am indebted to the *Journal of Chinese Literature* at National Cheng Kung University, the *Bulletin* of the Department of Chinese Literature, National Chengchi University, the *Journal of Chinese Studies*, and the *Tsing Hua Journal of Chinese Studies*. Their generosity enabled me to revisit and refine these pieces for a new audience.

My deep appreciation is also extended to my editor, Matthew Tibble, whose professional editing and thoughtful feedback helped shape this manuscript. During the early phases of manuscript preparation, Allan Bariman also provided concrete and nuanced writing guidance. Furthermore, I am deeply appreciative of the professional assistance provided by the team at Hong Kong University Press. Their collective expertise and dedication were instrumental in bringing this manuscript to fruition.

Lastly, I owe the deepest gratitude to my wife, Wei-chia Li, for her steadfast support throughout the writing process. Her faith in my work was a constant source of strength, making her a central pillar in this endeavor.

A Note on the Text

The Travels of Lao Can comprises multiple parts, including: the text proper (*chubian* 初編), presented in twenty chapters, first serialized in 1903 and reserialized between 1905 and 1906; plus an unfinished nine-chapter sequel (Liu 1907), also referred to as the second volume (*erbian* 二編), which is how I reference it in this book; and fifteen remnant pages of a fragment (*canbian* 殘編), written in 1906 or 1907. In this study, I reference the following translations with adaptation: Harold Shadick's translation of the twenty-chapter text proper (Liu 1990); Lim Gi-tong's 林語堂 (aka Lin Yutang) translation of the first six chapters of the second volume in Lin Yutang, *A Nun of Taishan (A Novelette) and Other Translations* (Liu 1936); and Timothy Wong's translation of chapters 7–9 of the second volume in *Renditions*, No. 32 in 1989 (Liu 1989). For the text and the closing commentaries (the commentaries at the end of each chapter) in Chinese, I use the annotated edition published by Liren Shuju 里仁書局 in 2013 (Liu 2013). For ease of reference, I refer to chapters 1–9 in the second volume as chapters 21–29. For a textual history of the novel, see Wong 1983 and Lupke 2007, 108–9. For an outline of the plot of the full novel, see Lupke 2007, 109–13.

Introduction

> We of this age have our feelings stirred about our life experience, about family and nation, about society, about the Chinese race and Confucian teaching. The deeper the emotions, the more bitter the weeping. This is why the Scholar of a Hundred Temperings from Hongdu has made this book.
>
> —Liu E, *The Travels of Lao Can*, preface (1905)

The Travels of Lao Can (*Lao Can youji* 老殘遊記, hereafter *The Travels*) is a novel about building a nation. Written by arguably the most talented but also most notorious late Qing (1644–1911) polymath, Liu E 劉鶚 (style name Tieyun 鐵雲, 1857–1909), this combination of travelogue, murder mystery, and political commentary follows a peripatetic physician protagonist as he travels through China's Shandong Province while treating patients, offering advice on local governance and flood control, and investigating an apparent murder. First serialized in 1903 (with a sequel begun a few years later), the novel is set in the contemporary present, referencing the recently concluded Boxer Rebellion (1899–1901) and the rise of the revolution that led to the collapse of the Qing empire in 1911 and the founding of the Republic of China the following year—less than a decade after it was serialized. To scholars, the novel offers a complex and nuanced perspective on the status of the Chinese nation at this critical historical juncture on the eve of its transition from a weakened dynastic imperium to a nascent republic. Yet to "the Scholar of Hundred Temperings from Hongdu" (Hongdu bailian sheng 鴻都百鍊生), Liu E's pen name, the work was more than a perspective. As his much-cited 1905 preface to the novel in the *Tianjin Daily News*, quoted above, makes clear, it was the emotional embodiment of his generation's greatest concern: the formation of a modern nation-state.

At the time of the novel's writing, Qing China had been undergoing a forced journey of transformation for over half a century—a journey triggered by Western aggression. And intellectuals from different camps held different views on its ideal direction. An ongoing debate raged on the relationship between individual and nation, which was the central issue for nation-building—how to create a sense of shared citizenship, common beliefs, and commitment to an imagined national entity.[1] Liu E's novel was a literary manifestation of these efforts. It was an expression that, although an imperial subject, a Chinese person is also an individual in a community, a citizen of the Chinese nation, and a member of the Chinese ethnicity.

For a work ostensibly concerned with national salvation, ethnic awareness, and nation-building, and whose title claims relation to a travelogue, the protagonist, Lao Can, barely ventures beyond the single province of Shandong. So how can this short journey within a single province represent an entire nation? Why did the author choose Shandong, rather than any other Chinese locality, as the central stage for putting on this show about the national crisis and nation-building? Are there any elements within *The Travels* set in Shandong that might offer insights into the novel's conceptualization of nation-building?

This book argues that *The Travels* by Liu E is a key work of modern Chinese literary history that intertwines environmental change, hydraulic engineering, nation-building, and literary creation. Set in Shandong, a region historically affected by the Yellow River floods, the novel sheds light on the role of water management in the process of nation-building. By examining these themes and their intersections, this study reveals the pivotal role of environmental degradation in shaping the formation of national literature in early twentieth-century China, going beyond conventional narratives that focus solely on political and cultural factors.

Issues of national identity and nation-building have been raised in a host of studies on early twentieth-century Chinese literature. Past scholarship has approached the question from various perspectives: the sense of national humiliation (Tsu 2005), the discourse of love (Lee 2007), popular sympathy (Lean 2007), historical violence (Braester 2003; Wang 2004; Berry 2008), and practices of translation (Liu 1995), among others. Those studies consider human beings the most important, if not the only, agent in the nation-building process. In contrast, recent developments in environmental history offer new insights into the part the environment played in literary nation-building. For instance, historians have identified the role of famine and relief in shaping national consciousness (Rankin 1986; Edgerton-Tarpley 2008). Moreover, as David Pietz and Mark Giordano (2009, 118–19) indicate, twentieth-century Chinese state-building efforts were concerned primarily with "how to effectively manage water to serve the goals of nation-building

---

1. As Duara (1988) points out, China's nation-building of the present day builds upon the ideas developed during the late Qing, a time that witnessed the elites' drive to build a Chinese nation with efforts in any form. The Qing court, in fact, participated in preparing the way for this effort of nation-building. The Qing court's interpretation of the concept of China (Zhongguo 中國) as a composite of multiethnic people in the late nineteenth century "provided twentieth-century Chinese nationalists with one of the major components of modern Chinese national identity: the multiethnic state" (Zhao 2006, 3–4).

Introduction

and modernization" and "the quest to establish a vigorous modern national identity among the peoples of the empire." The present book explores this connection to water in the literary nation-building of *The Travels*.

China had already struggled for thousands of years with Yellow River floodings when a course shift in 1855 brought this curse to the northern province of Shandong—a threat that would potentially lead to the collapse of the Qing empire. From the age of thirty-three to thirty-seven, Liu spent the best five years of his fifty-three-year-long life as a successful hydraulic engineer in Shandong, working to survey and regulate the unruly river. Undeniably, as this book will show, Liu's 1903 novel is deeply rooted in Yellow River floods and flood control in Shandong, the sociocultural-historical context in which Liu E's literary nation-building literally takes place, and the floods of the mid-nineteenth century present us with the nonhuman agent that animates Liu E's turn-of-the-century novel.

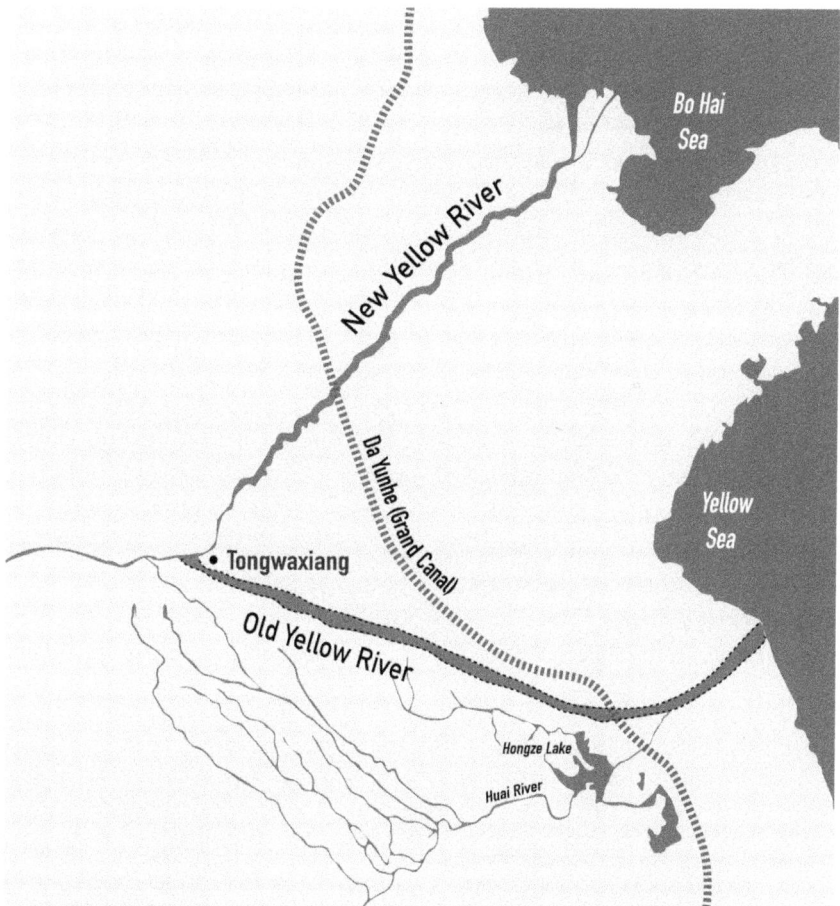

Figure 0.1: The 1855 course change of the Yellow River

The connection between flood control and nation-state formation in the late Qing, compared with that in the Republican period, has received little attention. The relatively small investment the Chinese state made in flood control before the twentieth century partially explains this lack of scholarly attention. Compared with China's national hydraulic projects in the twentieth century, the Ming (1368–1644) and Qing dynasties saw far less direct state intervention in flood control.[2] When the Yellow River changed course in 1855 after major flooding, the Qing government, for instance, chose to adopt a passive attitude toward its management. It delegated flood control responsibilities in the north to provincial authorities (Pomeranz 1993). This lack of direct state intervention partly explains why few scholars have noted the impact of Yellow River management on late Qing nation-building.

However, as Kathryn Edgerton-Tarpley (2008) demonstrates, national identity need not only be formed through direct state intervention in natural disasters; it can also be formed by the relief efforts sponsored by the local gentry. As they did in other disasters, the local gentry played an active role in flood control and disaster relief in the Yellow River floods of 1855 (Jia 2019). The local gentry could serve as a critical point of departure for understanding the relationship between Yellow River flood management and nation-building initiated by private citizens rather than the state. Liu E, who came from a gentry family, is a typical representative of this non-state effort to respond to disaster and form a national identity. By obtaining a series of low-ranking offices through donations, Liu entered the flood control bureaucracy and oversaw fundraising for disaster relief. As such, *The Travels*, set in flood-ravaged late nineteenth-century Shandong and embodying Liu's nation-building insights, provides a perfect literary perspective to probe the connection between Yellow River management and nation-building during the late Qing dynasty.

Past scholarship has tended to classify *The Travels* as the offspring of late Qing intellectual thought—Chinese or Western. Scholars have noticed the novel's autobiographical nature and deep political concern (Hsia 2004; Wong 1989). They have also explored how these features relate to the Taigu school (Taigu xuepai 太谷學派), a folk syncretic religious society that combined Confucianism, Buddhism, and religious Daoism and encouraged the pursuit of political ideals, of which Liu E was a lifelong adherent (Tarumoto 1983, 187–90; Wang X. 1990; Wang X. 1993a, 2000; Kwong 2001). These scholars see the Taigu school of thought as the driving

---

2. The Ming and Qing state governments, as pointed out by Pierre-Etienne Will (1985), acted mostly as an arbitrator in hydraulic management. The central authorities were inclined to limit the scope of direct intervention and the function of the bureaucratic apparatus. Instead, they endeavored to strike a basic balance among different conflicting regions and parties and encourage local communities to take care of their own welfare and safety. As a result, state presence in daily maintenance kept subsiding except for major catastrophes, and a sort of automatic local hydraulic management community started to play an increasingly dominant role. Thus, Will believes that the private sponsorship is more powerful than state intervention.

force of the novel's nation-building narrative. Similar views also frequently appear in recent studies on Liu's novel and late Qing nation-building.[3] Scholars have noted the relationship between the national sentiment promoted by Liu and the Confucian structure of feeling (Lee 2010) and the influence of Western sociological theories on the novel's imagination of the citizen-nation relationship (Guan 2014). These scholars generally consider nation-building in *The Travels* as based on abstract and immaterial philosophical concepts. Furthermore, although these varied analytical lenses have considerably expanded our understanding of the nation-building in Liu E's novel, they lack a unifying conceptual framework for comprehending the many themes that run throughout *The Travels*.

This book takes a different approach, one rooted firmly in environmental and fundamentally material concerns, to propose such a framework. Focusing on the case of *The Travels*, it examines the role of water in literary nation-building in early twentieth-century China. It looks at how floods and Liu E's embankment design provided him with the conceptual resources to imagine a new relationship between the individual and the state, propose a unique governance model, and mobilize national sentiment through concrete political and literary practice. As such, this study explores how Liu's real-world, hands-on experience as a hydraulic engineer contributed to the novel's breakthrough in literary form and how the novel, celebrated as exemplary in its new form of landscape writing, contributed to a new national consciousness in the early Republican period based in the water and earth of China's environment itself. Finally, in terms of the novel's narrative structure, the book elucidates the relationships between Liu's plans for hydraulic engineering and his discourse on the history and the future of China at the novel's plot center.

Such a broad-roaming scope naturally entails a thematic division of chapters. This book's five chapters examine the relationship between medical and political discourses, between discourses of water regulation and governance, between emotion and national sentiment, between river engineering and landscape description, and between the syncretic religious teachings of the Taigu school and the tenets of flood control. And while such a collection initially appears idiosyncratic, it reflects the complex and multifaceted approach of Liu E himself and is unified by the one concept at the heart of his identity: hydraulics. Accordingly, this book argues that *The Travels* presents us with a literary response to the political *and* environmental crises of late Qing China. Its narrative drive stems not only from Liu E's human-centered psychological anxiety for national salvation and his abstract philosophical beliefs but also from the urgent need to find a resolution to China's environmental crisis, the Yellow River floods. Flood disasters and river engineering are the overarching pivots that connect the novel's narrative and thematic elements and the discussions in this assessment of it. This novel allows us to discern a new way

---

3. For reading *The Travels* as a national allegory, refer to Holoch 1980; Huters 2005; Rojas 2015.

of conceptualizing nation-building: one that was, in every sense, shaped by the hydraulic technology Liu E had spent more than a decade developing to counter the deadly environmental collapse of the mid-nineteenth century.

Liu E: Successful Engineer, Failed Entrepreneur

The half century between Liu E's birth and his writing of *The Travels* in 1903 witnessed frequent flooding of the Yellow River, one of the most disastrous environmental degradations in Chinese history. This period also experienced the political turmoil of the late Qing dynasty and the ambitious beginning and frustrating end of the Self-Strengthening Movement (Ziqiang yundong 自強運動, 1861–1895), also known as the Western Affairs Movement (Yangwu yundong 洋務運動). This was a series of institutional reforms undertaken by the Westernizing faction (Yangwu pai 洋務派) to promote industrialization in response to China's military defeat in the Opium Wars (first 1839–1842, second 1856–1860). As such, flood control and Western affairs together formed the pivotal sociopolitical context for Liu E's literary nation-building.

Yellow River flooding has occurred regularly throughout Chinese history.[4] Floods were deeply associated with the ruler's ability to command resources, the mandate to rule, and thus the state's destiny. This is evident in the myth of Da Yu 大禹 (Yu the Great; traditional dates of reign 2205–2197 BCE), China's first river "engineer." According to legend, Da Yu guided the constantly flooding Yellow River into the sea by dredging and redirecting its course. This great accomplishment won him the right to the throne. He went on to found Xia (2205–1766 BCE), the first traditional Chinese dynasty in recorded history, laying the foundation for China as an agricultural civilization. Da Yu's rise to power also passed on an important message to subsequent Chinese rulers—their legitimacy to rule largely lay in their ability to tame the daunting Yellow River.

The intertwining of government and environment was especially pertinent for the Qing, the last imperial dynasty. Environmental degradation, such as the lack of soil conservation and deforestation caused by explosive population growth since the mid-Qing period, contributed to an increase in the magnitude and frequency of Yellow River floodings. The year 1855 finally ushered in a disaster with long-term implications. After a dike breach at Tongwaxiang 銅瓦廂 in Henan Province in the summer, the Yellow River changed course: it no longer followed the original southeastern river channel through Jiangsu to the Yellow Sea but moved north and flowed to the Bo Hai Sea through Shandong Province. This was the most serious breach and largest avulsion of the Yellow River since 1128. The course change of

---

4. On the problem of controlling the Yellow River in Chinese history, see Needham, Wang, and Lu 1971, 229–41; Elvin 1993, 2004; Elvin and Liu 1998; Dodgen 2001; Pietz 2015; Mostern 2021.

the Yellow River relieved Anhui and Jiangsu of centuries of afflictions but dragged Henan, Zhili, and Shandong into a new nightmare. Since the Yellow River's new course primarily shifted to Shandong, the unfortunate province became the region most ravaged by the river's floodings.[5] Between 1855 and 1884, when dike construction along the new river course was finally completed, the Yellow River flooded almost annually. Although the situation improved after 1884, dike failures of various magnitudes continued occasionally. More than a looming threat to the local people's lives and properties, the floods also dealt constant blows to the Qing Empire's national economy and social order. The floods made transport on the Grand Canal difficult and disrupted grain shipping to Beijing from the south. They led to crop failures, forcing the central government to grant tax relief to the affected regions, which further aggravated the state's already stringent finances. In turn, the food shortages and deteriorated environment led to a rise in poverty, sparking waves of peasant revolts in affected localities. Scholars generally consider such flood-related privations to be the main cause of the famous Boxer Uprising of 1900 and 1901, which, uncoincidentally, started in Shandong Province before spreading throughout the empire (Esherick 1988). The social, economic, and political domino effect of the Yellow River floods further degraded the Qing Empire's power, which was already struggling with internal strife and foreign military threat.

Liu E was a witness to late nineteenth-century Yellow River management, as well as an insightful and active participant.[6] He was born to an elite family in Luhe in 1857, and his ancestral hometown was Zhenjiang, Jiangsu Province. Liu E moved in adulthood to Huai'an, another Jiangsu city and, moreover, the center stage of Yellow

---

5. After the course change, the most affected province of Shandong insisted that the change be reversed, but the southern provinces, freshly rescued from the accursed flooding, opposed the proposal. The central government took the side of the southern provinces for reasons of strategic defense. Had the river been reversed to its old course and the new course been allowed to dry up, the emerging Nian rebels 捻軍 would have been granted a quick way to swarm into southwestern Shandong, endangering the safety of the capital, Beijing. Thus, the new river course, as a key natural moat, received the central government's connivance. In 1887, a dike breach on the river's south bank at Zhengzhou led to a course shift once again. Through the breach, the river flowed southward to its old course, reasserting its disruptive presence in the southern provinces after a three-decade lapse. The northern provinces—Henan, Zhili, and Shandong—were thus rescued from its afflictions. A new round of blame shifting ensued. The Qing government still favored the Shandong course to support increasing industrial activities in the southern provinces during the Western Affairs Movement. The movement ushered in modern maritime transport, which marginalized the canal transport that depended heavily on Yellow River flood control. Consequently, Yellow River management was no longer high on the imperial government's agenda (Jia 2019). After the river turned northward, its original channel ran dry and left behind what seemed like stretches of plains. One of the long-term impacts of the river course shift was that bandits, without having to deal with the natural barrier made by the Yellow River, became rampant throughout Shandong Province, and numerous locals took to banditry after the floods ravaged their homes and property.
6. The biographical details of Liu E presented in this section and elsewhere, unless otherwise specified, are derived from Lupke 2007 and Miao 2017.

River management in pre-1855 Qing China.⁷ Liu E's interest in river control stemmed from his family history. Liu E's father, Liu Chengzhong 劉成忠 (1818–1883), was typical of the traditional Chinese literati elite. Liu Chengzhong held a *jinshi* 進士 degree, the highest in the imperial examination, was well versed in the Chinese classics, particularly *Book of Changes*, and had shown great interest in Western knowledge. Liu Chengzhong had spent years managing the Yellow River in Henan and Shandong Provinces. He contributed noticeably to river engineering and published several monographs on the topic. Liu E's multifaceted education, enriched by his father's legacy in river engineering and a blend of Eastern and Western knowledge, uniquely positioned him to contribute to Yellow River management.

Liu E's most fateful engagement with flood control occurred in the summer of 1887, when a dike breach on the Yellow River at Zhengzhou in Henan Province led to devastating flooding, killing at least 930,000 people (Wang 1995, 41). It was the single deadliest flood in Chinese history and one of the deadliest environmental disasters in human history (*Encyclopaedia Britannica* 2021). This crisis offered Liu E an opportunity to test the ideas he had developed from his father's engagement with flood control and his own research. In 1888, with the nominal official title of expectant subprefect (*houxuan tongzhi* 候選同知), which he had purchased, Liu E traveled to Henan to offer his consulting service to Wu Dacheng 吳大澂 (1835–1902), director general of the Yellow River Conservancy. With his demonstrated ability in river regulation, Wu commissioned Liu E to lead the surveying and mapping of the Yellow River in Henan, Zhili, and Shandong Provinces. The result was *A Chart of the Course of the Yellow River through the Provinces of Henan, Zhili, and Shandong* (*Yu Zhi Lu san sheng Huanghe tu* 豫直魯三省黃河圖, hereafter *Chart of the Course of the Yellow River*). In 1890, Zhang Yao 張曜 (1832–1891), governor of Shandong, brought Liu E to the province to help manage flood control. After Zhang Yao's death while in his post in 1891, Liu E continued his service under Zhang's successor, Furun 福潤, until 1893. Between 1888 and 1893, Liu E proved himself a capable river engineer in Henan and Shandong Provinces. Ten years later, these experiences would inspire the chapters on Yellow River flood control and disaster relief in *The Travels*.

Although Liu E had achieved dazzling success in his work on river control, he had no intention of stopping there. As Harold Shadick (Liu 1990) has noted, Liu had two commitments—Yellow River management and political reform. Liu's demonstrated knowledge and contribution to flood control served as the best letter of

---

7. Before the 1855 course change, Huai'an occupied a key position in Yellow River management. Floods had been a headache since ancient times. In the early fifteenth century, the construction of the north-south Grand Canal for grain transport further complicated the Yellow River hydraulic engineering, as the Grand Canal intersected with the Yellow River. This raised two requirements for Yellow River management—preventing flooding and ensuring the canal transport. Qingkou 清口, the crossing where the Yellow River met the Grand Canal, became the focus of Yellow River hydraulic engineering (Dodgen 2001; Elvin 2004).

recommendation, earning him a chance to participate in national industrial development. In 1895, Shandong governor Furun recommended Liu E to the Foreign Office (Zongli yamen 總理衙門) and helped him earn the title of expectant prefect (*houxuan zhifu* 候選知府). Although the prefect title was nominal only and brought Liu E no power, he apparently capitalized on the opportunity to build connections and develop his influence in coal mining and railroad construction—industries he saw as the key to building national wealth. In 1896, Liu E proposed a plan to build a railway from Beijing to Hankou, Hubei Province, and later he proposed another railway construction project, this time from Tianjin to Zhenjiang. Neither proposal came to fruition because of the lack of support from higher-power echelons and the conflict of interest.[8] However, Liu kept trying to get involved in railway construction. In 1897, while still an official of the Foreign Office, he started to work for the foreign enterprise Peking Syndicate Limited (Fu gongsi 福公司) as a comprador, seeking rights to coal mining and railway construction for the company. The contract, drafted to be signed by the Peking Syndicate Limited and the Qing government, stipulated that the coal mines and railways would be returned to China after sixty years. That was how Liu strove to build the modern coal mines and railways that China needed but lacked the capital or expertise to develop. However, Liu's activity enraged a pack of powerful conservative officials headed by Gang Yi 剛毅 and Yu Xian 毓賢, who accused Liu of selling out his nation and later got him stripped of the nominal title of expectant prefect. (In *The Travels*, the characters Yu Xian 玉賢 and Gang Bi 剛弼, the so-called incorruptible officials [*qingguan* 清官], are based on these two officials.) Thwarted, the Peking Syndicate Limited had to shelve its coal mining and railway construction plans. Liu E's enthusiasm for coal mining and railway construction, however, was undiminished, and he continued to work behind the scenes. In 1902, he helped the Peking Syndicate Limited carry out successful investments in coal mining and railway construction in Henan. Despite

---

8. In 1895, Liu E tried unsuccessfully to bribe high-ranking officials to qualify for participation in the railroad construction project (Liu and Liu 2019, 285). In 1896, Zhang Zhidong 張之洞 (1837–1909), the viceroy of Huguang, oversaw the construction of the Lu-Han Railway (from Beijing to Hankou, Hubei). According to the emperor's instructions, the railroad was to be constructed by means of domestic investment. Liu E met with Zhang Zhidong for this purpose and expressed his wish to undertake the railroad construction. However, before Zhang Zhidong invited domestic investment, he had already decided to entrust the railroad construction to Sheng Xuanhuai 盛宣懷 (1844–1916), a late Qing tycoon and politician who played a major role in China's industrialization (Liu and Liu 2019, 295–96). In 1897, Liu E requested the authorities to build a railroad starting in Tianjin and ending in Zhenjiang, his ancestral hometown. However, trains could not cross the Yangtze River and could only reach Guazhou, a town across the river from Zhenjiang. Beijing officials from Zhenjiang were highly dissatisfied with this, fearing that Guazhou would replace the importance of Zhenjiang, which had been prosperous, by becoming the railroad's terminus. As a result, they rose against Liu E's proposal and stated that they would not recognize Liu E as a Zhenjiang native (Liu and Liu 2019, 316).

these later accomplishments, we can hardly regard Liu's reformist activities during 1896–1902 as successful.

Liu E's industrial plans may have failed, but the comprador post at the Peking Syndicate Limited helped him acquire significant power. The company provided substantial funding for public relations, which included bribes to officials and other illicit activities, to secure contracts and avoid legal repercussions. These practices, combined with lucrative commissions, brought him great wealth. As a comprador, he retrieved his lost title of expectant prefect with the help of the British ambassador, and with his newly accumulated wealth, he even bought a promotion from prefect to circuit intendant (*daoyuan* 道員). Liu also indulged in antique and art collections, often splurging on stone rubbings or pottery inscriptions. For Liu, selling and gifting art was an effective way of networking. His wealth also enabled him to build political connections and fund political lobbies and propaganda in the news world. One of his investments was the *Tianjin Daily News*, founded in 1898, where Liu serialized *The Travels*. Using his well-funded political and business connections, Liu built shopping malls and textile mills; he smuggled sea salt and invested in maritime transport, tap water, steel factories, electrical streetcars, and electrical lamps. Despite the money Liu E threw into these projects, none came to fruition. Furthermore, his attempt to bring in foreign investment to fund coal mining in Zhejiang and Sichuan continued to be branded as selling out the country and was blocked by conservative officials, zealously patriotic overseas students in Japan, and members of the local gentry. His only profitable investment was land, whose value skyrocketed after the railways were completed. Yet before Liu had a chance to enjoy the benefits, he was arrested and sentenced for smuggling sea salt (Liu 2018a, 2018b). After starting out as an aspiring patriotic entrepreneur committed to national salvation (who just happened to smuggle sea salt and profit from a very uncomfortable and close relationship between public and private interests), Liu died a much-despised traitor in exile at Dihua (today's Ürümqi), Xinjiang. Ironically, he had by then successfully achieved his aim of promoting China's national identity by arousing negative national sentiment against himself.

The Yellow River floods were the second catastrophe to hit the tottering Qing empire in the second half of the nineteenth century, after domestic and political security threats. For the central government, the biggest problem was how to stretch its limited financial means to fund civil and foreign wars, carry on the fledgling Western Affairs Movement, and tackle the Yellow River floods. The floods brewed ecological and social crises, while disaster relief efforts further strained the already stringent state finances, depleting the government's resources for coping with the overall political crisis. It was this historical reality that spurred the publically minded Liu E. In flood control, he delivered excellent outcomes, but his industrial and business endeavors were total failures, bringing him only disgrace and ruin. Few would doubt his talent, aspirations, and consistent devotion to helping build a modern

Chinese nation-state, but his approaches caused great controversy, and he ended up paying a heavy price.

Taming the River, Building Industry, and Discovering China's Origins

Liu E's career change from river engineer to the Western Affairs Movement reflected the effort of late Qing intellectuals to balance traditional Chinese and Western knowledge frameworks in an era of upheaval and transformation. While upholding Chinese traditions and knowledge systems, these scholars also sought solutions to contemporary Chinese issues based on Western knowledge. As Liu E saw it, neither indigenous nor foreign knowledge alone could build a new Chinese nation-state. The Western Affairs Movement greatly impacted how Liu E, who grew up during the movement's height, viewed traditional Chinese knowledge. The movement's basic logic was to exploit natural resources and adopt modern machinery to pursue maximum productivity, empowering and enriching the nation. Liu applied the logic in his river engineering and incorporated it into his coal mining and railway construction activities. Liu's inclination to engage and exploit natural resources as part of his engagement in modern nation-building also found expression in a seemingly more playful realm of academic engagement—deciphering and publishing oracle bone scripts. Yet to truly understand Liu E's twin engagement with both the Chinese tradition and modern, often Western forms of science, we need to better understand his approach to flood control and hydraulic engineering.

The innovative flood control strategy developed by the Ming statesman and river engineer Pan Jixun 潘季馴 (1521–1595), which was widely adopted during the Qing dynasty, provides a key foundation for understanding Liu E's approach to flood control and hydraulic engineering.[9] By focusing on controlling the river's current and harnessing its silt-carrying capacity, Pan's approach aimed to mitigate flooding and maintain the stability of the riverbed. Pan proposed a dike system designed to narrow the river's main channel, which would speed the river's current, scour the sediment, and thus prevent the riverbed from continuing to rise. This approach came to be known by the phrase "restrict the current to attack the silt" (*shu shui gong sha* 束水攻沙). The flood control approach involved two sets of dikes—the "thread dikes" (*lüti* 縷堤) close to the riverbank and the "distant dikes" (*yaoti* 遙堤) built farther away—to confine the river current and prevent floodwaters from spreading inland. The area between the two sets of dikes, known as *jiahe* 夾河, was levee protected, containing additional "screen dikes" (*geti* 格堤) that divided the

---

9. Pan Jixun is usually credited by hydraulic historians with the invention of the river contraction method, but it might in fact have been in existence since the Han dynasty. Nonetheless, Pan was the first to explicitly propose it and use it widely. See Lin 2006, 95n10.

space into grid pattern to further restrict flood inundation. Through this strategic use of dikes, Pan's flood control system effectively managed floodwater by guiding the water, depositing silt to form natural barriers, and ultimately confining the river to its central channel.[10]

The 1855 course change brought a new challenge to the existing method of managing the Yellow River. As the river now flowed along a completely new bed, local residents and the official government responded by constructing dikes ad hoc. While local residents built numerous small dikes near the riverbank, known as "people's dikes" or "*minnian* 民埝*,*" the government had begun constructing its own system of dikes, called "government dikes" or "*guanti* 官堤" or "*dati* 大堤," farther from the riverbank. However, the unplanned construction of small dikes by local residents became a problem. The people's dikes were not built with unified planning or standards and functioned poorly in conjunction with the government dikes. Instead of confining the river's current to attack the silt, as in Pan Jixun's embankment design, they created problems for flood control. Furthermore, residents planted crops in the levee-protected areas, which turned these flood-prone areas into densely populated residential districts and created obstacles to effective flood control. Any breach of the people's dikes could, as a result, lead to heavy human and financial losses, and when these dikes did fail, the local people tended to intentionally break the government dikes to drain the floodwater trapped in the dike-protected areas, relieving the flood between the dike but flooding all the lands beyond. The frequent debates about whether to retain or demolish these private dikes in late Qing Yellow River management reflect the challenges of managing flood control when dikes are not well planned and located.[11]

In addressing this dilemma, Liu followed Pan's river contraction method but with modifications. Liu felt that although this method was effective at washing away the silt, the narrow riverbed also caused frequent overflow. Meanwhile, few residents living in the areas between were willing to move out. As a solution to these two problems, Liu developed a new embankment system based on the traditional river contraction method. He suggested that the past embankments were designed to keep floods within the channel, while his new embankment system, inspired by the flood control methods attributed to the mythical Da Yu, would deliberately guide overflows into the in-between areas to achieve a better result.

Liu E's plan called for oblique dikes (*xieti* 斜堤), which, unlike earlier perpendicular dikes, would be constructed at an angle. Also, additional overflow dams

---

10. For the historical development of the Yellow River control system in late imperial China, see Dodge 2001 and Pietz 2015.
11. The relationship between government and local people in river management in the Qing dynasty was not always one of confrontation. As Jiayan Zhang (2014) observes, in the Qing dynasty, the local government and peasants in rural Wuhan area in Hubei Province developed a hydraulic community on the basis of mutual benefit.

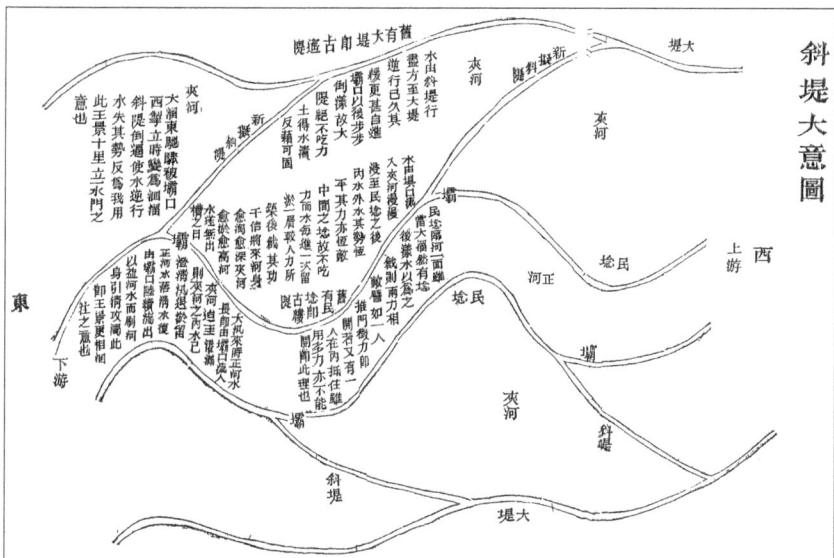

Figure 0.2: The deployment of the oblique dikes. Illustration from Liu E's *Five Essays on River Management* (*Zhihe wu shuo* 治河五說, 1889). Courtesy of Bukkyo University Library, Kyoto, Japan.

would be constructed inside the people's dikes. When the river overflowed the dams in this system, the system would ideally create a mechanism that could strengthen the dikes, scour the riverbed, and benefit agriculture. This mechanism was complicated. First, when water flowed into the *jiahe* area and met the oblique dikes, it either flowed backward to the mainstream of the Yellow River through overflow dams or, with its speed decreased when confronting the angled oblique dikes, moved slowly along the oblique dikes in the *jiahe* area toward official dikes. As the low-speed water flow reached the official dikes, their foundation, saturated with water, was solidified. Furthermore, as water continued to run over the dams into the *jiahe* area and finally became level with the mainstream of the Yellow River, the pressure of the water within the *jiahe* area provided support to the people's dikes and helped them withstand the impact from the other side. Liu called this mechanism a "water buttress" (*shuiqiang* 水戧), arguing that it "defended water with water" (*yi shui di shui* 以水敵水). Meanwhile, the longer the water stayed in the *jiahe* area, the more silt it deposited. Once the flood retreated, the water in the *jiahe* area, now cleared of much silt but with a high capacity to carry silt, flowed through the overflow dams to rejoin the Yellow River, helping to scour the silt from the riverbed. Liu E described this approach as "attack water with water" (*yi shui gong shui* 以水攻水). When the flood flowed into the in-between areas, the silt carried by the water was gradually deposited, becoming rich fertilizer for crops. Thus, Liu's new embankment system, first, turned the devastating flood into a powerful tool to control flooding and, second, made the overflow water an irrigation source and the silt a land-enriching element.[12] To Liu E, sustaining land use and its economic output was just as important in river management as saving lives. This was the main economic concern underlying Liu's river regulation approach.

The new embankment system featuring oblique dikes reflected Liu E's adoption of a Westernizing mentality of precise economic cost-benefit measurement. While the focus was on government-led military-industrial projects in the earlier stages of the Western Affairs Movement, in the 1890s, government interference decreased in the industrial sector to increase profitability. As a result, the exact estimating of profitability based on machine efficiency became the feature of the movement in this period. The way Liu E presented his oblique dike system reflected just that. When estimating crop production, efficiency, and cost after implementing the new system, Liu showed a strong interest in math in estimating production cost and return, which had never been seen in earlier river control documents.[13] This tendency to present detailed numbers for cost and return also featured prominently in his later investment in industrial projects. Since 1895, Liu had invested extensively in coal mining, railway, light industry, and commerce. In his 1902–1905 diaries, Liu more than once exhibited his fascination with highly efficient automated machinery and noted the production rate, cost, and possible return of various machines.[14] As with

---

12. On the question of how to avoid inundating villages and crops in the *jiahe* area, Liu E argued that the act of steering floodwaters into this land comes with a built-in solution: in the first two years, the villages and crops might suffer from flooding for only around two weeks per year. From the third year on, siltation in the *jiahe* area would rise and ward off incoming floodwaters, keeping the households and farms immune from them (Liu 2007, 1:45).

13. Liu defended the feasibility of his design with a meticulous budget proposal: "I hear that yearly maintenance now costs around four hundred thousand with an annual cost of two hundred thousand for building material, and yet deficit persists. If we adopt this design, after three years, labor costs will run less than thirty thousand annually and material procurement only a hundred thousand or so. This amounts to an annual savings of over twenty to thirty thousand—not including the saved costs from disaster relief and dike repairs. Total expense for three years runs below a million, saving about two to three million in ten years. Counting an additional one to two million savings in disaster relief and dike repairs adds up to five to six million saved in total. There is no denying that the proposal is impeccable" 聞現在每年歲修四十萬，備〔料〕二十萬，恆若不足。倘如此辦法，三年之後，薪水勇糧等項不過二十餘萬，購料買土等項不過十餘萬足矣，每年所省不下二三十萬，而放賑堵口所省之數，不在此內統計。三年之用，不足百萬，而十年之間，約省二三百萬。放賑堵口，又省一二百萬，共省五六百萬，不可謂非至計也 (Liu 2007, 1:44–45). When calculating the total cost of flood control, Liu's estimation often uses units smaller than the *tael*, like *qian* 錢, *fen* 分, and *hao* 毫.

14. For instance, in a diary entry dated November 25, 1902, Liu E expressed strong interest in the manufacture of a new type of handgun that could fire ten bullets in a row. He made the following comment: "This clever device can fire eighty shots a minute and as far as 1,800 yards. It can penetrate a thin iron sheet at 600 yards. Making one of them will cost no more than two *liang* of gold, and building a factory would cost only 30,000 *liang* of gold. The device is really simple: a bullet

his meticulous calculation of the manufacturing cost, productivity, and return of various machines, Liu's close attention to the construction cost, crop production increase, and cost efficiency in discussing his embankment system fully illustrates his industrialist mentality.

In the eyes of Liu E, flood control was a symbol of the origins of Chinese civilization. From early 1892 to late 1893, Liu, based on his studies of ancient literature, produced *Maps and Studies of Changes to the Yellow River through History* (*Lidai Huanghe bianqian tukao* 歷代黃河變遷圖考, hereafter *Maps and Studies of Changes*). *Maps and Studies of Changes* comprises maps of the Yellow River's course during various dynasties, from Da Yu's age to the late Qing. While his previous supervisor Wu Dacheng had commissioned him to produce *Chart of the Course of the Yellow River*, the creation of *Maps and Studies of Changes* was purely Liu's own initiative. Unlike *Chart of the Course of the Yellow River*, which contains clear, detailed instructions for its use and an explanation of the purpose, *Maps and Studies of Changes* comes with no such explanatory text. Apparently, the latter was not created for practical flood control. In fact, in the explanatory note to *Chart of the Course of the Yellow River*, Liu points out that since its course change in 1855, the Yellow River had actually turned into a new river, rendering past maps of the river valueless. A comprehensive, detailed mapping of the new Yellow River was badly needed to provide a valid reference for current river engineering (Liu 2007, 34–35). Arguably, studying the Yellow River's course in Da Yu's age served no purpose for contemporary Yellow River management. Why, then, did Liu E painstakingly produce *Maps and Studies of Changes*? The only explanation for this seemingly self-contradictory action is that Liu produced *Maps and Studies of Changes* as a symbolic reference. It suggests a comparison and link between the internal strife and foreign invasion of Liu's own time, symbolized by the ravaging Yellow River floods and similar circumstances faced by Da Yu, who had turned the crisis into an opportunity to build a great civilization. For Liu E, *Maps and Studies of Changes* represented his comprehensive reexamination of contemporary Chinese social maladies, through the lens of ancient history, as well

---

is sent forth simply by pulling and releasing the trigger. Very ingenious" 其機甚靈，每分鐘可八十發，及遠一千八百碼，六百碼內能穿薄鐵片。若製造，本銀不過二金，造廠不過三萬金。機器極簡，每一鉤則彈發，一縱則銅殼自出，誠至巧也。 (Liu 2007, 1:713). In another entry dated July 30, 1905, he described a visit to a towel-weaving factory where weaving machines were used: "A fast worker can weave sixteen pieces a day whereas a slow one can weave eight; average output fell at around ten or twelve. Each dozen output costs about twenty *liang* of cotton yarn.... If there are ten workers in total, 2,000 towels can be produced in a month, which is 166 plus a half dozen *liang*. It is profitable in Qinhuai because each dozen sells at one *yuan* and three *jiao*. However, it will not profit in Shanghai because there, cotton yarn costs five *jiao* five *fen*. Sell it at one *yuan*, and you earn only seventy-five *yuan* a month, which will not be able to cover housing, food, and wages" 快手一日可織十六條，慢手織八條，大概十條、十二條者居多也。每打費棉紗二十兩。……如有十人，則每月可出毛巾二千條，為一百六十六打半也。在清淮做則有利，因每打批價一元三角。若上海則必無利，因紗本需五角五分，若批價一元，則一月僅得餘利七十五元，以開支房、飯、工資，必不足也。 (Liu 2007, 1:728).

as his confidence in the nation's rebirth in a manner similar to the great and mythical Yu.

Liu's reexamination of China's maladies and his quest for the nation's rebirth continued after his 1895 departure from flood control in Shandong and well into his next important engagement—coal mining in Shanxi. China has a long history of mining coal and other minerals as commodities, but it was only in the late Qing dynasty that the Chinese came to view coal as the fuel most essential for strengthening the nation. The shift accompanied the introduction of modern mining technology, but it was more the result of a change in the conceptualization of natural resources—coal became an essential fuel of imperialism and the key to an industrial economy. Coal mining has been wielded as an essential means of nation-building by successive Chinese regimes, from the late Qing to the People's Republic of China (Wright 1984; Wu 2015; Seow 2022). Liu E's early involvement in coal mining in 1897 therefore makes him a pioneer in this long twentieth-century history of nation-building.

Liu's deep involvement in the coal mining industry allowed him to envision a new China, yet at the same time, he was equally inquisitive about the nation's past. Thanks to his involvement in coal mining, Liu E became a key figure in rediscovering the origin of Chinese civilization. Through his service for the British company Peking Syndicate Limited, Liu managed to accumulate immense wealth, which enabled him to spend lavishly on antiques. One of his most valuable acquisitions was the recently unearthed oracle bones previously owned by Wang Yirong 王懿榮 (1845–1900), a high official who committed suicide during the Eight-Nation Alliance's occupation of Beijing. In 1903, Liu drew on his newly acquired collection to compile and publish *Tortoise Shells in the Collection of Tieyun* (*Tieyun cang gui* 鐵雲藏龜), China's first lithographically printed catalog of oracle bone scripts and a remarkable contribution to the early study of these objects. In his publication, Liu was the first person to identify the oracle bone scripts as "writing records of the Three Dynasties of Antiquity" (*san dai wenzi* 三代文字), namely the Xia, Shang, and Zhou, and his characterization pointed to a correct direction for subsequent interpretation (Xu 2014; Ren 2018).[15] Liu's interest in the earliest forms of Chinese writing was driven by his passion for reconfirming, at a moment of national crisis, the potential of Chinese civilization to revitalize itself on the basis of these earliest origins. His two occupations after 1895—oracle bone cataloging and publication, and coal mining coordination—symbolize the fusion of his effort to explore the nation's highly civilized past and his quest for its modern rejuvenation.

Liu E saw China's natural environment as supplying material resources for his nation-building activities. Meanwhile, he understood it also to hold immense

---

15. In the preface to *Tortoise Shells in the Collection of Tieyun*, Liu notes that the oracle bone inscriptions apparently come from an age earlier than Zhou.

cultural deposits on which he could draw for his nation-building campaigns. The most remarkable contributions in his life—flood control, coal mining and railroad construction, and oracle bone study—all involved investigation, excavation, and utilization of the natural environment.[16] These activities looked for solutions to the imminent environmental and political crises facing China, but also carried his hope to reconfirm the nation's potential of rejuvenation in the bedrock of its glorious past. It is unsurprising, then, to find each of them to surface in some way as themes in *The Travels*.

Yellow River and Liu E's Literary Nation-Building

Scholars exploring literary nation-building in early twentieth-century China find *The Travels* a particularly valuable subject of study, not merely because the author has explicitly identified nation-building as his main purpose of writing or because he devoted much of his life to nation-building activities. Most importantly, the novel presents Liu E's effort to conceptualize the plight of the Chinese nation from multiple perspectives, offering discourses associated with medical treatment, political criticism, sentimental expression, landscape writing, and philosophical thought, to name a few. Over the past century, studies of Liu's novel have probed these dimensions to varying extents. Like jigsaw pieces, they each offer remarkable insights individually but fail to piece together a whole picture. This absence of an overall understanding is largely because we lack an interpretative perspective rooted in the historical and social reality of Liu's time and in Liu E's life experience that is also broad enough to encompass the novel's core dimensions. I argue that appreciating the Yellow River flooding and its management in late Qing Shandong solves this jigsaw, forming a unifying framework by which we can understand, organize, and represent the core themes of *The Travels* identified in previous scholarship as a coherent agenda of literary nation-building. Furthermore, only by doing so, I argue, is it possible to fully comprehend the novel's literary-historical significance.

The process of nation-building begins, naturally, with a way to conceptualize the nation-state. Only with that in mind is it possible to address its problems and construct its future. Consequently, the first chapter of the book explores how Liu E understood China and the issues it faced in the early twentieth century. For this conceptualization, we turn to medicine. Discourses on medicine, traditional or

---

16. Flood control involves both hydraulic engineering and civil engineering. The conversion and utilization of earth is not only a purpose of Liu E's oblique dike design, but also a general focus of flood control. Civil engineering plays an essential role throughout the implementation of a hydraulic project. In the beginning, land measurement constitutes an important part of the preparatory work. As the project progresses, dredging, embankment, and breach repair all rely on the transport and utilization of earth and stone. In fact, flood control can be viewed as a process of land and earth and stone investigation, utilization, and rescheduling.

modern, are unavoidable for scholars exploring nation-building in China in this period, including that of Liu E. The novel's discourse on medicine and nation-building should be understood in the context of a developing idea of public hygiene in the early twentieth century, which played a crucial role in China's modern state-building and nation-building.[17] The emergence of public hygiene at the beginning of the twentieth century was inextricably linked to the rivalry between Chinese and Western medicines (Rogaski 2004). Traditional Chinese doctors diagnose illnesses, treat diseases, and administer medication based on the theories of the yin and yang and the five elements. When missionaries introduced Western medicine into China in the early nineteenth century, a debate on the superiority and legitimacy of Chinese medicine and Western medicine arose, continuing to this day. On the surface, the debate is about medicine. It entails a conflict of two sets of views on the human body, often interpreted as a clash between two cultures. In the past, scholars were inclined to describe the encounter between Chinese and Western medicines in the early twentieth century as a confrontation. More recent research on the history of medicine has started challenging this binary paradigm by exploring the interplay of these two medicines and their mutual incorporation of ideas during their coexistent development in China (Andrews 2014; Pi 2019).

That medicine is the appropriate lens through which to explore the conception of the state in *The Travels* is evident in the purposeful correspondence between the professions of the protagonist, Lao Can, an itinerant medical practitioner, and the author, Liu E, a former practicing doctor.[18] As a traditional Chinese medical practitioner and entrepreneur engaged in Western affairs, Liu E adopted a view on medicine that blended Chinese and Western approaches. Liu believed Chinese and Western medicines have respective strengths and weaknesses. Chinese medicine excelled in diagnosis, medical theory, and therapies, while Western medicine was more advanced in systematic medical training, medical apparatuses, and medical drugs. According to Liu, a patient should first be diagnosed according to Chinese medical theory and then treated with Western devices and drugs for the best outcome. In the long run, he believed, China must establish a complete training and qualification system for cultivating medical doctors.[19] Liu's view obviously echoes

---

17. For the difference between nation-building and state-building, see Linz 1993.
18. From his mother, Lady Zhu 朱, Liu E learned traditional Chinese medicine, which allowed Liu to practice medicine for a time after repeatedly failing the imperial exams, though the business did not work out well.
19. In a letter dated 1895 to Sheng Xuanhuai, Liu E made the following observation: "Western medicine lacks a solid theory but boasts high barriers of entry for practitioners (who have to pass exams and earn a license before practicing), well-made drugs (which are not allowed onto the market without experts' verification), and a strict discipline mechanism (which would suspend the licenses of doctors for malpractice until their qualifications being reaffirmed). When such a system has been enforced for hundreds of years, how could there be no remarkable outcome? In treating external injuries, Western medicine indeed performs better (such as open surgeries, and wound and fracture

the principle that Zhang Zhidong 張之洞 (1837–1909), a leading figure of the Western Affairs Movement, proposed for guiding the movement—"Chinese learning as fundamental structure, Western learning for practical use" (*zhongxue wei ti, xixue wei yong* 中學為體，西學為用). Liu E's similar view of medicine serves as the basis for how we understand medicine in relation to his literary nation-building in *The Travels*.

Previous scholars have been inclined to regard the narrative of medical treatment in *The Travels* as part of the nation-as-body analogy, introduced from the West by late Qing constitutional reformists such as Liang Qichao (Guan 2014). Indeed, Liang's argumentation immensely influenced discussions about nation-building in the late Qing and early Republican eras. He was also an acquaintance of Liu E. However, since Liu believed in "Chinese medicine as the fundamental structure," we must understand the relationship between medicine and nation-building in the novel not only as influenced by Liang's new concepts of medicine but also in the context of longer-standing notions derived from Chinese medicine. The first chapter of this book addresses this question by examining the dominant political rhetoric in the early twentieth century as represented in the narrative of illness and healing in *The Travels*. The chapter maintains that unlike readings that only emphasize the modern notion of the nation as a body, Liu E actually frames his storytelling about national crisis and salvation in terms borrowed from traditional Chinese pathology and river control terminology. The chapter traces trends in late Qing political rhetoric, particularly the nation-as-body analogy. It shows how Liu E's training in traditional medicine allowed him to conceptualize the analogy and the nation's healing differently from Liang Qichao, who built his national healing agenda on Western concepts. This chapter further shows how the interplay between hydraulics and medicine, which dates to ancient China, shaped the nation-as-body analogy underpinning the novel's narrative of national healing. Chapter 1 also examines the political stance that Liu E reveals in the novel, illustrating how he analogizes Chinese revolutionaries of the time to the floods on the Yellow River and diseases

---

treatment) than Chinese medicine (because they have better trained doctors, more advanced apparatus, highly effective drugs, and advise more appropriate diet and daily care). In medical theory and therapies, Chinese medicine is not inferior to Western medicine. Only the practitioners have no interest in self-improvement and standardization. . . . They should study ancient masters' theories like transformation of *qi* (*qihua* 氣化) and tip and root (*biaoben* 標本) until achieving full mastery. Meanwhile, they should also read translated Western books (like *Anatomy to Human Body* 形體闡微, *Complete Guide to Abscess Surgery* 割瘡全書, *Elementary Medicine* 醫學入門, and *Foreign Medicine* 萬國本草), study them thoroughly, and incorporate the understanding into their expertise. Then they would gain full confidence in practicing medicine. . . . There is no need to discriminate against Western medicine (because their drugs for treating are indeed better, although the usage is too strong) or abandon Chinese medicine (as for internal disharmony and deficiency caused by the disorder in transformation of *qi*, Chinese medicine and therapies are much more effective, but truly skilled doctors are rare). Both offer something valuable to draw from" (Liu and Liu 2019, 317–18).

caused by liquid imbalances in the human body. It goes on to analyze the novel's criticism of the Boxer Uprising and the abuse of power by local governmental officials. Liu depicts these as the cause of national illness, something to be cured by medical means analogous to flood control. The chapter's argument that the novel's narrative of national crisis and salvation is based on flood control addresses the main concern of this book—the important role that water played in Liu E's literary nation-building.

With his novel conceptual framework for the state established, Liu E leveraged the analogical and intertwined relationship between the river, body, and polity to address political concerns. This is the subject of Chapter 2. *The Travels* recounts how the so-called incorruptible officials impose extremely rigid, harsh governance at the cost of the lives of local people and how Lao Can intervenes out of righteous indignation to rescue innocent people from torture. Liu E saw this exposure of such reputation-obsessed "incorruptible officials" as his proudest accomplishment in the novel. Likewise, it is this aspect of the novel that first attracted scholars' attention.[20] Even though the novel undoubtedly includes Liu E's scathing criticism of late Qing local bureaucrats, it is, as David Der-wei Wang correctly suggests, a variation of the court case and chivalric genre. The novel's reexamination of incorruptible officials marks an ironic departure from traditional court case and chivalric novels such as *The Three Heroes and Five Gallants* (*Sanxia wuyi* 三俠五義, 1879). A fresh understanding of political power and the concept of justice began to take shape in *The Travels*: the deep-rooted sins do not lie in the rebels who subvert state order but in the officials authorized by the state to maintain the order (Wang 2007, 93). By challenging the justice and authority of the officials representing state power, the novel calls into question the legitimacy of the regime's rule. As such, the challenge represents Liu's attempt to fundamentally reexamine state power.

To make this reexamination and critique of state power, the second chapter argues that Liu E ties his political discourse to the earlier nineteenth-century floods. He was not the first to do so. David Der-wei Wang shows that this link between political discourse and the floods is observable in the figurative language in the 1879 novel *The Three Heroes and Five Gallants*.[21] However, in *The Travels*, the floods do

---

20. Lu Xun (2011), for example, propounded his famous idea of the "novel of exposure" (*qianze xiaoshuo* 譴責小說) by taking as its example the criticism of harsh local governance in Liu E's novel.
21. In studying *The Three Heroes and Five Gallants* and *The Travels*, David Der-wei Wang borrows the idea of chronotope from Mikhail Bakhtin to read the flood disasters in the two novels as a literary configuration of the historical drive. In the former, the flooding of Lake Hongze 洪澤湖 that threatened the Song regime is closely linked to the traitorous Prince Xiangyang, while in the latter, the devastating Yellow River flood disaster that leads to numerous injuries and deaths results from a wrong decision made by the actually honest, upright Governor Zhuang. In either disaster, a hero stands up to fight for justice amid the engulfing waves of political and social transformation but in vain (Wang 2007, 96–97). Lake Hongze, whose dike breach induces a flood in *The Three Heroes and Five Gallants*, played a crucial role in Ming and Qing Yellow River management. Pan Jixun and Jin

not merely serve as a literary configuration of the historical drive toward political and social reform; these floods are the very historical drive itself, directly shaping social and political transformations. As Chapter 2 will show, the novel directly links its criticism of incorruptible officials to state governance and to the environmental collapse of the late nineteenth century. The Yellow River floods and his innovations in hydraulic engineering molded Liu E's sociopolitical critique and his agenda of governance and statecraft.

To make this point, this chapter begins by understanding the novel's criticism of the incorruptible officials. This criticism, it argues, implicates the Qing government's methods for addressing the public security challenges caused by the frequent Yellow River floods. The chapter further analyzes the solutions for public security suggested in the novel as an alternative to the mode of governance adopted by incorruptible officials. Chapter 2 then shows how Liu E's designs for hydraulic infrastructure served as conceptual resources for his challenge to the Qing government's defensive and rigid bureaucracy and in his blueprint for nation-building. From Liu E's perspective of river engineering, the novel redefines the very idea of incorruptibility and considers the concepts on which the idea of incorruptibility has historically been based. This chapter ends by looking into the underworld scene in chapter 28 of the novel, exploring how river engineering plays a significant role at the novel's close. Here, Liu E addresses his accusation of a national traitor, which was brought upon him due to his conceptualization of ideal governance. Like Chapter 1, this chapter examines the role of water in nation-building in *The Travels*, but now in the light of Liu E's agenda of governance and statecraft.

As should already be evident, Liu E's nation-building agenda and methodology stem from his very identity as a river engineer and political reformer. Unsurprisingly, then, *The Travels* is wrought with emotion and must be understood within the broader discourse of emotion and national sentiment within late Qing literature. This is the subject of Chapter 3. Emotion has been a key force driving China's nation-building activities since the late Qing, and *The Travels* is a quintessential case of this. In his 1905 preface to the novel, Liu E drew on the power and literary history of weeping and cited the various sentiments shared by contemporaneous Chinese people about nation, society, ethnicity, and civilization as the reason for writing the novel. Liu's opening statement has since become a core text that scholars must engage with when exploring the modern forms of Chinese people's emotions. Most notably, Liu's preface features centrally in Haiyan Lee's study of the relationship between the discourse of love and literary nation-building in nineteenth- and twentieth-century China. In it, Lee detects a sentiment that levels social hierarchies

---

Fu 靳輔 (1633–1692), the celebrated hydraulic engineers of the Ming–Qing period, implemented an embankment system at the lake to wash away silt with the lake's water and prevent deposits, to ensure the operation of the Grand Canal.

and distinctions and posits a new principle of ordering human society. It is a sentiment that springs up from human nature, associates one with the world, and transcends all boundaries, and the celebration of it bears characteristics of the late Ming cult of passion or feeling (*qingjiao* 情教) (Lee 2007). Lee posits that this sentiment of belonging was the key element of nation-building in Liu's preface.

While Lee's observations have merit, extending this understanding to the core content of the novel's discourse of emotion would risk oversimplifying. Instead of a transcendental, abstract sentiment of belonging, Chapter 3 argues that what Liu depicted most in the novel is the postdisaster trauma caused by the Yellow River embankment failures. While mapping the Yellow River in 1889, Liu witnessed a dike breach that rendered tens of thousands of people homeless or separated them from their loved ones. The firsthand experience of trauma was the basis for the novel's writing of emotion, and Chapter 3 identifies the trauma associated with the Yellow River flooding as the resource on which Liu E drew to develop the idea of nationally shared sentiment. It argues that Liu E's novel establishes the discourse of emotion by transforming flood trauma through symbolic healing on the narrative level and conceptually combining disaster relief, trauma healing, and nation-building with newspaper editing.

The chapter begins with a discussion of the novel's allusion to earlier literature, illustrating that the novel develops the idea of saving the nation through flood taming by rooting the idea in canonical works in poetic and narrative traditions. It then analyzes how the ancient analogy between water flow and emotion informed Liu E's way of crafting a narrative of national salvation through a story about flood trauma and its healing. It goes on to investigate the expression of flood trauma as shaped by hydraulic criticism and a technology-based morality before examining the novel's narrative of trauma healing as resonant with river engineering technology and the history of hydraulics of the Yellow River. The chapter concludes by exploring how the novel's narrative of trauma and healing participates in the literary national identity construction executed through newspaper layout editing in reporting a 1907 flood in northern China and its aftermath. Whereas Chapters 1 and 2 deal with the political aspects of the novel, Chapter 3 takes the thesis of nation-building in a new direction by addressing the discourse of emotion. Its primary argument is that it is only possible to appreciate this integration of emotion into the political discourse by recognizing the unifying hydraulic framework employed by Liu E. That is, this chapter discusses the novel's construction of national identity by establishing a connection between the flood experience and national sentiment.

Having established the link between emotion and hydraulics in Liu E's nation-building, we then use this framework in Chapter 4 to reconsider the novel's most lauded aspect: its landscape writing. *The Travels* holds a special place in the literature reforms of the 1910s. After the founding of the Republic of China in 1912, Chinese intellectuals saw it as their mission to promote a new national language and new national literature. In formulating new literary standards and envisioning modern national literature, Hu Shih 胡適 (1891–1962), the leading literary reformer, cited *The Travels* as an important case study. Vernacular Chinese, Hu advocated, should be the standard form of writing. In his 1925 preface to the Yadong Library Press (Yadong tushuguan 亞東圖書館) edition of *The Travels*, the first serious literary study of the novel, Hu praised the novel's exceptional literary techniques, focusing on its accomplishments in vernacular landscape description. It was the vernacular depiction of landscape, Hu Shih argued, that distinguished the novel from traditional Chinese novels, providing an example of vernacular fiction writing that could be followed by all subsequent vernacular literature (Hu 2013, 1045–48).

As C. T. Hsia (2004) pointed out, Hu's focus on the novel's landscape writing led him to miss out on the novel's more significant breakthroughs in literary form and narrative techniques. However, Hu's observation still alerts us to a highly important but easily neglected fact: *The Travels* marks the emergence of a new type of landscape writing in Chinese novels. This contribution made *The Travels* not only a cornerstone of Hu's national literature construction but also a forerunner of modern Chinese literature. Since the publication of Hu Shih's preface in 1925, *The Travels* has been regarded as a classic exemplar of landscape writing. For generations, high schools in the People's Republic of China, Hong Kong, and Taiwan have utilized excerpts from the novel as teaching materials to instruct literary techniques of landscape description. Chapter 4 asks, what brought about this history-shaping emergence of landscape writing? Although numerous studies have been devoted to the novel's innovative landscape writing ever since Hu first called attention to it, surprisingly few have probed the root causes of its emergence. Chapter 4 explains the emergence of a new type of landscape description from the hydraulics perspective. It argues that Liu E's landscape description was premised on a new perceptual mode informed by his profession as a hydraulic engineer.

The chapter starts by showing that due to his engagement with hydraulic engineering, Liu E considered natural landscapes as enigmatic and unable to be depicted through conventional literary and artistic forms. The chapter then discusses how the technical problems Liu E encountered in flood control and the optical knowledge required to solve them shaped his writing on water landscapes. It further explores how Liu E's landscape writing relates to his concern for visual illusions and the mechanisms that shape visual experience—an inquiry arising from his anxiety about the limits of human visual capacity to deal with the instability and unpredictability of the untamed Yellow River. The chapter concludes by demonstrating how Liu E's landscape writing embodies his interest in the perception of light, his critical understanding of philosophy, and his contemplation of Chinese political prospects. Ultimately, Chapter 4 shows that the novel's innovation in landscape description is more than an innovation in the craft of writing. It is a more complicated one that incorporates flood control, visual perception, and philosophy into literary nation-building—one that we can appreciate only by understanding his identity as a river engineer.

The first four chapters of this book analyze *The Travels* from the perspectives of body imagination, political governance, discourses of emotion, and literary techniques—the four focuses of past scholarship on late Qing literary nation-building—by positing Liu E's attempts at controlling the Yellow River floods as the central idea uniting them. Yet as Chapter 5 argues, such an assessment would be incomplete without examining Liu E's engagement with the philosophy of the Taigu school, a secret religious cult banned by the Qing government. As scholars have noted, the Taigu school, to which Liu was a lifelong adherent, served as an essential spiritual drive for his exploits in industrial and commercial activities, and even literature. The final chapter discusses how the theme of the Taigu school and that of river regulation together form the very core structure of the novel. Specifically, Chapter 5 explores the connection between Taigu philosophy, flood control, and the nation-building themes of the novel by addressing one of the most puzzling aspects of *The Travels*: the episode in chapters 9–11 involving a gathering of a hermit prophet, a female philosopher, and a Confucian scholar. This gathering, at the structural center of the novel's twenty-chapter first volume, has usually been regarded as an interlude irrelevant to the main plot and even a rupture in the narrative. This chapter disagrees. It contends instead that this episode is the very center of the novel's narrative logic and Liu E's imagination of nation-building because it embodies his belief in the Taigu school and concern for Yellow River governance.

The final chapter identifies the Taigu school and flood control as distinct but highly interrelated themes in *The Travels*. Chapter 5 first illustrates that the music playing during the gathering, the most representative scene in the interlude, encapsulates the Taigu school at its crucial historical moment of revival and articulates Liu E's vehement call to perpetuate the school's legacy. The chapter further explores the connotation of political resistance in the music-playing scene by discussing the link between the fictional music piece and a music score Liu E printed for circulation. Aside from the Taigu school, Yellow River regulation is another legacy that Liu E deemed in danger of being lost and which he, therefore, needed to pass on. The chapter delves into the intellectual resources shared by the Taigu school and the long history of Yellow River regulation, indicating that Yellow River governance, like the Taigu school, serves as a hidden context for the novel's imagination of China's rejuvenation, as suggested in the political prophecy of the hermit Yellow Dragon (Huanglongzi 黃龍子), a character with strong reference to the Taigu school leaders. The chapter ends by analyzing Yellow Dragon's explanation of his prophecy, pointing out that Liu E bases his political imagination on the model of hydraulic engineering at the very core of the narrative structure. This chapter argues that Yellow Dragon, in the most enigmatic episode at the novel's center, embodies the Taigu school's legacy and the history of Yellow River regulation. Chapter 5's most important contribution is to consolidate the overall thesis of the Yellow River as the driving force of Liu E's literary nation-building on a structural level by incorporating the Taigu school's significance.

In sum, this book presents a new approach to a critical work of modern Chinese literary history. It identifies the single, unifying driving force behind *The Travels*'s innovations in political imagination, the discourse of emotion, and literary form and explains the driving force that brought them about. By examining the confluence of devastating floods, hydraulic engineering, nation-building, and literary creation, this study explores the relationship between environmental change and the birth of modern Chinese literature. Conventional narratives depict literary nation-building in the late Qing as induced primarily by political and cultural collision. This book goes beyond human factors to show the pivotal role of environmental degradation in forming national literature and literature about the nation in early twentieth-century China.

1
Hydraulics and Medicine
Remedying Body and Nation

> The world lies ill and slumbers deep. Should the path to healing be obscured, sound the stringed bell to rouse it from its sleep. Know this: no cure for any affliction may be found until one stirs from their slumber.
>
> —Liu E, *The Travels*, commentary on chapter 1

Early twentieth-century Chinese intellectuals primarily used the analogy of a body to conceptualize the relationship between citizen and state. Liang Qichao, arguably the most well-known reformist leader during the late Qing, exemplifies this tradition in the introductory passage of his 1902 landmark treatise *On New Citizen* (*Xinmin shuo* 新民說). He wrote, "A nation is composed of its citizens. Citizens are to a nation just as limbs, organs, veins, and blood cells are to a body. A body cannot live with its limbs cut off, organs damaged, veins impaired, and blood dried out" 國也者，積民而成。國之有民，猶身之有四肢、五臟、筋脈、血輪也。未有四肢已斷，五臟已瘵，筋脈已傷，血輪已涸，而身猶能存者 (1998, 46). Liang likens the nation-state to the anatomy of its citizens, with individuals envisioned as an extension of the state's body, which is believed to reflect Johann Kaspar Bluntschli's (1808–1881) ideas (Shen 2006; Liu C. 2011, 62–66). In Liang's view, the health or illness of the individual body is thus indicative of the strength or feebleness of the nation. From the late Qing onward, nation-building discourses leveraged this conceptual relation to discuss the bodies of the masses and how to cure and transform them to ensure national fortitude. Prescriptions include hygiene, physical drills, and abstinence from opium. Their primary concern was how to convert the weak, sluggish, numb, and even paralyzed body of the "sick man of China" into a strong and healthy one.

Liu E wrote *The Travels* between 1903 and 1907, precisely when biological nationalism took hold in China, and calls for building a stronger body and nation took shape. Consequently, the novel is often considered part of this trend (Guan 2014, 214–16; Sen 2015, 106–7). In the closing commentary of chapter 1, Liu E, who also assumes the role of commentator, makes explicit the purpose and method of Lao Can's healing practice. He explains Lao Can uses a string of bells to rouse his ill and somnolent fellow Chinese. That is, the patient Lao Can intends to treat is none other than the nation that Liang Qichao considered sick, drowsy, and in desperate need of awakening and treatment—China.[1]

Despite employing biological nationalism, Liu E's writing does not necessarily share an ideological heritage with that of Liang and his compatriots. The body-state analogy has a longer provenance in China than scholars of late Qing novels generally suggest. The metaphor was not merely a twentieth-century Western import to late Qing literature but also a traditional rhetorical device used, mostly in the form of allegory, in both Chinese political discourse and traditional theories of medicine and pharmacy since ancient times.[2]

Consequently, ideas of illness and healing according to traditional Chinese medicine also demand consideration when trying to understand how Liu E conceives the individual-state relationship. Lao Can, Liu's literary surrogate, is a long-serving practitioner of traditional medicine. And Liu E was a famous physician of the "warm disease school" (*wenbing xuepai* 溫病學派), having published a monograph on medicine and pharmacology.[3] While he credited Western medicine for its efficacy in medication and anatomy, he warned of its limits and potential harm, maintaining Chinese medicine's theoretical superiority (Liu and Liu 2019, 317–18). Accordingly, we should be cautious of reading the allegory of curing and the narrative of national crisis and salvation in his novel through the same lens scholars use to read Liang's apparently similar analogy.

The Travels, however, does more than simply incorporate traditional Chinese medical concepts into its narrative of national salvation. The discourse of national salvation is also highly associated with the issue of water control. According to traditional Chinese medicine, the human body comprises five elements—wood, fire,

---

1. The sleep metaphor in Liu E's commentary can be traced to the 1887 article "China, the Sleep and the Awakening," published in the British periodical *Asian Quarterly* by the late-Qing diplomat Zeng Jize 曾紀澤 (1839–1890). It was later translated into Chinese and caused a sensation among Chinese readers. Liang Qichao cited it several times in public and developed it into his celebrated metaphor for China, "the sleeping lion." For a discussion of the metaphor of sleeping and awakening in the late Qing, see Yang 2016.
2. Examples can be seen in Ge Hong's 葛洪 (283–343) *Master Embracing Simplicity* (*Baopuzi* 抱朴子), Liu Yuxi's 劉禹錫 (772–842) "Inspecting Medicines" ("Jian yao" 鑒藥), Zhang Lei's 張耒 (1054–1114) "Caution on Medicine" ("Yao jie" 藥戒), Liu Ji's 劉基 (1311–1375) "An Analogy of Governance" ("Yu zhi" 喻治), and Fang Xiaoru's 方孝孺 (1357–1402) "The Enlightenment from a Sick Thumb" ("Zhi yu" 指喻). See Ge 1990, 145b; Liu 1990, 76–77; Zhang 1990, 817–19; Liu 1987, 37; Fang 1967, 124–25.
3. The school of warm diseases, whose approach to understanding epidemic diseases was fully developed by Ye Tianshi 葉天士 (1667–1764), focuses on the clinical manifestations of epidemic diseases marked by fever caused by heat and fire in the body. In dealing with high fever, the warm disease school uses herbs that are cold and cool in nature. For a discussion of the warm disease school, see Cheng 2017.

earth, metal, and water—whose proportions must be kept in balance to maintain health. As Epstein points out, Confucian ideals of restoring political order are especially represented in late imperial Chinese fiction by the literatus doctor who can restore order to the bodily imbalance (2001, 261). Specifically, this literatus doctor comes to be related to the theme of river control (Schonebaum 2004, 116–17). The literatus doctor and the water control expert Lao Can, who seeks to heal the nation, is part of this narrative tradition.

An expert in river control and a practicing doctor himself, Liu E, however, was not content with simply drawing an analogy between controlling floods, curing illness, and restoring order to the government. In *The Travels*, Liu consciously incorporates his knowledge of medicine and water control into the novel's narrative of treating the nation's illness, deftly intertwining medical treatment, river regulation, and national salvation to address the Boxer Uprising and the revolutionary movement. As this chapter explores, Liu E analogizes Chinese revolutionists to both floods on the Yellow River and diseases caused by water imbalances in the human body. He criticizes the Boxer Uprising and the local government's abuse of power by depicting them as a national illness—an illness that must be cured by traditional medical means analogous to flood control.

Hydraulic Engineering and Medicine

The novel's narrative of national salvation begins with and hinges on an analogization of medicine to hydraulics and thus medical treatment to flood control. This analogy further connects the objects of these treatments—the human body, rivers, and by extension, the state. Chapter 1 begins by narrating the first medical case that the itinerant physician, Lao Can, attends. Arriving at Shandong, Lao Can treats a patient from the house of Huang. The ill man, named Huang Ruihe 黃瑞和, suffers every summer from a festering body, riddled with open sores. Lao Can cures this disease using a method he claims was passed down from Da Yu, the legendary cultural hero celebrated for his prowess in flood control. The patient's name and the invocation of Da Yu's authority hint at the Yellow River (Huanghe). Huang Ruihe's place of origin alludes furthermore to the Yellow River in Shandong, which overwhelms its dikes every summer just as Huang's recurrent disease overtakes his body. The story of Lao Can treating Huang Ruihe's skin disease thus is an allegory of the regulation of the Yellow River.

The Yellow River has every reason to be the first patient Lao Can treats. As Liu E's aforementioned commentary on chapter 1 makes clear, the physician targets a larger concern than the festering body of an individual patient; he aims instead to treat his sleeping fellow countrymen and his country. Management of the Yellow River has been closely associated with the management of the state throughout Chinese history. The earliest river control literature in China, "Tribute of Yu" ("Yugong" 禹

貢) from the *Documents of Antiquity* (*Shangshu* 尚書),[4] describes Da Yu's success in flood control, which prepared him to succeed the legendary leaders before him and found the Xia dynasty. "Tribute of Yu" is also the first literature to propose the Nine Provinces (Jiuzhou 九州) and Five Domains (Wufu 五服) as a geographical way to conceive of and plan the Chinese world. Taming the Yellow River floods thus not only symbolizes the genesis of Chinese civilization but is also paramount to domestic affairs—a relationship still prevalent when Liu was writing his novel. It is therefore understandable that Liu E chooses the Yellow River as Lao Can's first patient in the allegory that launches the novel's narrative of national salvation.

While the analogy Liu E establishes between flood control and medical treatment relies on his professional engagement in both fields, it also reflects the interweaving of ideas in these two fields throughout history. Traditional Chinese hydraulics and medicine had long borrowed ideas from one another, as we can see in the term *weilü* 尾閭, which has had both hydraulic and medical usage since ancient times. The term appears in "Autumn Floods" ("Qiushui" 秋水) from *Zhuangzi* 莊子 in reference to the place where all waters converge and leak away. It also appears in the earliest surviving Chinese medical text, *Inner Cannon of the Yellow Emperor* (*Huangdi neijing* 黃帝內經, after 168 BCE), referring to an acupoint located at the coccygeal end of the spinal cord and associated with treating diarrhea. *Inner Cannon of the Yellow Emperor* very likely borrows *Zhuangzi*'s hydraulic meaning of the term in referencing an acupoint used to treat the excessive leaking of water from the body. In turn, hydraulics discourse has borrowed *weilü*. Because of *weilü*'s location at the end of the vertebral column, Ming–Qing river engineers used the term for the lower reach of a river; they likewise used the bodily terms *tou* 頭 (head) and *fu* 腹 (abdomen) for a river's upper and middle reach, respectively. This example represents a long-established phenomenon in Chinese intellectual history, and it is this borrowing of ideas between the two fields that informed the novel's allegory of Huang Ruihe's treatment.

We find the most elaborate materialization of the hydraulics-medicine analogy in the medical theory of treating blood and dampness. In traditional Chinese medical theory, the meridians of the human body are analogous to river channels, and blood flows through the meridians as water through channels. Accordingly, practitioners treated blood disorders similarly to managing rivers. In his *Detailed Analysis of Epidemic Warm Diseases* (*Wenbing tiaobian* 溫病條辨, 1798), the famous Qing physician Wu Jutong 吳鞠通 (1758–1836) argues, "River management and blood treatment [are the same]: to increase the flow by excavating side channels; to restrict the flow by building dikes" 治水與血之法，間亦有用通者，開支河也；有用塞者，崇堤防也 (Wu 1995, 745). Similar expressions appear in Wu's discussion of what is

---

4. The *Documents of Antiquity* is one of the *Five Classics* in Confucianism and the foundation of Chinese political philosophy.

considered the root cause of all diseases: uncontrolled dampness. Wu believes that mountain springs, rivers, soil moisture, and human body dampness are all the same substance, although taking different forms and names.[5] Internal dampness, in other words, is not merely analogous to river water; it is essentially identical. To drain the body of dampness, Wu proposes "digging through ditches to enable the middle energizer (*jiao* 焦) to transform the *qi* and strengthen the spleen [which bears the feature of earth] as if consolidating the dikes" 開溝渠，運中陽，崇剛土，作堤防之治 (1995, 715).[6] To treat diarrhea and oliguria arising from the disorder of internal dampness, he suggests "dividing water and dampness into branches from the screen gate [the junction between the large and small intestines] and directing them through the bladder to avoid overflow in the large intestine" 分闌門，通膀胱，開支河，使邪不直注大腸.[7] With its conceptual affinity to hydraulics, traditional medicine borrows hydraulic expressions in its theoretical and clinical discourse on blood and dampness.[8]

Wu Jutong's dampness theory illuminates the significance of the episode in which Lao Can treats Huang Ruihe's sore-riddled body. Liu E, a seasoned physician of the warm disease school, regarded Wu Jutong's *Detailed Analysis of Epidemic Warm Diseases* highly and knew his approach to treating dampness.[9] If Liu under-

---

5. According to Wu (1995, 715), "Dampness, as a substance, takes the form of rain and dew in yang-dominant weather, frost and snow in yin-dominant weather. It becomes springs in the mountains, water in the river, and moisture in the soil. It blends with the lungs in the upper energizer, with the spleen in the middle energizer, and with the *gui* water of lesser yin in the lower energizer. This summarizes the embodiment of dampness in the universe and the human body, which all comes from the same origin. It shows that earth is made up of mixed *qi* whereas water is created by the One and can blend in anywhere . . . It blends with the spleen in the middle energizer because the spleen is endowed with the property of moist earth and is inclined to hold dampness, and thus most damp diseases derive from the middle energizer" 濕之為物也，在天之陽時為雨露，陰時為霜雪，在山為泉，在川為水，包含於土中者為濕。其在人身也，上焦與肺合，中焦與脾合，其流於下焦也，與少陰癸水合。此統舉濕在天地人身之大綱，異出同源，以明土為雜氣，水為天一所生，無處不合者也……中焦與脾合者，脾主濕土之質，為受溼之區，故中焦濕症最多。
6. The middle energizer (*zhongjiao* 中焦), one of the triple energizers (*sanjiao* 三焦), is located between the diaphragm and navel and includes the spleen, stomach, liver, and gallbladder. The *sanjiao* serves as a pathway for *qi* and water circulation and dominates *qi* transformation. See World Health Organization 2022, 18.
7. Flood control metaphors are also used to describe other, or even opposite, treatments. For example, the preface to *Answers to Questions on Medicine* (*Yixue dawen* 醫學答問, 1895) suggests, "A doctor who tries to stop diarrhea without trying to identify its cause is like an engineer building dikes to prevent flooding. The riverbed builds up year by year, and over time it can no longer be remedied" 醫者但知止泄，不揣其病所從生。譬如治河者，築堤捍水，歲歲增高，久且決不復可治矣. See Liang and Tao 1994, 3.
8. Chinese medicine not only likens dampness-induced disorders to river flooding on a conceptual level but also applies flood control principles to pharmaceutical practice. This explains why traditional medications for swelling and water retention, such as "Yu's achievement powder" (*Yugong san* 禹功散), "river-dredging powder" (*junchuan san* 濬川散), and the "water diversion pill" (*daoshui wan* 導水丸), received the names they did.
9. Liu E even composed verses (*gegua* 歌括) to promote Wu Jutong's book.

stood floods and dampness to work and be managed by similar mechanisms, we should then understand Lao Can's treatment of Huang Ruihe's skin ulcers not just as Liu's assertion of an analogy between taming floods and healing illness but also as involving similar diagnosis and treatment.

Chapter 1's heading indicates the Huang Ruihe allegory's complexity: "The land does not hold back the water; every year comes disaster" 土不制水歷年成患 (Liu 1990, 3).[10] Aside from the first part's literal meaning—"earth failing to control water"—we also find a pathological term. In traditional Chinese pathology, "earth" refers to the spleen, the earth-associated organ that regulates water metabolism. When the spleen malfunctions, excess fluid accumulates in the body and can generate symptoms such as edema, excretory disorders, and even skin ulcerations and exudate overflow—the symptoms Lao Can observes in Huang Ruihe's body. Based on this understanding, Chinese medicine treats excessive dampness by enhancing spleen function, a treatment described in traditional Chinese medicine as "nurturing the earth to boost water metabolism" 敦土利水. Translated into flood control, this approach entails building dikes to regulate river water—the very method Lao Can claims to have inherited from Da Yu and uses to cure Huang Ruihe's disease. The Huang Ruihe episode thus entwines hydraulics and medicine in two ways: it is an allegory that analogizes illness treatment to river regulation[11] and a medical case of treating excess body water and dampness. That a narrative of treating an ailing state begins with a medical case of treating a water disorder clearly illustrates how Liu E understands the issue of China's salvation: the nation suffers from dampness syndrome and requires treatment accordingly.

The allegory of curing the sick Huang Ruihe/Yellow River demonstrates the intertwining of traditional Chinese medicine and its theoretical sibling—hydraulics. We can view Lao Can's expertise in both disciplines not only as his autobiographical presence in the novel but also as a token of the commonality between the two knowledge spheres. This commonality urges us to rethink the relationship this allegory reveals between the body and nation. Although the body's health relates closely to the nation's health, the Huang Ruihe allegory is inconsistent with the Western state-as-organism analogy popular when Liu E wrote the novel. Instead, he built his

---

10. All references to the main text (i.e., excluding commentary) of the novel's first volume are based on Harold Shadick's translation (Liu 1990), sometimes with slight adaption. When no other source is given, translations are my own, in which case, the page numbers of the Liren Shuju edition (Liu 2013) are provided.
11. Allegories depend on metaphors, which help us understand one thing through another—using tenor and vehicle. What necessitates and enables such comparison is that the tenor and vehicle must be different objects. This, however, is not the case for the allegory of Huang Ruihe. The allegory's uniqueness lies in the fact that despite the ostensible difference between the vehicle (skin ulcers) and the tenor (Yellow River flooding), they are in fact the same thing. Skin ulceration is a sign of excessive internal dampness, which signifies the same loss of control over water as the frequent floods that plagued the Qing empire.

framework around the complexly analogical and interwoven relationship between the river, body, and state.

Sweeping Revolution, Surging Floods

Liu E was typical of the "Westernizing faction" of late Qing intellectuals, who advocated for adopting Western knowledge and producing Western tools and machines. Yet, in the complex political spectrum of intellectuals, the Westernizing faction was too radical for the conservative gentry and officials but too conservative for the revolutionists. Since 1897, Liu had thrown himself into railway and coal mine projects with foreign companies, believing they held immense promise for the people's livelihoods and the empire's prosperity. However, his close relationship with the West soon landed him on the firing line, with many calling him a traitor. Even more than the conservative gentry and government officials, revolutionists both at home and abroad denounced him especially loudly. *The Travels*, written during this turmoil, is Liu E's defense of his views on national salvation. This defense rests on linking the revolutionists and devastating floods: Liu E identifies the revolution as the nation's most deadly disease and himself as the one to cure it.

Liu E's clash with the revolutionists happened in the newspapers. Beginning in August 1903, newspapers and journals such as the *Shaoxing Vernacular News* (*Shaoxing baihuabao* 紹興白話報) and *Zhejiang Tidings* (*Zhejiang chao* 浙江潮) frequently published articles accusing Liu of treacherously selling out the railway and local collieries and urging him to respond (Ji Ming 1903, 3; *Zhejiang chao* 1903a, 1–2; 1903b, 159–61). Both newspapers were founded by the revolutionists to propagandize for revolution.[12] On November 24, 1903, Liu confronted these attacks by publishing "Clarification on Mining Affairs" ("Kuangshi qi" 礦事啟) in *Chinese and Foreign Daily* (*Zhongwai ribao* 中外日報), a newspaper supporting the Westernizing faction. He argued that the revolutionists' attacks against him "would be harmful to the general interest" (Liu 2007, 1:667), which to him was the prospect of bolstering national power by building railroads and developing the mining industry. Liu E hoped the "sagacious men out there would determine the verdict and together decide on the rights and wrongs [of this case]" (2007, 1:667). Liu expected the newspaper debate to replace a court trial and its judicious readers to return a just verdict.

Liu E incorporated his self-defense campaign into the novel by comparing the revolution to floods. He builds this connection in a lecture by a character who is the book's spiritual center. Chapters 9 to 11 relate a nighttime dialogue in which

---

12. Members of the Restoration Society (Guangfuhui 光復會) and the United League (Tongmenghui 同盟會) founded *Shaoxing Vernacular News* in 1903. The Zhejiang regional student association in Tokyo founded *Zhejiang Tidings*.

Yellow Dragon, an enlightened hermit representing the highest level of spirituality in the novel, diagnoses China's major illnesses as revolution and the Boxer Uprising. He alludes to *Book of Changes* and examines the etymology of the word *geming* 革命 (revolution), which is derived from the *ge* hexagram (*gegua* 革卦). According to Yellow Dragon's interpretation, this hexagram implies great misfortune.[13] He explains that the inauspicious *ze-huo ge* 澤火革 hexagram is associated with the *yin* virtue of *dui* water, which is linked to frustration, jealousy, and destructiveness. He then compares revolutionists to a jealous and destructive woman endowed with the property of *yin* water, indicative of disastrous floods. In doing so, Yellow Dragon reinforces the novel's initial diagnosis that river flooding is the nation's malady. Put another way, it is within the narrative of "flood as national malady" that Liu E associates revolution, which he considered the national malady, with flood.

Furthermore, Yellow Dragon's analysis identifies revolution as a deadly flood-related disease requiring eradication. Yellow Dragon makes this connection through a relatively free association of ideas. He begins his discussion with the original definition of the character *ge* in *geming*, "animal hide," and progresses to its extended meaning, "human skin." He then warns that a minor skin disease, if neglected, will lead to a deadly skin condition. Similarly, any association with the revolutionists, he suggests, will lead to festering and death. For readers, Yellow Dragon's statement doubtlessly immediately calls to mind the allegory of Huang Ruihe's skin ulcers and the associated Yellow River dike breach. Liu E therefore suggests the illness caused by revolution is as *highly contagious and fatal* as the epidemics in the wake of floods. The galvanizing fervor, infectious appeal, and overpowering pathos of revolutionary discourses show exactly how easily this disease can spread. By invoking the allegory of Huang Ruihe, Yellow Dragon links revolution and the disease related to the Yellow River flooding that Lao Can, the doctor and river engineer, aims to quell.

Two years before his death, Liu E returned to novel writing to clear his name and conclude the case. At the end of the novel's second volume, written in 1907, Lao Can, serving as Liu E's literary surrogate, visits the underworld in a dream to seek justice against the defamatory accusations directed at Liu E. In the underworld, Lao Can witnesses criminals suffering brutal punishments. According to King Yama, the ruler of the underworld, defamation is the most vicious of all vices because "[w]hen there are many who destroy people's reputations, then the world becomes one which cannot distinguish between good and evil . . . good people will diminish by the day and bad people increase, until all humankind in the world is destroyed" (Liu

---

13. This interpretation, though grounded in the exegesis tradition of *Book of Changes*, is not unbiased. *The Tuan Commentary* has a different explanation for the hexagram *ge*: "Heaven and Earth oppose [each other] and the Four Seasons are completed. [King] Tang and Wu changed the Mandate [*geming* 革命], complying with Heaven and responding to their people. The time of change is great indeed!" See Zhu 2019, 214. This is the most auspicious use of the hexagram *ge* and the root of the Chinese word for revolution (*geming*).

1989, 35). This warning against careless accusations recalls a similar commentary in the sinking ship allegory in chapter 1 of the novel—another instance of Liu E responding to his revolutionists critics. In this episode, a hate-mongering, riot-inciting "hero" accuses Lao Can and his friends of treason for using Western nautical equipment in their attempt to rescue a sinking passenger ship. Through King Yama's subtle yet convincing allusion to the revolutionists' attacks on Liu and the smooth-talking hero in the sinking-ship allegory, we can discern that those glib, propaganda-savvy revolutionists are among the most detested people in hell.

In Lao Can's dream visit to the underworld, where he represents Liu E's quest for justice, King Yama compares revolutionists, who are portrayed as defamers, to those who cause floods, emphasizing the potential destruction they can inflict. His comparison mirrors Yellow Dragon's analogy between floods and revolutionists: "When a Yellow River flood comes, a single person causing a dike to burst can result in calamity for hundreds of thousands" (Liu 1989, 34). This comparison alludes to the significant damage a single person can deliberately cause in river works, which likely reflects a darker side of these projects. The deliberate destruction of dikes for personal profit had long been a rampant problem in the construction of river embankments. Just as common were construction foremen who intentionally damaged dikes before flood season so that job opportunities and gains would flow their way with the inevitable deluge. Contemporary works, such as Li Boyuan's 李伯元 (1867–1906) novel *Present-Day China* (*Zhongguo xianzaiji* 中國現在記), shed light on the corruption and malicious practices within river works.[14] Liu E's first-hand knowledge of the underbelly of river works provides the context in which King Yama's analogy illustrates the potential harm that revolutionists can cause.

King Yama's implicit comment on the revolutionists reveals Liu E's understanding of the relationship between the individual and the state, grounded in his experience with river management. Firstly, the analogy reminds readers that human action, not just heaven, plays a critical role in natural disasters—the conventional wisdom that there is no truly "natural" disaster. Yet the analogy also shows how, when such human-made environmental catastrophes become an empire's Achilles' heel, one destructive individual can be responsible for the fate of the entire empire. In King Yama's analogy, "hundreds of thousands" of human lives being lost due to the actions of a single person is possible only with the scale of Yellow River flooding. This reference to the Yellow River allows Liu E to convey the concept of one

---

14. In his novel, Li Boyuan (1998, 76) exposes the corruption in river work: "There is a kind of person who works as a construction foreman and worries that he would have no income if all is well with the river. Therefore, he gathers a few folks to make some holes in the dike. The holes get bigger and bigger when water floods in, and it bursts the dike in less than a day. Now that the dikes have burst and require repair, these people have money to earn again" 還有一種做夫頭的，愁著河工平安，他沒處弄錢混飯吃，便約幾個人，把大堤上挖幾個洞，等到水勢盛漲的時候，這個洞口愈刷愈大，不到一日，就潰堤而出了。等到水沖開了大堤，又要修築，這些人也有處賺錢混飯了。

impacting hundreds of thousands in the relationship between the individual and the state. In this sense, King Yama's analogy does not merely emphasize the environment as the nexus between an individual and the state. It also analogizes the maintenance of a state and the maintenance of a river, implying that the individual is responsible for the health of both. Liu E establishes his understanding of the individual-state relation based on his hydraulic engineer's perspective on the healthy maintenance of fluid systems.

The pairing of the allegories of river regulation and the revolutionists' accusation of treason is not incidental. They were the two main concerns in Liu E's life when he wrote the novel. More importantly, their combination in chapter 1 demonstrates that the novelist understands the revolutionists as closely related to the destruction of flooding. Likewise, the approach for dealing with the revolutionists is likened to taming the floods. *The Travels* incorporates Liu E's professional concerns in responding to the revolutionists' charge of treason. Liu depicts the revolutionists as analogous to the floods and the subsequent epidemics that have devastated the nation. And he presents himself, a river engineer and physician, as responsible for quelling these threats. Liu E further identifies the revolutionists as triggering the floods, understanding the individual-state relation from a hydraulic perspective.

The Boxers: Control Lost and Regained

In addition to the revolutionists, *The Travels* addresses a second major national crisis: the Boxer Uprising. An officially supported peasant uprising in China between 1899 and 1901, the Boxer Uprising campaigned to expel all foreigners in northern China, especially in Shandong. Calling themselves the Righteous and Harmonious Fist (*Yihequan* 義和拳), the Boxers practiced spirit invocation and martial arts to "support the Qing and destroy the foreign" (*fu Qing mie yang* 扶清滅洋). The uprising invited the assembly of international forces that captured Beijing in 1900, resulting in the death of tens of thousands or more, including Chinese Christians, foreign missionaries, and soldiers, and leading the empress dowager to flee westward to Xi'an in Shanxi Province. The novel addresses the danger the Boxer Uprising posed thematically: as a loss of control. The theme of loss of control, as exemplified by the uprising, informs an additional dimension of *The Travels*'s exploration of the body-nation relationship. This dimension is present in the scenes depicting the uncontrollable nature of these events and the novel's proposed symbolic remedy for this issue, which can be found in chapters 5 to 7.

The Boxers' incapability to control their body manifests in a story involving one of their victims in chapter 5. Arriving in Caozhou prefecture, Lao Can learns from an inn servant that Prefect Yu Xian has given a local villain and Boxer leader known as Wang the Third free rein as the town's bully.[15] According to the servant, Wang the Boxer killed the innkeeper's brother-in-law for gossiping that Wang had engaged in Boxer spirit possession. Specifically, the innkeeper's brother-in-law claimed that Wang had called upon shrewd Great Monkey Sage to possess him but instead invoked lustful Pig of Eight Vows—a mistake that was an obvious sign of Wang's lustful intentions.[16] As a religious practice, possessive invocation dictates yielding control over one's body to the invoked spirit.[17] The uncertain outcome of possessive invocation described by the innkeeper's brother-in-law deepens this sense of loss of control. According to the gossip, Wang not only lacks control over his desires, like Pig of Eight Vows, but he cannot even control which deity he summons. The worst possible outcome is death by the very deity he attempts to invoke: "The Great Sage will lift up his Gold-Bound Staff and give him a blow that he won't survive" (Liu 1990, 61). The servant's story reveals the horrific and lethal outcome when such witchcraft backfires and the spirits gain control.

While the Boxer threat takes the form of a local bully in chapter 5, subsequent chapters and the novel overall identify it explicitly as a national disaster. In chapter 11, Yellow Dragon describes the Boxers—which the royalty and higher officials hope to instrumentalize and thus plan to fully support—as a fist from within that is utterly beyond control. He considers this uncontrollable fist as one that swings at the country and the country as a victim who nearly dies from the attack.[18] Yellow Dragon's characterization of the Boxers recalls the story of Wang the Third, the spirit-invoking Boxer leader in chapter 5. The "country-smashing blow," as Yellow

---

15. The prefect alludes to the historical figure Yu Xian 毓賢 (1842–1901). Known for his iron-fisted rule as Caozhou prefect in Shandong in 1889, Yu Xian played a crucial role in inciting the Boxer Uprising.
16. Great Monkey Sage and Pig of Eight Vows are legendary deities and the main characters in the sixteenth-century novel *Journey to the West*. The lethal gossip shows not so much the absurdity of Wang the Third's purported divine possession as the gossipers' own credulity concerning those claims. Not only do the gossipers readily buy into Wang's possession story, but they also judge Wang's moral character based on that belief, rendering them prey to Wang's tyranny.
17. After the Boxers swallowed Taoist talismans (*fu* 符), recited incantations, and were possessed by a spirit, they displayed eccentric behaviors. For example, they "danced with their eyes closed as if deranged . . . lay stiffly supine and, after some while, abruptly rose to their feet like lunatics, dancing and panting heavily" (Liu 2008, 24).
18. Although the Boxers claimed to "support the Qing and destroy the foreign," Liu E held a different and more complicated view of them. In commenting on the Boxers and the revolution, Yellow Dragon states that the court in the north supports the Boxers to suppress the Han ethnic group, while the politicians in the south support the revolution to expel the Manchus. Liu E understands the Boxers and the revolution in terms of internal ethnic conflicts, which should be considered against the historical context of racial politics in the Qing court and provincial regions. Although the Boxers consisted entirely of Han peasants, the uprising was widespread in the northern provinces; the governors there were mostly conservative Manchu officials, who were much friendlier to the Boxers than their Han counterparts in the south. This explains why Liu E understands the court and northern provinces as lending support to the uprising to suppress the Han officials from the south.

Dragon describes the Boxers, paraphrases "a blow that he won't survive," the fatal strike by the Great Sage's Gold-Bound Staff that Wang risks with his unruly spirit invocation. Yellow Dragon's comments imply that just as the Boxer leader was possessed and lost control, China has been possessed by the Boxers and has in turn relinquished control to the intractable deities. Yellow Dragon considers this loss of control, potentially leading to self-destruction, China's greatest menace—second only to revolution.

Although the Boxers' introduction in chapter 5 unleashes a threat to local public security, the novel soon presents a symbolic antidote to the national menace brought by the Boxers. This occurs in chapter 7 when Lao Can suggests to county magistrate Shen Dongzao that he invite Liu Renfu, a much-revered martial arts master, to tackle the bandits plaguing the county. Lao Can asserts he would provide an alternative to the draconian methods of Shen's supervisor Yu Xian. Aside from suppressing crime, we soon discover Liu Renfu has a larger significance for the theme of countering national threats. Read from the perspective of the body-nation relationship, Lao Can's proposal represents both an alternative to Yu Xian's callous governance and a contrast to the magistrate's loss of control over the Boxers and their bodies, as had happened under Yu Xian. The Boxers represent a collective loss of control over the body, an unrestrained fist that will "go near to smashing the country" (Liu 1990, 123), which threatens to spread rampantly with the Boxers' proliferation. Liu Renfu sharply contrasts this runaway expansion; he is the epitome of control. He received secret martial skills from an old monk, and he upholds the same discretion in passing down the legacy. He represents a much more reserved and prudent actor that helps to quell the uncontrollable forces bringing disaster to China.

Liu E presents Liu Renfu's countering of the unbridled Boxers as a cure for China's illness, using medical language. The author makes Liu Renfu's role as symbolic medicine clear when magistrate Shen thanks Lao Can for proposing to invite the martial arts master: "To hear you talk about these things is like waking from a dream, or recovering from sickness" (Liu 1990, 76). Shen's comment echoes the theme of rousing a sleepy patient—the Chinese nation—in the novel's beginning. A similar conceptualization of Liu Renfu appears in the closing commentaries of chapter 7. Invoking an allegory from *Zhuangzi*, Liu E, as a commentator, compares Liu Renfu's martial art to a protective salve used by soldiers defending a country.[19] This allegory accentuates the value of Liu Renfu's martial art, a reserved and prudent

---

19. The allegory appears in "Free and Easy Wandering" ("Xiaoyao you" 逍遙遊) in *Zhuangzi*. The allegory tells how a traveler bought the salve's recipe from a silk bleacher for a hundred measures of gold. The traveler introduced the salve to the king, who needed it in naval battles. In return, the king rewarded the traveler with a portion of the conquered territories as a fief. "The salve had the power to prevent chapped hands in either case," Zhuangzi concludes, "but one man used it to get a fief, while the other one never got beyond silk bleaching—because they used it in different ways." See Zhuangzi 2013, 5–6.

use of the body, which Liu E believes will benefit the state in countering Western hegemony. Liu Renfu is thus both a symbolic alternative and solution to the Boxers, whose ungovernable attempts to "support the Qing and destroy the foreign" led to devastation. The plan Lao Can puts forward to Shen Dongzao is a remedy, not just for the local disorder but also for the Boxer Uprising—the nation's malady, according to Yellow Dragon.

The novel's criticism of the Boxers (and revolutionists) constitutes Liu E's exploration of the relationship between the individual and the state. Like the revolutionists, the Boxers in the novel are diagnosed as China's illness, and their loss of control is the symptom of that illness. From chapters 5 to 7, the novel narrates a progression from loss of control (by an individual Boxer over his own body) to the symbolic regaining of control (by Liu Renfu over the Boxers' corporate body). Throughout, Liu Renfu, a faint presence that exists almost only in Lao Can's recounting, nevertheless holds paramount significance as the remedy for the country's weakness and vulnerability.

Unrestrained Flows: Storytelling and the Yellow River

Liu E also incorporated the loss-of-control theme into the novel's storytelling form. Such narrative unruliness is visible in chapters 12 to 16, which involve Lao Can's friend Huang Renrui telling a story about a flooding event on the Yellow River and a murder trial. Lao Can encounters Huang in a telling location: while waiting to cross the frozen Yellow River. Huang narrates the events in a flowing and loose manner, following his whims. Although seemingly haphazard, this storytelling style is not a defect in narrative. Rather, it is the manifestation of the ongoing theme of loss of control.

Huang Renrui is narratively important. He claims the role of an omniscient narrator in his conversation with Lao Can and is crucial to advancing the storyline. Huang first describes a flood two years earlier on the Yellow River in Shandong, caused by the provincial governor's misguided river control policies. Huang claims he only arrived in the province a year after the flooding and therefore does not know for certain the policymaking that led to the disaster. Nonetheless, he provides a vivid and detailed report of policymakers' dialogues, as though he were one of them. After relating the flooding event, Huang recounts a murder trial, including the interior monologues of trial participants—elements that would exist only in omniscient narration. Further, his recounting of the murder trial inspires Lao Can to intervene and investigate the case at the end of the novel. Accordingly, we can safely say Huang Renrui drives the plot and is arguably the most crucial character in the latter half of the novel's narrative.

Crucially, Huang Renrui is a clear reference to the Yellow River. This symbolic meaning derives first from his official position. He is an officer charged with procuring construction materials for Shandong river works. Even more noteworthy is his name. His courtesy name Renrui differs from the name of Lao Can's skin ulcer patient—Huang Ruihe—by only one character. Beyond this, he has the given name Yingtu 應圖, which alludes to the legendary King Wen of the Zhou dynasty (1152–1056 BCE). King Wen was believed to have been bequeathed from heaven the Yellow River Chart (*hetu* 河圖), the auspicious diagram illustrating the mandate of heaven, to which the king's virtue corresponded (*yin* 應).[20] The Yellow River, after debuting in chapter 1, again enters the spotlight under another alias.

The novel's portrait of Huang Renrui echoes his symbolic identity as the flooding Yellow River. Liu E describes him first as a heavy opium smoker. In chapter 12, he invites Lao Can to smoke opium with him, contending that smoking with restraint is an excellent time-passing pleasure that will do no harm to his livelihood. In response, Lao Can makes his anxiety about smokers' inability to control their opium use clear. However, Huang Renrui's invitation and Lao Can's refusal concern more than opium smoking itself. In the late Qing, Yellow River flooding and opium smoking drained the state treasury more than any other issue. Contemporary intellectuals used the image of a leaky wine vessel (*louzhi* 漏卮) to describe both opium smoking and river work on the Yellow River,[21] which they considered identical in terms of their disastrous economic consequences. Huang Renrui, therefore, embodies the coupling of opium addiction and dike failure. And through that character, the novel addresses issues of control related to both opium and water.

Huang Renrui's storytelling is characterized by poor control, flowing forth inconsistently and paradoxically. He first mentions "a most amazing law case involving a great many lives" (Liu 1990, 140) and insists he must consult with Lao Can about the case before dawn. While Huang Renrui claims that the case is urgent, his constant need for opium continually interferes with his storytelling and denies its purported urgency. Huang asks Lao Can to wait until he takes his two puffs of opium, which will raise his spirits so he can tell the story. However, after his two puffs, Huang instead chats with the courtesans in their company about the Yellow River flood that led to innumerable deaths. The recounting of the urgent and "amazing" case, which Huang Renrui was so eager to share with Lao Can, is thus further delayed, to be finally told two entire chapters later.

The delayed narration of the murder case is not the result of the story's loose organization. Contrarily, this arrangement conforms to the internal narrative logic.

---

20. For further discussion of the Yellow River Chart, see Cammann 1960, 116–24; 1962, 14–53; Zhao 1988, 755; Zhou 1997, 50; Ho 2003; 2005, 45–60. See also the discussion in Chapter 5.
21. The comparison between opium smoking and management of the Yellow River dates to the early 1840s. Wei Yuan 魏源 (1794–1857), one of the most influential late Qing thinkers and a pioneer of the reform movement, stated that "the foreign drug is a major leaking vessel to the people's wealth, as is river work to the imperial treasury" 是夷煙者，民財之大漏卮，而河工者，國帑之大漏卮也 (1976, 367).

Storytelling is the process by which a story flows from a narrator to listeners. That Huang Renrui needs opium to start recounting his story suggests opium smoking drives his storytelling.[22] Since opium smoking has a reputation as a "leaky wine vessel," as does the endless costly work on the Yellow River, Huang Renrui's storytelling is driven, in an analogous sense, by the flooding of the Yellow River—that is, of Huang Renrui himself. That Huang recounts in detail a flood event on the Yellow River from two years prior before finally recounting the supposedly urgent murder case is therefore no casual narrative arrangement. Rather, Huang as a storyteller draws the drive and content of his narrative from himself, the Yellow River. As the metaphorical persona of the river, he prioritizes a story in which he is the subject. On a narrative level, then, Huang Renrui's delay in recounting the murder case is a pertinent choice.

The image of Huang Renrui as a heavy opium smoker underlines a conflict in the novel's narrative. Lao Can is the listener of Huang's storytelling. Yet listening to Huang Renrui's story means Lao Can, who opposes opium, must endure opium smoking—a symbolic flooding of the Yellow River. These two uncontrolled flows present an unbearable situation for Lao Can, who is an expert in river regulation. This narrative conflict finally resolves when Lao Can compromises. In chapter 16, as Huang Renrui nears the end of the murder trial story, Lao Can waits eagerly to learn the trial's outcome. But Huang Renrui deliberately leaves Lao Can in suspense, saying, "The more impatient you become, the less impatient I am! I want to have a couple of pulls at my pipe!" (Liu 1990, 173). Ultimately, Lao Can relinquishes his earlier objections. He urges a courtesan, "Quickly roast two pipefuls so that he can talk" (173). Instead of asking Huang to abstain from opium, Lao Can prods the storyteller to hasten his smoking to speed up the storytelling. Satiated with opium, Huang Renrui finally finishes recounting the case he promised to tell four chapters earlier. Lao Can's initial vigilance against opium and unwavering commitment to bodily control eventually gives way to narrative demands.

Throughout the novel, the Yellow River serves as the hidden context of Liu E's discourse on the relationship between an individual's body and the nation-state. Yet in the novel's latter half, the river assumes key narrative functions. It becomes the omniscient narrator. Frequently characterized as the cause for one of China's leaky vessels, the Yellow River, appearing in the guise of Huang Renrui, smokes yet another leaky vessel, opium, telling the story of its own illness. By portraying Huang Renrui as an opium addict, Liu E creates a character that symbolizes the loss of bodily (and riverine) control. Huang's loose storytelling in turn enhances this sense of runaway flow, which Lao Can attempts to correct. This attempt, ironically, is successful only

---

22. The novel's description of Huang Renrui's opium smoking provides a unique perspective of investigating the relationship between opium smoking and modern Chinese fiction. On opium smoking and Chinese modernity, see McMahon 2002.

when Lao Can allows the narrator to satiate his addiction. Huang Renrui's storytelling thus shows the novel derives its narrative drive from the tension between flooding and the (unsuccessful) attempt to regulate it.

Quickening the Sleepers and Taming the Flood

After presenting the problems related to the loss of control through Huang Renrui's storytelling in chapters 12 to 16, the novel provides a symbolic treatment for this symptom in its final three chapters (18 to 20). This treatment takes the form of Lao Can investigating a murder case—the case Huang Renrui finally finishes recounting to Lao Can in chapter 16 after satiating himself with more opium. The narration of the murder investigation, which happens at the end of the novel, is an allegory that illustrates the novel's central concern: the relationship between an individual's body and the nation-state.

The murder case involves Mrs. Jia and her father, Old Wei, residents of Qinghe County in Shandong Province, who were wrongly accused of poisoning and killing thirteen members of the Jia family and whom the willful judge Gang Bi tortured to extract confessions. To save them, Lao Can requests the Shandong governor assign the sagacious judge Bai Zishou to hear the trial instead of Gang Bi. While Judge Bai vindicates Mrs. Jia and her father, key questions about the case remain unanswered. The poisoner's identity is still unknown. Also unknown is the poison used, which caused highly uncommon effects: the poisoned individuals looked deathly pale, were breathless, and had no heartbeat, but their bodies did not stiffen, and all their joints stayed soft. Requested by Judge Bai to assume the role of "Holmes," the legendary fictional detective from the West, Lao Can begins an independent investigation to identify the murderer and the mysterious poison. Lao Can first enlists the help of a Roman Catholic priest with deep knowledge of Western medicine and chemistry, but the priest's Western knowledge fails to help the investigation. Lao Can then tries to continue his investigation using his knowledge as a medical practitioner to gather pertinent information. He rings the stringed bells to announce his service on the street where Mrs. Jia and her father live. Fortunately, Old Wei invites him into the house to provide medical treatment to Mrs. Jia, who suffers from injuries sustained under torture. Lao Can capitalizes on this chance to learn key details about the case from Mrs. Jia and Old Wei and subsequently brings the true criminal—the rogue lover of Mrs. Jia's sister-in-law—to justice. When questioned, the culprit also divulges an important truth about the case: the thirteen victims from the Jia family are still alive. They have simply fallen into a coma after being forced to drink a potion made from an herb known as "thousand days' sleep" (*qianri zui* 千日醉), which grows on Mount Tai (泰山). Only a small amount of the herb will send a person to sleep for a thousand days. The antidote to this soporific is "quickening incense" (*fanhun xiang* 返魂香), obtainable only from a hermit known as Green

Dragon. Lao Can sets out to find the antidote, and he is eventually able to awaken all thirteen members of the Jia family from their long sleep.

The novel's narration of Lao Can's investigation is an experiment in modes of storytelling. It begins as a Sherlock Holmes whodunit, and true to his inspiration, certain Holmesian hallmarks emerge at the outset. Holmes is known for calling upon his rich knowledge of medicine and chemistry in his investigations, and Lao Can similarly enlists the help of a priest with the same knowledge. Yet that is where similarities with a detective story end. Specifically, the investigation violates a key expectation of early twentieth-century detective stories: there is no unveiling of the criminal at the end. The reader knows the poisoner's identity from the outset.[23] Instead, Lao Can's investigation better fits the category of traditional Chinese court-case story in which a wise judge finds a way to prove a suspect's guilt. This generic heritage is most obvious in the episode where Lao Can, after failing to find clues using medicine and chemistry, turns without hesitation to gather key information using the opportunity to provide medical treatment to Mrs. Jia. This episode echoes the story of Gongsun Ce 公孫策, private adviser to the legendary Judge Bao in *The Three Heroes and Five Gallants* (*Sanxia wuyi* 三俠五義, 1879), the classic chivalry court-case novel (*xiayi-gong'an xiaoshuo* 俠義公案小說) in which Gongsun investigates a murder in the guise of an itinerant doctor who rings a stringed bell. Liu E presents Lao Can's investigation—which returns to the court-case tradition after failing as a Holmesian detective story—first through a Western storytelling mode, only to discard it for a Chinese one.

Initially, Lao Can's investigation resembles that of judicial adviser Gongsun Ce in *The Three Heroes and Five Gallants*. In that novel, Gongsun's bell ringing and the doctor's call, according to Paize Keulemans (2014, 141), extend imperial power and the universal morality he stands for into private spaces normally beyond official reach, thereby reestablishing imperial moral order. As the temporary deputy of Judge Bai Zishou, Lao Can likewise performs this infiltration of official power by ringing bells, which gains him an invitation into residences to ply his medical trade. Both the stories of Gongsun Ce and of Lao Can depict the patient's symptoms as the key to solving the murder case, and both characters' diagnoses help restore imperial moral order. In both investigations, moral order is intimately related to the order in the human body.

---

23. Readers do not need Lao Can's sleuthing to ascertain that Mrs. Jia is innocent. Her innocence is verified through the sympathetic voices of the narrator and other characters long before she is finally proven innocent. For example, Huang Renrui describes Mrs. Jia's reaction as she comes home to find the entire family dead, thus: "Without really knowing what it was all about, she gave herself up to bitter weeping and wailing" (Liu 1990, 164). In addition, when the Qihe County magistrate hears Huang Renrui prod Lao Can to help in the case, he exclaims with joy, "Mrs. Jia's deliverer has come. Marvelous! Splendid!" (Liu 1990, 167). The novel further tells readers through Judge Bai's judgment that it is Mrs. Jia's sister-in-law who fabricated charges against her. Attentive readers would even infer that the sister-in-law's rogue lover must also have been involved in the setup.

While drawing upon *The Three Heroes and Five Gallants,* Lao Can's investigation presents a different way of understanding the relationship between the body and the state from its predecessor. Gongsun Ce's need to gain recognition as a private adviser and prove his value to the state drive the investigation: he uses his knowledge to read information from his patient's body and convert it into intelligence that will help the state uphold the moral order. In Lao Can's investigation, however, the patient's body reveals injuries resulting from the abuse of official power. By treating those injuries, Lao Can exposes and symbolically heals the bureaucratic state's illness. Emphasizing the damage inflicted by bureaucrats (the representatives of the state) upon the body of citizens (the extensions of the state), Lao Can's investigation presents the state as a patient suffering from an autoimmune disease.

As the last medical case in the novel, Lao Can's treatment of Mrs. Jia, like that of Huang Ruihe, the patient of his first medical case, is allegorical. It reveals how Liu E envisages the relationship between medicine, the state, and river management. This allegory rests on a medical term Lao Can uses in Mrs. Jia's diagnosis. The physician takes Mrs. Jia's pulse and discovers that she suffers from blood stasis, or *tingyu* 停瘀, which in Chinese medicine refers to blood that has stopped flowing or has stagnated in the vein. Liu E plays again with the shared terminology between hydraulics and medicine. The character *yu* 瘀 (blood stasis in blood vessels) shares the same phonetic compound *yu* 於 with the character *yu* 淤 (siltation in river channels), a term describing inadequate river transport capacity leading to sediment buildup and eventually flooding. In his official report on river survey and mapping, Liu E himself used the term *tingyu* 停淤 to refer to siltation, which he viewed as the most vital issue in Yellow River management (2007, 1:40). By assigning its symptomatic equivalent to Mrs. Jia, Liu E conceptualizes the state's bureaucratic illness—evidenced by Mrs. Jia's physical illness—from a hydraulic perspective. In doing so, he binds medicine, the state, and river management just as in the Huang Ruihe allegory.

Liu E further develops the theme of treating the illness of the body and the state in the episode where Lao Can awakens and cures the seemingly dead members of the Jia family. Lao Can burns the quickening incense, which can awaken those who have fallen into a coma caused by the herb "thousand days' sleep." Scholars often read this story allegorically.[24] Such readings see this episode as echoing Liu E's commentary to chapter 1 in which he considers the Chinese as dormant patients waiting to be woken, then treated. The awakening episode represents, in this view, a full-circle return. Liu E might also intend this allegory to suggest the cause of China's illness comes not from without but from within the country (Wei 2020, 78), since the soporific drug is a local product, not a Western one, as Lao Can at first presumes. However, attributing the national illness to internal factors is more than a gesture of self-analysis—it proclaims the insufficiency of Western medical knowledge to

---

24. For an allegorical reading of this story, see D. Wang 2000 and Wei 2020.

cure China. As suggested by the failure of the priest versed in Western medicine and chemistry to diagnose the victims' symptoms, Liu E believes that his nation's illness is beyond the understanding and capacity of Western knowledge to solve. The diagnosis and remedy are discoverable, as the quickening incense allegory makes clear, only in Chinese intellectual traditions.

What, then, is the traditional knowledge that remedies China's illness, according to the allegory of quickening incense? It could be the Taigu school of which Liu E was a lifelong follower.[25] However, evidence suggests the remedy lies also in the regulation of the Yellow River. David Der-wei Wang (1997, 154–55) juxtaposes Lao Can's quest for quickening incense with his treatment of Huang Ruihe in chapter 1, pointing out that the novel both opens and concludes with a medical allegory. What lies beneath the two medical allegories is their common connection to the Yellow River. The relationship between Lao Can's quest for quickening incense and the Yellow River is suggested by the names of the places he encounters on his journey to find Green Dragon and obtain the quickening incense. Lao Can learns that Green Dragon lives in Black Pearl Grotto of Inner Mountain (Li shan 裏山). "Li shan" is likely derived from "Limao shan" 狸貓山 (Mount Civet), which is located southeast of Ji'nan, the seat of Shandong Province (Liu 2013, 360). One of Limao shan's peaks, Mount of Yu's Ascent (Yudeng shan 禹登山), is allegedly the mountain that Da Yu ascended to inspect the floods and arouse a dormant dragon to help tame the rivers.[26] Mount of Yu's Ascent, also known as Dragon Cave Mountain (Longdong shan 龍洞山), is home to Dragon Cave and Hanging Pearl (Xuanzhu 懸珠) Spring. The latter is a homophone of "black pearl" (*xuanzhu* 玄珠), as in Black Pearl Grotto (Liu 2013, 360), where the hermit Green Dragon resides in the novel. The residence of Green Dragon thus alludes to the Da Yu legend through a cluster of highly related place names. Further, the visit of river management expert Lao Can to Green Dragon in Black Pearl Grotto alludes to the legendary river tamer's rousing of the dormant cave-dwelling dragon. The story of Lao Can's quest for quickening incense, therefore, revives the legend of the first river regulation in Chinese history.

---

25. Yan Wei (2020, 78–79) argues that the quickening incense that awakens the Chinese represents the thought of the Taigu school—the syncretic religious organization of which Liu E was a lifelong follower. Some evidence supports this. The image of Green Dragon, who provides the quickening incense, is typical of Taigu followers. And undeniably, Taigu thought helped motivate Liu E's passion for national salvation. For studies on the Taigu school in connection with Liu E, see Yan 1985; Wang X. 1992, 1993a, 2000. More general studies on the Taigu school can be found in Wang 2003; Han 2017; Zhou 2010, 2014. See also chapters 2 and 5 for a discussion of Taigu thought and its political significance.
26. In the record by Li Yuanying 李元膺 (active 1100), a Northern Song official, Dragon Cave Mountain is described as follows: "Legend has it that Yu the Great once ascended this mountain and aroused the dormant dragon to tame the rivers. Hence it is called the Mount of Yu's Ascent to date." See Ye and Ye 1640, 27b–28a.

In the first volume's final chapters, Lao Can, as a practitioner of Chinese traditional medicine and expert in river regulation, takes over martial arts master Liu Renfu's efforts to heal China's malady (the Boxers) and conducts another symbolic treatment. In his investigation of the Jia murder case, Lao Can diagnoses and treats China's bureaucratic illness. By rewriting a classic scene from a traditional court-case novel, Liu E connects medicine, governance, and river work to explore the relationship between the individual's body and the nation-state. Further, he renders the quest for the antidote to the nation's illness, in an allegory, as a recapitulation of Da Yu's journey to subdue an epic flood. Ultimately, strategies for treating the sick nation rely on those the ancient sage king used to control a legendary flood. Liu E's own river management work is the inextricable undercurrent beneath these allegories and his search for a means to save the nation.

Diagnosing a Leaky Nation

Informed by Liu E's professional expertise, *The Travels of Lau Can* addresses the relationship between the individual and the state from two perspectives: traditional medicine and hydraulics. Liu E diagnoses China as suffering from a loss of control over the body and, by analogy, over water. Stemming from various uncontrolled flows, the nation's illness takes the forms of revolution, the Boxer Uprising, and the abuse of governmental power. To heal these illnesses, the novel provides symbolic remedies that enable the regaining of lost control. The tension in this analogy between restrained and unrestrained flows drives almost every aspect of the novel: its plot, narration, characters, and even linguistic choices and nomenclature.

The intertwining of hydraulics and traditional medicine enables Liu E to uniquely explore the body-nation analogy embedded in late Qing political discourse on the nation-state. The treatment narrative's emphasis on the body's link with the natural environment—specifically, the Yellow River—is nonexistent in an understanding of the individual-state relationship based on Western physiology, as typified by Liang Qichao. This emphasis on the human-nature relationship sets Liu E apart from many other late Qing novelists, who conceived of the individual's relationship to the state according to a body-nation analogy based on this Western idea of the physiology of the state.[27] Despite this radical difference—and even Liu E's repeated expressions throughout the novel of the inadequacy of Western medicine and, by implication, the Western conception of the state's physiology—scholars of Western biological nationalism still categorize Liu E's work alongside that of Liang Qichao, thereby deploying an incomplete, or at worst incorrect, critical lens through which to understand Liu E's nation building.

---

27. For a discussion of the conceptualization of the body-nation relationship in late Qing novels, see Guan 2014, 209–44.

As the central theme in Liu E's exploration of the individual-state relationship, the connection between failure in state affairs and the loss of control over body water is fully developed in the novel's first volume. Furthermore, this connection manifests in an unpublished fragment of the novel.[28] The fragment features a conversation regarding a high-ranked police officer who was caught urinating in the street but escaped punishment. Public urination indicates not only incivility but also, more profoundly, inadequate control over the body and its flows. In both colloquial Mandarin and the tradition of Chinese fiction, urination has long been glossed with the metaphor of flood discharge. One of Lao Can's friends argues that while the discipline of the police force is an indicator of national promise, the officer who "took a leak" in public without being punished bodes a bleak future for the nation. Whether in the first volume of *The Travels* or the idle unpublished manuscript from 1907, Liu consistently builds his imagination of the nation upon the control of floods.

By creating a novel conceptual framework dependent on a complexly analogical and intertwined relationship between the river, the body, and the state, Liu E can subsequently leverage that framework to express his ideas for healing the sick nation-state of China. Liu E establishes this purpose early in chapter 1 through the treatment of Huang Ruihe's skin disease, which becomes an allegory for the regulation of the Yellow River and, by extension, for the government of China, given the long historical association between the river and the state. This complex framework works only through an appreciation of ancient Chinese hydraulic and medical literature, such as the "Tribute of Yu" and the *Inner Cannon of the Yellow Emperor*, and an understanding of the shared semantics between the disciplines. In the broadest sense, Liu E understands China as suffering from dampness syndrome and requiring a treatment drawn from the tradition of hydraulics: flood control. This framework develops throughout the novel as Liu E introduces characters and events that correspond to those he deemed responsible for China's disease, such as the revolutionists, Boxers, and abuse of government power. Specifically, as we will now explore, Liu E uses the Yellow River floods and his innovations in hydraulic engineering as conceptual resources to challenge the Qing government's defensive and rigid bureaucracy, explore ideas of corruption and incorruptibility, and present solutions for public security.

---

28. The unpublished fragmented manuscript is only fifteen pages in length. Liu E dismissed this work as unsuccessful soon after he started it in late 1906 or early 1907. See Liu and Liu 2019, 655–56.

2
Governance, Hydraulics, and the Vice of the Incorruptible

> It is known to everyone that corrupt officials are detestable. Much less known is that incorruptible officials are particularly detestable. Corrupt officials know of their own misconduct and thus would not dare to blatantly do wrong. Incorruptible officials, however, think they can do whatever they want as long as they don't take bribes, and therefore they act entirely according to their own will. This could result in people getting killed or a whole nation being put in peril.... Novels in the past have exposed the vice of corrupt officials, whereas *The Travels of Lao Can* is the first to expose the vice of incorruptible ones.
>
> —Liu E, *The Travels*, commentary to chapter 16

Core to Liu E's literary nation-building in *The Travels* is an exploration of corruption and incorruption within the Qing government. Since the Song (960–1279) dynasty, the term *qingguan*, or incorruptible official, described local officials invulnerable to corruption who enforced the law justly and impartially. Both rulers and authors of traditional court-case novels praised these officials as model local bureaucrats. And the novels mainly modeled their incorruptible officials after historical figures such as Bao Zheng 包拯 (999–1062), Hai Rui 海瑞 (1514–1587), and Shi Shilun 施世綸 (1659–1722)—all local officials reputed for their incorruptibility. Such depictions did not just become the center of everyday political discussion among commoners. They also shaped the evaluative criteria by which elite scholar-officials assessed political figures and informed their conception of political ideals.

In a departure from traditional court-case novels, *The Travels* offers a critical portrayal of incorruptible officials, highlighting their conservative nature that hinders progress. Liu E's novel bases its depiction of incorruptible officials on historical figures. Yet crucially, it rejects the idealization of incorruption present in traditional examples of the genre. The novel excoriates these typically lauded officials, describing them as iron-fisted, bull-headed conservative bureaucrats. Yu Xian 玉賢 and Gang Bi 剛弼, the two local incorruptible officials in the novel, are roman-à-clef versions of Yu Xian 毓賢 (1842–1901) and Gang Yi 剛毅 (1837–1900), two conservative late Qing officials infamous for their support of the Boxer Uprising.[1] They appear in the novel as the embodiment of the rigid, conservative form of statecraft that impeded the kind of innovation Liu E believed was necessary.

The Travels's criticism of incorruptible officials has unique aspects, but it also follows a critical tradition of political discourse dating to the Ming dynasty. For example, in his criticism of Song politician Wang Anshi 王安石 (1021–1086), late-Ming thinker Li Zhi 李贄 (1527–1602) wrote, "the harm done by a corrupt official affects the common people [only temporarily], but the harm done by an incorruptible official can last for generations" 貪官之害但及於百姓，清官之害並及於兒孫 (1975, 217). As Li Zhi argues, incorruptible officials consider themselves to be men of honor superior to all others. Believing themselves to be infallible, they become intolerant. Their reputation for incorruptibility also made wielding public opinion against them difficult (217). Similar criticism even came directly from the emperors. For example, Emperor Kangxi 康熙 (r. 1662–1722) indicated that an ideal official is at once incorruptible and sympathetic, contrasting one who is only incorruptible and often unbearably harsh to subordinates (Ma et al. 1985, 381, 568, 576). The bureaucracy itself also offered penetrating observations on these figures. Wang Huizu 汪輝祖 (1730–1807), a famous private adviser during the Qianlong 乾隆 reign (1735–1796), explains why incorruptible officials are undesirable and easily subject to public criticism: they are as morally harsh to others as themselves (1939, 8). These criticisms share one common argument: a truly incorruptible official should be simultaneously incorruptible and lenient—upright and magnanimous rather than willful and harsh toward others. As this chapter will explore, Liu E advocates for the same duality among local governors and centers his criticism on those who fall short of this ideal.

While Liu's novel engages with this long-standing critical tradition to address the general vice of incorruptible officials, it also responds to specific governance issues in Liu E's own time. Large-scale floods had afflicted the northern part of the empire from the 1850s onward; especially destructive was the 1855 dike failure on the Yellow River, which caused the significant course shift that created disastrous economic consequences for a once-fertile region (see Introduction). These disasters exacerbated the deterioration of public security resulting from the rapid population

---

1. Yu Xian, installed as the magistrate of Caozhou prefecture in Shandong Province and then serving as governor of Shanxi Province, was known for his cruelty, rigidness, and radical jingoism during the Boxer Rebellion. Gang Yi, who served as Shanxi governor and as a military secretary, was also famous for supporting the Boxer Rebellion and gained the favor and trust of Empress Dowager Cixi 慈禧 (1835–1908). Although the incorruptible officials are based on historical figures, the novel can hardly be read as a faithful record of these two people. Yu Xian did enjoy a repute of incorruptibility, but Gang Yi, to whom the incorruptible Gang Bi alludes, was infamous for his greed and avarice even in his living days (Cai 1978, 462; Institute of Modern History of the Chinese Academy of Social Sciences 1982, 156; Xiaohengxiangshi zhuren 1971, 479).

increase beginning in the mid-eighteenth century. Western Shandong Province, where the novel's stories of the incorruptible officials are set, was subject to the most devastating flooding catastrophes and social order deterioration in the latter half of the nineteenth century. It was under such circumstances that the imperial administration came to rely on disciplinary measures to maintain local order—incorruptible officials who were familiar with laws, free of corruption, and willing to optimize efficiency at all costs. The novel's criticism of incorruptible officials, in this sense, is directed at the attempt to solve the local public security problems caused by the long-term flooding of the Yellow River.

However, by referring to the two notorious conservative officials with national influence as incorruptible officials, *The Travels* also considers late Qing politics in a much broader context than might be expected in a story about local officialdom. While literary scholars often focus on incorruptible officials as the problems of local bureaucratic governance themselves, it is crucial to understand that these officials are not the issue per se, but rather represent a problematic effort by the central government to address broader local sociopolitical problems. Incorruptible officials symbolize the central government's effort to restore social order and establish a moral model amid sociopolitical turmoil, which ultimately aimed to maintain imperial rule (Chen 2010, 321–27). In this sense, the novel's criticism of incorruptible officials, although seemingly centered exclusively on poor local governance, also targets the national malady stemming from the central government's flawed approach.

For Liu E, China was brought into crisis at local and national levels because of the very same rigid and stringent way of governance. As Liu E (1990, 70) himself comments on the character of Yu Xian, "If he controls a prefecture, then a prefecture suffers; if he governs a province, then a province is maimed; if he rules the empire, then the empire dies!" 守一府則一府傷，撫一省則一省殘，宰天下則天下死。As an alternative to what he viewed as a dysfunctional mode of governance, Liu E promoted a more flexible one, informed primarily by his professional knowledge in hydraulic engineering. This alternative mode proposed a blurring between the government and civilian/private affairs, which Liu E presents as a remedy for local public security problems as portrayed in the novel and the national crisis that he had tried to help resolve, even at the cost of his reputation and life. The impact of the Yellow River floods and Liu E's river control techniques deeply shaped the novel and its criticism of local bureaucratic failure and Liu's lifelong engagement in national rejuvenation. Accordingly, *The Travels* shows how Liu E, a seasoned river engineer, understands China's crisis of governance and its appropriate remedy in a manner resembling his understanding of the Yellow River.

Hydraulics and the Making of the National Traitor

Like many of his late Qing intellectual peers, Liu E's most significant concern was securing the Chinese nation's survival, which Western powers were threatening, by boosting its industrial and commercial development. Among the many intellectual resources, Yan Fu's translations of Western works of social science, particularly T. H. Huxley's (1825–1895) *Evolution and Ethics* (1893) and Adam Smith's (1723–1790) *The Wealth of Nations* (1776), provided arguably the most powerful language for expressing concern for the demise of the state and the extinction of the "Chinese race."[2] Liu E believed that national wealth was the key to China's survival and that productive efficiency was the key to national wealth. In his diary entry dated March 8, 1905, where Liu E recorded that he had read *Evolution and Ethics*, he also recorded a visit to a paper factory run by a Japanese owner. Liu E (2007, 1:717) describes how he was impressed with the productivity of the factory machinery and took elaborate, remarkably precise notes on coal consumption, machine horsepower, daily paper output, paper price per package, and so forth. This diary entry illustrates the close association between Liu E's agenda of racial survival and his interest in industrial productivity. His way of engaging in national salvation projects, however, sparked a strong backlash and earned him infamy as a national traitor. The resulting political uproar is an important context for *The Travels*. Although the novel criticizes the failure and vice of local governance, it also represents Liu E's response to this unbearable personal and national scandal. Contrary to the common belief that this scandal stemmed from Liu E's political naivety, the true cause, as this section will demonstrate, lies in his effort to integrate hydraulic knowledge into political philosophy.

Although scholars often read the novel's criticism of incorruptible officials as targeted at local bureaucracy, the historical figures on whom the novel's two incorruptible officials are based were significant to Liu E for more reasons than being local. To remedy China's dire economic situation, Liu E had been engaged in various industrial businesses from the mid-1890s. Among his ventures were foreign-funded coal mining and railroad construction, which Liu E considered crucial for strengthening the country's ailing economy. The two major obstacles to the projects were Yu Xian and Gang Yi—these were the very officials alluded to by the novel's two incorruptible characters and were responsible for Liu E's infamy as a national traitor.[3] To implement the mining and railroad projects, Liu E raised funds from Peking Syndicate Limited, a British holding company, and took on the role of a comprador. This move infuriated local officials and the gentry, who accused him of collaboration. In 1897, Yu Xian pleaded with the government to shut down the Shanxi railroad and mine projects, ostensibly out of concern for national security and the negative

---

2. Huxley's *Evolution and Ethics* was introduced to China through Yan Fu's adapted translation titled *Tianyan lun* 天演論 (1897). For a discussion of Yan's adaptation, see Wang 2013; Lu 2020.
3. For research on Liu E's arrest for alleged treason, see Liu 2018a, 80–92; 2018b, 20–38.

impact on the local economy.⁴ In early 1898, amid mounting objections from local officials, the Qing government reprimanded Liu E and revoked his official title and right to participate in Shanxi mining (Liu and Liu 2019, 340). Again in 1900, Gang Yi accused Liu E of selling away the country and called for the government to severely punish him (Liu and Liu 2019, 337). Yu Xian and Gang Yi were among those Liu E hated most for their role in subverting his grand project of national salvation. The detailed portrayal of the incorruptible officials in *The Travels* is significant, as it underscores their negative role within the novel's narrative of national salvation.

Yu Xian's and Gang Yi's attacks on Liu E constituted an ideological battle. Within the late Qing political spectrum, Liu E belonged to the Westernizing faction, or the constitutional reformers (*weixin pai* 維新派), which was more liberal than the conservative faction to which Yu and Gang belonged but more conservative than the revolutionists. Supporters of diverse political ideologies attacked Liu's conception of the state. This included conservative officials like Yu and Gang, who strived to secure the absolute monarchy from challenges. He conveys his understanding of this diverse opposition in the sinking ship allegory that opens the novel. As discussed in Chapter 1, the allegory involves Lao Can, in a dream, attempting to help a storm-beaten passenger ship pull ashore with the aid of Western navigational instruments. Lower-ranking seamen fight this effort, accusing Lao Can of being a national traitor who has already sold the ship to the Westerners. This scene refers to the conservative bureaucrats' attack against Liu E's Westernizing position.

In addition, the allegory's structure reveals Liu E's understanding as a constitutional reformer of the relationship between citizens and the state. He analogizes China in crisis as a ship—that is, the property of a passenger ship company—while he likens citizens to passengers, who are also company shareholders, and the emperor to the captain. In other words, the relationship between citizens and the state is portrayed as that between shareholders and a ship company. According to this analogy, the relationship between the emperor and citizens is not one of coercion between ruler and ruled. Instead, it reflects the idea of contractarianism in which political authority is derived from the people's consent, and the state's purpose is to serve those who have entered into a social contract with the government. This perspective on governance is closely associated with constitutional reformers. A year after Liu E's death, the constitutional reformer and famous historian Xu Xusheng 徐旭生 (1890–1976) stated similarly that the state's legitimate authority derives from the idea of a contract, with the governor serving as a manager of a company and the people as shareholders entrusting their lives and property to the manager (Li

---

4. Yu Xian argued that Shanxi Province was a natural barrier (*tianxian* 天險) against the enemy from the western borderland. He insisted that building the railroad would eliminate this natural barrier, turning it instead into a smooth road for the enemy, besides depriving local workers who make their living providing traditional means of transport (Liu and Liu 2019, 338).

2019, 106). This view of the state and governance aligns with the thinking of Liu E. The allegory illustrates his recognition that the accusation of treason against him was the result of an ideological battle the conservative faction waged against the Westernizing faction and constitutional reformers.

While the structure of the sinking ship allegory suggests Liu E was a constitutional reformer, it also reveals his conceptualization of state governance from the perspective of commercial management. The passage implies the Chinese state is a tool (a ship) for making profits for the Chinese people (shareholders of the passenger ship company). Liu E understood state governance in terms of commercial logic—as a comprador for a British holding company, he proposed to weaponize international commerce to create mechanisms of force dynamics in international relations. In his fundraising proposal for coal mining and railroad construction projects in the latter half of the 1890s, Liu E suggested "drawing on commercial power to resist military power" 引商力以禦兵力 (Liu and Liu 2019, 325).[5] He maintained that opening to foreign powers and ushering in foreign capital would help the Chinese market prosper and prompt foreign countries to fend off other invading forces in defense of their interests. According to this model, China would open as a commercial arena where foreign players would claim their part until a balance of rivalry is achieved. Liu E raised funds to promote this model, whereby China profits from the rivalry and countervailing influences among Western powers. In his view, the secret to state governance when facing foreign threats is to operate like a company, which benefits the most when it receives the most bids.

Liu E also applied his strategy of countervailing forces to the management of foreign-funded construction projects. Instead of the government acting as the debtor and the agency in charge of implementing the projects, Liu E suggested adopting what resembles today's build-operate-transfer model. Under this model, foreign corporates would build and manage railroads and collieries; after a set period, China would take over all construction, management rights, and a portion of the earnings without liability for any deficit. Liu further insisted that, instead of the state, Chinese businessmen should commission the entire process from negotiation and contracting to overall supervision. According to his analysis, local Chinese businessmen would "see to financial details with fastidious care and are exceptionally shrewd about the stakes and interests involved; therefore, their business stratagems and maneuvers are bound to be ten times cleverer than anything the government could come up with" 朝夕審計，其利害奧竅知之較詳，故其操縱之術，必勝官家十

---

5. From the 1970s, newspapers often contained discussions of military and commercial powers, presented as antitheses. Newspaper articles in Shanghai and Hong Kong examined how foreign countries defended their interests in China with the strategy of "enhancing military power with commercial power; assisting commercial power with military power" 以商力裕兵力，以兵力佐商力. See *Shen Bao* 1876, 1885, 1887, 1888, 1891, 1892, 1904, 1908. Liu uses the same terminological pair but completely differently.

倍 (Liu and Liu 2019, 323–24). Local businessmen, Liu E argued, would compete against their foreign counterparts to protect their interests and thus counterbalance foreign forces. Involving foreign corporates and local businessmen in national construction projects without governmental interference, Liu reasoned, would create a win-win scenario for the Chinese government, Chinese businessmen, and foreign businessmen.

 Liu E extended this logic of commercial management to his proposition for national border issues. Due to the increasing foreign threats and the Qing's limited military resources, borderland protection had been a controversial issue for the government since the 1870s. The national crisis caused by foreign threats in the decades surrounding the start of the twentieth century made border protection even more urgent. In February 1905, soon after the Russo-Japanese War (1904–1905), Liu E published his unique perspective on borderland management in major newspapers such as *The Times* (*Shibao* 時報) and *Northern China Journal* (*Huabei zazhi* 華北雜誌). He proffered two strategies to protect China from foreign invasion: the vassal states strategy and, as a compromise, the land mortgage strategy. The former involved relinquishing control over the borderland provinces and making them vassal states cogoverned by foreign countries' fiscal and administrative bureaucracies. Each vassal state would enjoy fiscal autonomy, and the mutual checks and balances between the cogoverning regimes would prevent the concentration of power. Ideally, these vassal states would become China's defensive barriers. The land mortgage strategy entailed mortgaging part of the Chinese territory. The state would temporarily yield governance and jurisdiction over the borderland provinces to different countries in exchange for foreign investments in domestic industrial infrastructure and borderland defense forces (Liu and Liu 2019, 582). Although the two strategies differ, both propose opening borders to foreign forces by parceling out ownership or governance over a region, contriving a balance of power in these areas, and making them the empire's barrier.

 Although Liu E's strategies may seem like the famous Qing scholar Bao Shichen's 包世臣 (1775–1855) proposed strategy of "subduing foreigners with foreigners" 以夷狄攻夷狄 during the first Opium War (1839–1842), they differ fundamentally. Bao advocated capitalizing on Britain's conflicts by forming alliances with its enemies, prompting those foreign powers to fight Britain outside of Chinese territories to win the privilege of trading with China. Liu E, though similarly capitalizing on conflicts among foreign countries, advocated completely opening the market for foreign powers that, he projected, would fight each other to protect their interests. Liu's views also differ from the revolutionists' stance, which proposed relinquishing the borderlands entirely. The revolutionists comprised Han nationalists, who emphasized the distinction between Manchu and the Han and cried enthusiastically for the establishment of a single nation-state restricted to the eighteen provinces populated mainly by the Han. Xinjiang, Tibet, Mongolia, and the three northeast provinces were relinquishable. This is a viewpoint that Liu E would not be inclined to endorse. Liu E advocated for a novel conception of international relationships and borderland governance.

Liu E's proposed governance strategies had an earlier origin. The river embankment system he developed as a river work expert in Shandong around 1890 inspired his proposal to redirect external threats inward and convert them into resources against themselves. In 1891, Liu invented what he called the oblique dike design to tackle Yellow River floods. He posited that dikes built to ward off water entirely would only heighten flood risk. Unlike past approaches that attempted to block floods, Liu E's oblique dike design redirects river water into the riparian area enclosed within dikes. The water pressure in the interior flood zone rises until it matches that of the river beyond, fortifying the dikes' resistance against the flood water. Liu called this "withstanding water with water." Once precipitation ceased, the water channeled into the riparian area would be redirected back into the riverbed, helping scour the silt deposited on the riverbed and preventing the water level from rising. Liu called this "attacking water with water." In brief, the oblique dike system maneuvers the flood water in a way that nullifies its own force.[6] Liu E's strategies of international commerce and politics operate under the same principle: they manipulate external threats against themselves, thereby protecting the nation. Liu E's hydraulic engineering viewpoint shaped his mining and railroad projects in the latter half of the 1890s and subsequently transformed into the guidelines for borderland governance he formally proposed in the mid-1900s.

Liu E's hydraulic conceptualization of state governance stems less from his professional bias as a river work expert than from the fact that the Yellow River is always the definitive site of state governance. The river embankment system, consisting of people's dikes built by locals along the riverbank and the official dike maintained by the central government and constructed farther from the riverbank, is a physical sphere where the power of state authorities and local civilian bodies are mediated and reconciled. The power dynamics of this mediation and reconciliation manifest in flood control policies demanding different approaches to the dikes. A

---

6. Only Liu E (2007, 1:44) mentions the actual efficacy of oblique dikes in *Five Essays on River Management* (*Zhihe wu shuo* 治河五說, 1889): "Past records have attested to the effectiveness of oblique dikes. Last year, Expectant Circuit Intendant Li, named director general of the lower reaches, asked for permission to build oblique dikes between Putai and Lijin. Governor Zhang assigned its execution to me. One oblique dike was built in Lijin and another was built in Putai. Although the height and thickness of the dikes deviated from the original design because of a lack of funds, over two hundred villages that used to suffer from annual floods now celebrate good harvests in both the wheat-harvesting season and fall. Over two thousand *qing* of previous drylands have now become fertile" 顧斜堤之效, 已有可考者焉。去年下游總辦候補道李稟請於利津之間補築斜堤, 宮保張委鶚承辦其事。利津修斜堤一道, 蒲台修斜堤一道。後雖因經費不足, 高厚未能如式。然二百餘村莊年年浸於水中, 而年年振濟者, 今已麥秋二季, 一律豐收矣。約涸復膏腴之地, 可二千餘頃.

flood control policy advocating the indispensability of the people's dikes champions the benefits to local civilians—the people's dikes allowed civilians to leverage the economic value of the riparian lands between the official dikes and the people's dikes. Contrarily, a flood control policy calling for the relinquishment of the people's dikes and placing the responsibility for flood prevention solely on the official dikes denies civilians' role in the construction of the embankment system and, naturally, of any chance to benefit from it. Therefore, the debate to use or to abandon the people's dikes involves not just technical issues but the financial interest of local people in state governance. Liu E's oblique dike design relies heavily on people's dikes. The design secures civilian involvement in state governance and grants civilians the chance to profit from it. Liu asserted that the oblique dike design would also strengthen the official dikes, benefiting both the central government and local civilians. The people's dikes and the politico-economic ideology they represent lay the foundation for how Liu E imagined the relationship between the state and civilians.

The Travels is more than a criticism of local governance. It is also a criticism of conservative statecraft, which Liu E believed had led to China's dire situation. As a comprador, Liu understood governing the state as like managing a company that puts business contracts out for tender—China would gain the most by leveraging competition among bidders, that is, foreign powers. This commercialized understanding of state governance derived from Liu's hydraulic engineering viewpoint. His application of river engineering knowledge to state governance was materially based—the structure of the Yellow River embankment system was the materialization of the relationship between the state and civilian society. Liu's governance tactic, which he saw as applicable to any governance situation, strategically eliminates boundaries and barriers to usher in foreign forces, defy government interference, and foreground the civilians' agency. His stance challenged governance marked by rigid binary opposition, which conservative officials who set the government against civilians and China against foreign nations gladly embraced.

Local Governance and River Regulation

With conservative officials attacking his hydraulics-informed imagination of the state, Liu E, ironically but unsurprisingly, built the novel's response on the same imagination. He believed the ossified binary mode of governance embodied by the incorruptible officials required correction—by a more flexible governance strategy informed by hydraulic engineering techniques. The novel explores this relationship between hydraulics and governance fully when narrating the incorruptible official Yu Xian's governance of Caozhou prefecture. At the end of chapter 3, the governor of Shandong province, who has been troubled by the Yellow River floods, invites Lao Can to offer guidance on river management. The governor highly appreciates Lao Can's erudite and insightful advice and invites him to stay in the office for further consultation. Lao Can nevertheless declines the governor's invitation and leaves for another commitment, embarking on a survey trip to Caozhou prefecture after learning about Yu Xian's controversial reputation as an incorruptible official. Through Lao Can's observations and experiences, the novel explores the relationship between the problems of local governance and the Yellow River floods in late nineteenth-century Shandong and indicates their common cause. The novel treats flooding and the governance of incorruptible officials as identical problems and presents an alternative strategy, built on hydraulic engineering knowledge, for addressing local governance issues.

As the novel progresses beyond chapter 3, the narrative of the incorruptible official emphasizes the local public security problems these officials face in relation to the Yellow River floods. This relationship manifests in the novel's description of the ceaseless criminal activities in Shandong Province. Caozhou prefecture, where "scarcely a day passed without a case of banditry" 幾乎無一天無盜案 (Liu 1990, 35) such that the incorruptible official Yu Xian sees the need to tackle banditry with unrelenting rigor, was one of the regions where social order broke down due to the Yellow River floods. And Chengwu, a county under Caozhou prefecture described as running a deficit because of futile efforts to hunt down bandits, was a particularly flood-stricken area. The novelist understands the criminal activities in Shandong as part of a larger problem of public security deterioration in northern China that the Yellow River course shift in 1855 had caused. Chapter 7 describes a conversation between Lao Can and his friend Shen Dongzao 申東造, magistrate of Chengwu County, about quelling the outlaws thriving in his area of jurisdiction. Lao Can observes that bandits abound in particular geographic areas: "The three provinces—Henan, Shandong, and Zhili—and the northern parts of the two provinces—Jiangsu and Anhui—together may be considered as making one area" 河南、山東、直隸三省及江蘇、安徽的兩個北半省，共為一局 (Liu 1990, 74). The areas Lao Can mentioned were those the Yellow River floods had most sorely affected in the latter half of the nineteenth century after its course change. Beforehand, the river's lower reaches passed through mid-northern Henan, southern Shandong, northern Anhui, and northern Jiangsu. Economic activities in these regions, which the Yellow River system had long sustained, suffered when the course change caused the original channel to dry out. Meanwhile, areas along the new river course, such as southern Zhili and northwestern Shandong, bore the bitter brunt of the floods. The hotbeds of public security problems Lao Can identifies are those that emerged following environmental changes resulting from the river's course shift. That Lao Can tackles banditry in these course shift–impacted areas reveals the novelist's comprehensive reflection on Yellow River management.

Liu E envisages the relationship between Yellow River management and local governance through the character of the Shandong governor, who first appears at the end of chapter 3. While the Yellow River flooding establishes the context for issues of local social order in the novel, Liu suggests that the floods are caused not so much by natural forces as human error—that of the Shandong governor. Speaking with the governor in chapter 3, Lao Can says the local leader's ill-advised approach to river regulation, though seemingly effective, would lead to irredeemable disaster in the long run. Chapters 13 and 14 bring more forthright charges against the governor, naming him accountable for a disastrous flood event in 1889 that killed hundreds of thousands. Further, the novel claims he provided the soil for crime and social instability to take root. Beyond suggesting the governor's poor decisions about flood control are the origin of the public security problems he faces, the novel also condemns his proposed remedies for these problems. Yu Xian and Gang Bi, the two incorruptible officials whom the governor puts in charge of dealing with local crime, epitomize this wrong solution. The Yellow River floods and the cruelty and harshness people suffered from the incorruptible officials, therefore, are not separate government issues. The latter is not only the consequence of the former; the two problems are different manifestations of the same problematic governance philosophy.

Yu Xian and the Shandong governor both adhere to a binary approach to governance. This mindset insists on an authority-civilian binarism in river management and an authority-criminal binarism in public security. In terms of river regulation, the governor's method of river expansion attempts to abandon the people's dikes, built along the riverbank with local civilian resources, and to move the line of flood defense to the bigger dikes constructed farther from the riverbank by the central government. To Liu E, this binary approach denies the significance of the locally built dikes and represents a total reliance on state resources to solve the flooding problem. Adopting this method, Liu E argues, creates more frequent and devastating floods. Prefect Yu Xian's local governance resembles the governor's river regulation strategy and suffers similar drawbacks. Yu Xian's binary approach to governance insists on eradicating banditry solely with the force of authority, leading to a direct confrontation between authorities and criminals that worsens public security. In chapter 4, for example, the bandits take advantage of Yu Xian's binary approach by framing the victims of banditry as bandits, reducing the prefect to an instrument to serve their own ends. Just as the Shandong governor's binary approach to river regulation invites devastating floods, Prefect Yu Xian's binary approach to local governance leads to disaster in public security.

After condemning the incorruptible official, the novel offers an alternative that works according to the opposite rationale. Liu E introduces this approach in a scene of political consultation, where Lao Can advises Shen Dongzao, the Chengwu County magistrate, that he can solve the banditry problem without the harsh measures Yu Xian advises. Lao Can suggests Shen invites the martial arts master Liu Renfu, whom the outlaws esteem highly, to be a guest of the county and provide Liu with resources to socialize with the bandit chiefs. As a result, Lao Can asserts, the bandit chiefs will "immediately issue an order that no man may make a disturbance" 立刻便要傳出號令，某人立足之地，不許打攪的 (Liu 1990, 75) and help Liu capture the lesser bandits and thieves. As Carlos Rojas points out, this philosophy of local governance echoes Liu E's interest in the force of water. Rojas (2015, 51) argues the novel shows this hydraulic view of governance in chapter 3 when Lao Can visits the Golden Thread Spring and observes how two springs of matching strength create the appearance of a thread on the water's surface. However, the mechanism of force dynamics that Lao Can's strategy aims to create is much more complex than simply water force. Like Liu E's proposal for managing international investment, this approach to local governance draws on the oblique dike system Liu designed when he was a river engineer, which used water to counteract water and involved civilian participation and aid. Following a similar logic, Lao Can's plan involves opening the bureaucratic system to civilians and resolving the threat of the outlaws by employing the force of the outlaws themselves. This tactic creates a mechanism in which bandits exercise self-discipline and self-supervision, effectively turning the bandits into a self-consuming force. Marked by counterpoise and coexistence, Lao Can's governance tactic strikingly contrasts the incorruptible officials' conservative measures; rather than forceful suppression, Lao Can's tactic affects a reversal, turning the bandits into the government's tool.

The story about the incorruptible official Yu Xian in chapters 4–7 is essentially a story about river regulation. Readers might easily consider Yu Xian's story as a departure from the theme of river regulation developed in the first three chapters of the novel—in the allegory of Lao Can's treatment of the sick Yellow River in chapter 1 and later in the Shandong governor's consultation with Lao Can on river work in chapter 3. After all, in chapter 3, Lao Can leaves for Caozhou prefecture before having provided the governor with all his river management advice. However, as demonstrated above, the novel's criticism of Yu Xian and its presentation of Lao Can's local governance agenda are extensions of the Yellow River management theme. The novel presents Yu Xian's harsh and annihilative measures as the embodiment of the Shandong governor's misguided philosophy of river regulation, which Liu E opposed. Lao Can's proposal for local governance, serving as an alternative to incorruptible officialdom, bears palpable traces of Liu E's flood control techniques. Although Lao Can cannot present his technical advice on river regulation to the Shandong governor before his travel, it emerges fully in the narrative of the incorruptible official.

Redefining the Virtue of *Gong* and Incorruptibility

The novel's criticism of incorruptible officials implicates both the officials and the traditional idea of incorruptibility. And to challenge the latter, *The Travels* wrestles with the concepts and traditions informing it. The idea of incorruptibility, as opposed to corruptibility, has been established since antiquity on the paired concepts of *gong* 公 and *si* 私, arguably one of the most powerful and complicated conceptual pairs in Chinese intellectual history. While the novel criticizes incorruptible officials from a hydraulics-informed political perspective, it simultaneously examines the political concept of *gong*, the basis of the identity of the incorruptible official, through its narration of a political consultation, a philosophical conversation, and a murder trial. Liu E undertakes this examination from his perspective of river engineering.

The term *gong*, since the pre-Qin period (221–207 BCE), has been one of the most important ideas in political discourse in China. The term *gong* was first associated with the idea of government affairs, whereas *si* was associated with civil (*minjian* 民間) and private (*siren* 私人) affairs. In terms of governance, *gong* has been used to refer to one holding public office—that is, the governor—and *si* to one who is not in office—that is, the governed or civilians. This conceptual pair is domanial. For those holding public office, the difference between *gong* and *si* also refers to the boundary between government affairs and private affairs. Avoiding the mixing of government money and private money is considered essential for public officeholders, who should be disinterested and thus free to act with perfect impartiality. In this second sense, this conceptual pair is ethical. Corruption, defined as abusing power for private gain, suggests confusion between government and private affairs. Incorruption, accordingly, suggests a separation of affairs to avoid using the government office for private gain. The term *gong* was later invested with the positive connotations of universality, entirety, and transcendence, as opposed to the negative ones of partiality, limitation, and interestedness. In the Song dynasty, the Neo-Confucian scholar Zhu Xi 朱熹 (1130–1200) and his peers adopted the term *gong* to refer to the goodness (*shan* 善) attained after the removal of overgrown human desire (*renyu zhi si* 人欲之私), or the universal and ultimate heavenly principle (*tianli* 天理), though, to them, only the teachings of the Confucian sages can be termed as *tianli*. It was not until the late Ming dynasty that a new idea of *gong* appeared. Although still defined by universality and entirety, this later conception confirms the value of *si*, arguing that *gong* is the fulfillment of everyone's desires and needs (*ju si wei gong* 聚私為公). Although this new idea was less popular after the early Qing dynasty, it regained popularity in the face of the intellectual challenges from the West in the late nineteenth century and found expression in the proposition that the state would acquire wealth when every individual seeks his own wealth.[7]

Lao Can's hydraulically informed proposal on local governance challenges the traditional understanding of *gong* and *si* in terms of the government-civil relationship. While traditional discourse demarcates government and civilians, Lao Can instead blurs the boundary, suggesting the government share power and resources

---

7. This description of the development of the concepts of *gong* and *si* is based on Chen Jo-shui's discussion (see 2005, 81–138).

with civilians. Specifically, he advises the county government to incorporate Liu Renfu, a civilian, to help address local crime by mediating between the government and the outlaws. Lao Can's proposal suggests that if properly harnessed in a strategic alliance, civilian power and resources do not necessarily encroach upon government power. Lao Can compares Liu Renfu's role in this alliance to the head of a private armed escort company (*biaoju* 鏢局), which enlists collaboration with bandits and gangs to secure the county government's property.[8] That the government must rely on a private escort company to operate demonstrates the impossibility of utter separation between government and civilians. Inspired by a river engineering approach, Lao Can's proposed tactic for local governance is an alternative to incorruptible officialdom that questions the division between *gong* and *si* as a political idea.

The novel morally rationalizes the amorphous distinction between governmental affairs and private affairs by philosophically investigating the concept of *gong*. Chapter 9 features a conversation about the idea of *gong* between a mysterious maiden named Yugu 璵姑 and the young Neo-Confucianist Shen Ziping 申子平, who is on a mission to find Liu Renfu and quell the bandits as advised by Lao Can after being sent by the county magistrate. The conversation occurs while Shen Ziping seeks lodging at the Peach Blossom Mountain and meets Yugu. The maiden maintains that the Three Teachings—Confucianism, Buddhism, and Daoism—all encourage man to be morally good and thus can all be described as *gong*. According to this spirit, all practices that serve the end of "encouraging man to be good, leading man to be disinterested" 誘人為善，引人處於大公 (Liu 1990, 98) should be tolerated and accepted. Although Yugu acknowledges that all Three Teachings conform to the value of *gong*, she asserts that Buddhism and Daoism are inferior in the level of *gong* to Confucianism, which shows unrivaled tolerance for opposite opinions and the least selfishness.[9] Yugu's idea of *gong* is therefore inclusive but hierarchical.

---

8. Private armed escort offices, or *biaoju*, arose in the late Ming and thrived in the Qing (Chen 2018). A private escort company's business relies simultaneously on resistance against bandits and diplomacy in building rapport with them and securing their influence. The government usually relied on escort offices for cash transport. High officials and nobles were also their clients. The renowned late-Qing politician Li Hongzhang 李鴻章 (1823–1901) was said to recruit private armed escorts from the famous Huiyou 惠友 Escort Office in Beijing as his household guard. In alleviating the conflict between the government and the bandits, these private escort offices stepped in as mediators (Chen 2018). The analogy between Liu Renfu and an armed escort in the novel is based on historical fact. Liu Renfu might be based on martial artist Wang Zhengyi 王正誼 , better known as Great Blade Wang the Fifth (Dadao Wang Wu 大刀王五), who had a close friendship with Liu E and established Shuenyuan 順源 Armed Escort Office in Beijing. See Liu and Liu 2019, 125.
9. Yugu's attempt to distinguish between the Three Teachings in terms of the level of *gong* is to conduct what Chinese philosophical tradition knows as "classifying the teachings," or *panjiao* 判教. Teaching classification was a major aspect of textual studies of Buddhism sutras by medieval Chinese monks. It was done by discriminating between different scriptures, commentaries, schools of thought, canons, and their level of perfection and interfusion. They aim not just to classify different theories but also to determine the practical order of self-cultivation practices. By following this order, one is said to eventually be enlightened to the supreme state of perfection and interfusion,

When applied to the political sphere, Yugu's idea implies removing the boundary between government and civilian affairs on which the traditional idea of *gong* in a domanial sense is based, to attain the goal of goodness. Within the overarching and inclusive perspective of *gong*, any effort, either from the government or civilians, to contribute to the wellness of the people should be encouraged. Yugu's new overarching framework thereby justifies the fusion between government and civilian affairs that Lao Can advises in chapter 8, just one chapter later.

Yugu's idea of *gong* is founded upon criticism of Zhu Xi's idea of Neo-Confucianism, the orthodox school of thought established since the Song dynasty. Yugu's idea that *gong* encompasses the Three Teachings, which have the shared purpose of promoting the pursuit of moral goodness, directly challenges the Neo-Confucian orthodoxy. Her conception, which stresses *gong* as goodness, universality, and entirety, points out the conflicts in the theoretical position of Neo-Confucianism: although Song Neo-Confucians defined *gong* as universality and entirety, they nevertheless denied that any thought other than Confucianism could be considered *gong*. Yugu also expresses her idea of *gong* by criticizing Neo-Confucianists' emphasis on the sharp dichotomy between the heavenly principle and human desires: she suggests Neo-Confucianists violate the original teaching of Confucius—the representation of the true virtue of *gong*. C. T. Hsia (2004) argues that the novel attributes the harshness and self-willingness of incorruptible officials to the Neo-Confucian ideas Yugu criticizes as biased, inflexible, and dichotomous.[10] Yugu directs her criticism, however, not merely at Song Neo-Confucianists but also at the idea of *gong* as framed by them. Yugu's criticism of the school's emphasis on the rigid dichotomy between the heavenly principle and human desires, for example, obviously reflects the new concept of *gong* that confirms the value of human desires, an idea arising in the late Ming and revived in the late Qing. The consummate virtue expressed by the tolerant and all-encompassing spirit in her conception of *gong* also chimes with that new idea of *gong*, which justifies the fulfillment of diverse agendas and needs. Yugu's criticism of Neo-Confucianism is essentially a claim for the revival

---

which is the ultimate goal for all practitioners. On that account, the point of classifying teachings is to determine which canon is the most perfect, interfusing, and inclusive. After the Song dynasty, Neo-Confucianists carried out teaching classification on Confucianism, Buddhism, and Daoism. They did so mainly in response to challenges posed by Buddhism and Daoism, particularly by their different views on human nature and cosmology. Therefore, their concerns lay not so much in the order of self-cultivation practices as in establishing, through classification, Confucianism as the sole orthodox teaching.

10. Yugu's criticism of the Neo-Confucian ideas of *zhujing* 主敬 (reverence) and *cuncheng* 存誠 (sincerity) in chapter 9 is clearly directed at the incorruptible official Yu Xian, a Neo-Confucianist who follows the principle of reverence and sincerity. Liu E further confirms the relationship between Neo-Confucianism and incorruptible officials in the commentary to chapter 16. There, he criticizes the obstinacy of incorruptible officials by naming the famous conservative official Xu Tong 徐桐 (1819–1900), who identified as an avid Neo-Confucianist.

of the late Ming idea of *gong* that challenges the mainstream idea of *gong* framed by Neo-Confucianism.

The redefinition of *gong* and *si* in the first half of the novel also appears in the second half via the narration of a murder trial, specifically the judge's manner of hearing the case. The innocent defendants foolishly try to bribe their way out of trouble. Consequently, the presiding judge, Gang Bi, as an incorruptible official with a rigid sense of morality, takes their bribery as solid evidence of their guilt and insists that they are guilty of murdering the Jia family by poison. To save the wrongly charged and convicted defendants, Lao Can requests that the governor assign Judge Bai Zishou, a sagacious official highly esteemed for his probity, to hear the trial instead of Gang Bi. Because of the governor's intervention, a lenient and truly incorruptible official replaces a willful and harsh one who enjoys an undeserved reputation as incorruptible. Moreover, governance marked by strict separation between government and private affairs is set aside in favor of governance that blurs the boundary between the two spheres. Bai Zishou's behavior in court further undermines Gang Bi's uncompromising morality. To raise funds to further investigate the case, Judge Bai borrows money from the defendants—the same money they used for bribery—in public view during the trial. As if it were not startling enough for Bai to borrow money from a briber, Bai turns to Gang with a joking smile. "I suppose you will scorn me for accepting a bribe in the court!'" 不免笑兄弟當堂受賄罷 (Liu 1990, 204). By doing so, Bai teases Gang about what he holds to be supreme moral doctrines. The narrator ends the description of the trial with the following line: "Gang Bi muttered, 'I wouldn't dare.' Then the drum was beaten, and the court adjourned" 剛弼連稱：「不敢。」於是擊鼓退堂 (Liu 1990, 204). The defendants' names are thus cleared, and the expedient appropriation of private funds for government aims is justified. This trial scene explicitly opposes the canonical separation between government money and private money. By identifying Bai Zishou as an official who is more reliably incorruptible than Gang Bi, the novel defines the idea of incorruptibility very differently from the traditional definition.

While Bai Zishou's hearing of the case challenges the traditional separation between *gong* and *si*, it is Lao Can who radically undermines it. The relationship between Bai Zishou and Lao Can interlocks: while Lao Can brings Bai into the trial, Bai later brings Lao Can into the investigation of the murder, which remains unsolved even after the defendants are vindicated in the trial. Bai Zishou then asks Lao Can, a civilian, to investigate the case on the government's behalf—an invitation that represents a governmental effort to erase the distinction between government and private affairs. Lao Can's response then shows an even more radical way of dissolving the distinction from a civilian perspective. He accepts Bai's invitation but proposes to fund the investigation with his money instead of the borrowed bribe money. Lao Can does so less because of his moral qualms and more because of his strong desire for a more active role in local governance. He asks the government to repay him only if he successfully solves the case. It is a political investment: Lao Can spends money to participate in governmental affairs. However, the financial issues highlighted in this exchange undermine the boundary between government and private affairs in a manner more complicated than it seems. We later discover that Lao Can's ostensibly private funds are not totally private. Chapter 17 describes the Qihe County magistrate Wang Zijin embezzling four hundred *liang* of silver from the county treasury for Lao Can's private use—to redeem a prostitute. The money Lao Can uses as his political investment (funding for the investigation) is, in fact, the four hundred *liang* of silver that he owed the Qihe County treasury and planned to repay. The money that Lao Can uses to gain an opportunity to participate in government affairs, therefore, is neither purely private nor purely governmental. Lao Can's invited participation in a government investigation shows the most extreme dissolution of the government-civilian boundary possible.

Lao Can's political investment in the investigation represents a mindset regarding resource management that Liu E developed as a river work expert. Although Liu had faced criticism for using bribery as a means of political networking since the mid-1890s,[11] his tendency to challenge political ethics concerning money likely came from a very familiar difficulty encountered during his river engineering career as early as around 1890. As one of the most urgent and costly internal state affairs, river work in the late Qing always ran short of money and needed additional fundraising, which was frequently nongovernmental and sometimes even unethical. River work attracted innumerable opportunists who gained posts through donations or bribery; capitalizing on their new positions, they embezzled river work funds (Dodgen 2001, 46–51). The resulting deficit in river work led to requests for even more donations and bribes, leading to a productive but vicious circle. This was not just an open secret but even normalcy, revealing a fluidity and ambiguity between government resources and private capital that we cannot simply summarize as corruption. Fully exposed to the culture of river work, Liu E makes this fluidity and ambiguity central to incorruptibility.

Chapters 7–18, in which Shen Ziping journeys to the Peach Blossom Mountain and the Jia family's murder trial is held, entail a quest to remedy local governance problems. Yet Shen Ziping's journey is ultimately one to explore how to undermine the strict separation between *gong* and *si*, or government and civilian/private affairs,

---

11. The late-Qing scholar and imperial tutor Weng Tonghe 翁同龢 (1830–1904) once criticized Liu E for bribing him to assist with the railroad projects. Weng wrote in his diary on June 12, 1895, "Liu E is a fellow Zhenjian-born who has more than once submitted petition memoranda to the Supervisory Office. He went to Beijing with fifty thousand *liang* of silver to press for the construction of railways. Yesterday, he even asked someone to send me dozens of calligraphy works and paintings. I hereby note it down as evidence of inappropriate offering" 劉鶚者，鎮江同鄉，屢次在督辦處遞說帖，攜銀五萬，至京打點，營幹辦鐵路，昨竟敢託人以字畫數十件餂余。記之以為邪蒿之據 (Liu and Liu 2019, 285).

by which incorruptible officials abide. This newly defined relationship between *gong* and *si*, then, further materializes in Bai Zishou's hearing of the murder trial and Lao Can's participation in the case's investigations. Liu E's hydraulic engineering knowledge deeply informs the new understanding of the relationship between government and civilian/private affairs proposed in the novel. Incorporating his philosophy of river regulation into the narrative of incorruptible officials, Liu E reexamines the nature of governance and the idea of incorruptibility.

Sin, Punishment, and River Work

In chapter 1 of the novel, Liu E uses the sinking ship allegory to describe the treason accusations he endured from conservative officials whose statecraft, he believed, had led to China's national crisis. *The Travels* ends with a scene in the underworld in chapter 28. There, Liu E wraps up his self-defense against the scandal of treason and ensures karmic justice for the conservative officials who had cost him his reputation. It is at the end of the novel that we find poetic justice—and river work again plays a significant role in securing that justice.

Lao Can's journey to the underworld echoes the theme of national salvation and defamation in the sinking ship allegory at the start of the novel. King Yama, lord of the underworld, comments on the vice of humanity in relation to the survival of the Chinese race. He suggests those who commit the crime of defamation cause the greatest harm because it can drive the world to the point of human extinction. The message cannot be clearer: the greatest vice of humanity is committed by conservative officials, whose rigid mode of governance and whose defamation of those, like Liu E, attempting to save China, would together lead to the failure of national rejuvenation and the extinction of the Chinese race. The hell scene combines Liu E's defense against the treason accusation (as discussed in Chapter 1 of this book) and his criticism of conservative officials—the two themes interconnected from the novel's very beginning in the sinking ship allegory. The novel thus ends where it begins and pronounces an ultimate moral judgment on conservative governance.

King Yama's moral pronouncement reflects Liu E's two interrelated concerns, hydraulics and politics. King Yama addresses the vice of humanity analogously, suggesting vice proliferates quickly and impacts profoundly: "When a Yellow River flood comes, a single person causing a dike to burst can result in calamity for hundreds of thousands" (Liu 1989, 34). To explain the vice of humanity with the example of the dike breach on the Yellow River does not merely apply trope but also reveals how the novel addresses the relationship between river work and politics. King Yama's reference to the broken Yellow River dike and its human cost easily reminds readers of the Shandong governor. In chapters 13 and 14, the governor is blamed for poor policymaking, which induced the flooding of the Yellow River and caused the death of hundreds of thousands. This parallel compares an individual's vicious deed that leads to the end of the world with an individual's bursting of a dike on the Yellow River that causes innumerable casualties. But more importantly, it also suggests the Shandong governor, who causes the dike to burst, causes the destruction of the world. After all, the governor is responsible for both environmental catastrophe and political disaster: he applies a misguided river regulation philosophy marked by ossified binarism, *and* he is responsible for political disaster at the local and national levels, caused by the incorruptible officials he assigns out of the same governance philosophy. The governor becomes thus the very symbol of the vice of humanity that King Yama criticizes. King Yama's comment on the vice of humanity illustrates the close relationship that Liu E saw between failures in state governance and river work.

The punishment that King Yama adopts to eradicate the ever-proliferating crime of defamation—and thus solve China's political malady—is built again upon Liu E's professional knowledge of hydraulic engineering. It adopts the same logic of Liu E's oblique dike design, *turning the undesirable into a constructive resource*. To purify the humanity of the sinners, the hell guards feed those condemned for defamation into countless huge millstones arrayed in rows for grinding; the sinners' bodies are subsequently transformed into products made from their flesh and bones. This instrument of punishment works similarly to the oblique dike system, transforming disastrous elements—the defamers, including conservative officials and those assigning them to the position—into productive material. Modeled after the oblique dike system, the millstones naturally serve as the best choice for punishing the defamers. King Yama analogizes these sinners and the countless deaths they caused by their vicious words or wrong decisions to the inducer of the dike burst on the Yellow River and the great flood that follows. This hydraulics-informed punishment aims to purge not only the conservative officials' crime of defamation but also their erroneous philosophy—in governance, which led to that crime, and in strategies for river work and local public security.

The millstone punishment illustrates Liu E's infatuation with the inexhaustible productivity and accuracy that typify industrial manufacturing processes. The way the hell guards execute the punishment, as the narrator observes, demonstrates the same smoothness and precision as seasoned factory workers. Liu E describes the operation of the millstones and the output of minced flesh and bones as highly standardized, as would occur on an industrial production line. This factory-like process, activated by none other than tremendous vice itself, operates ceaselessly, for "after the grinding, the wind will blow on the remains and restore them to their original shape, ready for a second go-round. There is no set number of times a person must undergo milling. The number depends on how many sins each has accumulated" 磨過之後，風吹還原，再磨第二回。一個人不定磨多少回呢！看他積的罪惡有多少，定磨的次數 (Liu 1989, 35). The more one sins, the greater the output of minced flesh and powdered bones. The giant machine of punishment does not merely eradicate the sinners' vice to save the Chinese race from extinction but also converts vice into productivity. The millstone in the underworld functions as a machine that embodies Liu E's concern for fixing governmental problems, promoting economic productivity, and securing racial survival.

Many readers have found the ending of *The Travels* to be incomplete. However, when considered through the appropriate lens, the novel's final chapters, in which Lao Can travels to the underworld, weave all threads together to create a powerful conclusion. The episode addresses the concerns Liu E raised at the beginning of the novel about the survival of the Chinese race, the criticism against incorruptible officials, and his self-defense against the accusation of treason. The novel's solution to all these concerns takes the form of the millstone punishment, a mechanism informed by Liu E's hydraulic engineering design that metaphorically transforms ethical vice into productive resources to help secure China's survival. As a river engineer, Liu E ends his novel by providing a hydraulic solution to all the political problems that he understands in relation to the Yellow River and conceptualizes hydraulically.

Hydraulic Remedies

In traditional court-case novels, the difference between corruptible officials and incorruptible ones is the basis of their narrative of political problems. However, in the late Qing, politics was beyond the issue of corruptibility and incorruptibility and involved a much more complicated political spectrum. Although *The Travels* is, first of all, Liu E's attempt to challenge the traditional narrative of incorruptible officials, it demonstrates the ambition to invent a new way to explore the late Qing political crisis by upending traditional political discourse on local governance.

Using his unique framework of hydraulics and medicine, Liu E deliberately conflates the problems of local governance and the Yellow River floods to expose the harm of the incorruptible officials. This conflation is most evident in the depiction of the Shandong governor tasked with river regulation and the official Yu Xian he appoints to deal with local crime in the wake of the flooding. Both share a rigid, binary philosophy of governance reliant on authority and state intervention that ultimately leads to disaster. Indeed, Liu E frames Yu Xian's harsh and annihilative measures against bandits as the embodiment of the Shandong governor's misguided river regulation. Perhaps more significantly, the novel keeps the same framework to propose a common cure built from hydraulic concepts—a cure emphasizing counterpoise, coexistence, and civilian involvement.

The significance of Liu E's proposal is to challenge the separation of government affairs (*gong*) and private ones (*si*) advocated for in traditional political discourse. Liu E establishes the philosophical rationale for this challenge in chapter 9, through the voice of the maiden Yugu. By establishing the superiority of the Confucian understanding of *gong*, Yugu, and thereby Liu E, promotes tolerance and inclusivity, criticizing the Neo-Confucian orthodoxy as biased, inflexible, and dichotomic. In a political spectrum, this new concept of *gong* promotes a fusion of government and civilian affairs without encroaching on government power. Liu E drives home the justice of this fusion in two primary ways: through Judge Bai Zishou's lenient hearing of a court case and through the collaboration of Lao Can and Bai Zishou in the investigation of the murder. Both of these actions hinge on the fluidity and ambiguity between government resources and private capital—a fluidity informed by Liu E's hydraulic engineering knowledge and his practical experience with river work funding. Indeed, Liu E had himself offered bribes to gain support for government industrial projects, adhering to the belief that the ends justify the means.

In his perspective, the Yellow River floods and the incorruptible officials' stringent governance are not only the problems of local governance but a microcosm of national problems. The crises that China faced related to the environment, public security, national economy, and even international relations were all the result of an ossified binarism in governance discourse. The hydraulics-informed, more fluid strategy of governance that Lao Can proposes to solve the problems of local public security is also the remedy he proposes for the multiple political crises in late Qing China. Yet this approach was also precisely what earned him a reputation as a national traitor when he received backlash from conservative officials. As Liu E's self-defense against accusations of treason, *The Travels*, ironically adopts as its foremost ideological resource the very hydraulic approach and river work techniques that caused his condemnation.

3
From Sediment to Sentiment
Transforming Flood Trauma into National Identity

> The game of chess is almost ended. We are getting old. How can we not weep?
> —Liu E, *The Travels of Lao Can*, preface (1905)

By incorporating hydraulics into the analogy of biological nationalism, Liu E created a framework to criticize the philosophy of incorruptible government and express his agenda for national salvation. However, this incorporation played a dual role: it enabled him to draw on earlier literature and an ancient analogy between water flow and emotion to develop the idea of national sentiment in the novel. That this was his intention is evident from the preface he wrote on the theme of weeping when the *Tianjin Daily News* (*Tianjin riri xinwen* 天津日日新聞) reserialized *The Travels* in 1905. He presents the novel as the expression of his tears for his troubled country's misfortune and his fears about the nation's indefinite future. Meanwhile, the overall sentiment in the novel is this deep concern and the sorrowful and overwhelming "feelings stirred about our life experience, about family and nation, about society, about the Chinese race and Confucian teaching" 有身世之感情，有家國之感情，有社會之感情，有種教之感情.[1] That sentiment is what the present chapter explores.

Referencing the metaphor of a chess game, Liu E pushes his readers to consider the current political climate. The "game of chess is almost ended" 棋局已殘 suggests the Chinese political system is about to collapse, and "we are getting older" 吾人將老 suggests it is too late to do the right thing. Using the words "end" (*can* 殘) and "old" (*lao* 老) to express a sentiment of doom, Liu also weaves the protagonist's name, Lao Can, into the text.[2] This associates the character with the then-prevalent

---

1. My translation.
2. For discussion on the name Lao Can, see also Wong 1989. For discussion on "can" in "Lao Can" as ruins, see Cheng 2007.

societal despair and anxiety concerning the nation's future, establishing the theme as integral to the protagonist's identity and, therefore, the novel.

Given the clear association between the protagonist's name and the sentiment of national misfortune, it is perhaps surprising that Lao Can is not the character who sheds the most tears in the novel. Instead, Liu E develops this sentiment of national misfortune through an analogical story about flood trauma and healing and the sympathetic portrayal of a courtesan named Cuihuan. Chapters 13 and 14 describe the great suffering that the 1889 Yellow River flood in Shandong caused Cuihuan, who was sold into prostitution because of her family's loss of fortune. Terribly victimized by the flood, Cuihuan is the novel's most lachrymose and sentimental character. Cuihuan cannot stop crying about her family's loss of fortune, her father's death, and her miserable fall to prostitution because of the flood. The huge volume of her tears is unrivaled. Of the fifty-one mentions of the word "weeping" (*ku* 哭) in the novel, thirty are found in chapters 13 and 14; of the twenty-one mentions of the word "tears" (*lei* 淚), eleven are found in these two chapters. The two chapters are saturated with the tears Cuihuan sheds for her misfortune. By letting these tears flow freely, Liu portrays her as the epitome of the flood victims, the carrier of traumatic memories, and the mournful victim who cries for the calamity.

Liu E's regret at failing to save people from perishing in the 1889 Shandong flood finds expression in Cuihuan. The depiction of the disaster in chapters 13 and 14 is based on Liu's witnessing the destruction while mapping and surveying the Yellow River as a river work official. As Liu clarifies in his commentary on chapter 14, nothing was more devastating to him than failing to rescue the victims of the flood. He "could not help but burst into bitter tears" 不禁痛哭 at the heartbreaking scene and his inability to help. It is the only occasion in the novel or accompanying commentary when Liu expresses his emotions so forcefully, showing the moral weight of his failure. Accordingly, as this chapter will explore, Cuihuan's trauma reflects the novelist's own state of mind.

However, as well as expressing his inner turmoil, Liu E's portrayal of Cuihuan's trauma enables him to address national sentiment by analogizing flood victims and the nation. Just as his tears for his country in the preface are expressed in the novel as the tears for the Yellow River flood victims and for his own failure to prevent the flood and save lives, when Liu writes about the flood and its suffering victims, he writes in fact about the suffering of his country. Fitting his broader hydraulic framework for understanding the nation-state, this analogy of flood trauma and national sentiment depended on water flow as a symbol of emotion. As this chapter explores, such symbolism was rooted in Chinese literary tradition and a long-standing Confucian-Buddhist conceptual model that enabled him to connect the trauma caused by the Yellow River floods to the idea of national identity. Furthermore, it enabled him to explore not just national mourning but also national salvation through the narrative of trauma healing. In the novel, the healing depends on river taming, enabling Liu

E to engage in national identity-making in a manner that he, a hydraulic engineer, could contribute to—the regulation of the Yellow River. That water was at the heart of this analogy charged his work with an emotional depth that few scholars fully recognize.

Evoking Floods in Earlier Literature

Although *The Travels* is not the first Chinese novel to describe devastating floods, it is the first to explore the relationship between floods and the shaping of national sentiment. Liu E explores this relationship by drawing on the greatest works in Chinese literary tradition. By alluding to the eighteenth-century novel *The Story of the Stone* (*Shitou ji* 石頭記, also known as *Honglou meng* 紅樓夢, or *Dream of the Red Chamber*), and the earliest Confucian canon, *The Book of Odes* (*Shijing* 詩經), Liu E justifies the relationship between the emergence of national sentiment and floods.

In his 1905 preface, Liu E justifies his claim that his tears for his country drove the writing of the novel by turning to Chinese literary tradition. He references its most important writers and identifies their works as their own crying (*kuqi* 哭泣). The long list of these writers starts with the slandered patriotic poet Qu Yuan 屈原 (340–278 BCE), who is regarded as the first poet in Chinese literature, and ends with Cao Xueqin 曹雪芹 (1715–1763), author of *The Story of the Stone*. Liu pays tribute to Cao by using highly sentimental references from Cao's novel, which appear at the end of the preface of *The Travels*, inviting humankind to weep and grieve with him for the country's fall and his inability to save it. These quoted phrases, taken from two beverages consumed by Cao's protagonist (a tea named "qianhong yiku" 千紅一窟 and a wine called "wanyan tongbei," 萬艷同杯), each reference "weeping" and "mourning" through a homophonic pun.[3] No other text in Liu's list of great works enjoys such privileged allusion.

With this connection to Cao's novel established, it becomes apparent that the emotional depth of Liu E's work is deeply influenced by *The Story of the Stone*. Marked by romantic and tragic sentiment, *The Story of the Stone* is arguably the most important resource on which later novels—including *The Travels*—have drawn to address affection. The sadness and regret Liu expresses for his uselessness in the face of tragedy is grounded in the beginning of Cao's novel. *The Story of the Stone* begins

---

3. In chapter 5 of *The Story of the Stone*, the protagonist Jia Baoyu 賈寶玉, the projection of Cao Xueqin himself, drinks a tea named *qianhong yiku*, which literally translates as "a thousand lovely ones are in one cave (*ku*)," and a wine called *wanyan tongbei*, which means "ten thousand beauties are in one cup (*bei*)." The word *ku* is a homophonic pun on "cave" 窟 and "weeping" 哭, while *bei* puns on "cup" 杯 and "mourning" 悲. The puns made by Cao Xueqin, as Liu E correctly points out in the novel's preface, mean "thousand lovely ones weeping together" 千芳一哭 and "ten thousand beauties mourning together" 萬艷同悲 (Liu 1990, 2).

by retelling a Chinese foundation myth about the goddess Nüwa 女媧.[4] Nüwa uses smelted stones to repair a hole in the heavens that had caused an apocalyptic catastrophe. The protagonist of Cao's novel is Jia Baoyu, the incarnation of the one stone Nüwa left unused in her heaven-patching task; and because of his uselessness, the stone "became filled with shame and resentment and passed [his] days in sorrow and lamentation" 自怨自愧，日夜悲哀 (Cao 1973, 47). Cao creates a figure unprecedented in the history of Chinese fiction, shedding tears for his inability to be of use to the world, or "all under heaven" (*tianxia* 天下). At the end of his novel's preface, Liu borrows the image of this crying stone to express resentment at his own incapability to save the country. His publicized sadness and sorrow, as well as the tears flowing for his country, find their source in the very beginning of *The Story of the Stone*.

By referencing the stone in the Nüwa myth, however, Liu E also empowers himself to save the country through his profession, river engineering. In the original myth, Nüwa's grand undertaking hinges on controlling floods and fixing breaches. These acts are the very contributions that Liu E, a renowned river engineer, could—and did—make when the Yellow River flooded in the latter half of the 1880s and in the early 1890s. By mending flood-damaged dikes, Liu successfully regulated the floodwaters. The reference to the Nüwa myth allows Liu E to identify with the heaven-patching stone used to save "all under heaven."

The name of the novel's protagonist, Lao Can, perfectly captures the self-empowerment suggested by the reference to the Nüwa myth. The narrator introduces Lao Can as follows:

> There was once a traveler called Lao Can. His family name was Tie, his given name was of one character, Ying, and his pseudonym, Bucan. He chose Bucan as his pseudonym because he enjoyed the story of the monk Lan Can roasting taros. Since he was a pleasant sort of person, people regarded highly of him and began to call him Lao Can, which eventually became a regular nickname. (Liu 1990, 3–4)[5]

---

4. The earliest textual version of the Nüwa myth appears in *Huainanzi* 淮南子 in the early Former Han dynasty (202 BCE–8 CE): "Going back to more ancient times, the four pillars were broken; the nine provinces were in tatters. Heaven did not completely cover [the earth]; Earth did not hold up [Heaven] all the way around [its circumference]. Fires blazed out of control and the people could not extinguish them; water flooded in great expanses and would not recede. Ferocious animals ate blameless people; predatory birds snatched the elderly and the weak. Thereupon, Nüwa smelted together stones of five colors to patch up the azure sky, cut off the legs of the great turtle to set them up as the four pillars, killed the black dragon to provide relief for the Ji area, and piled reeds and cinders to stop the surging waters" 往古之時，四極廢，九州裂，天不兼覆，地不周載，火爁炎而不滅，水浩洋而不息，猛獸食顓民，鷙鳥攫老弱。於是女媧鍊五色石以補蒼天，斷鼇足以立四極，殺黑龍以濟冀州，積蘆灰以止淫水 (Liu 2010, 223–24). Translation slightly adapted.
5. In Chinese, *lao* is often added to a (usually male) name to show familiarity and express fondness.

> 卻說那年有個遊客，名叫老殘。此人原姓鐵，單名一個英字，號補殘。因慕
> 懶殘和尚煨芋的故事，遂取這「殘」字做號。大家因為他為人頗不討厭，契重
> 他的意思，都叫他老殘；不知不覺，這「老殘」二字便成了個別號了。

The name Tie Ying literally means "pure iron"—that is, smelted iron ore; it refers both to Liu E's style name, Tieyun, and the smelted stones Nüwa used to seal the heavens. The pseudonym Bucan, literally meaning "to mend (*bu*) the broken (*can*)"—that is, to patch up holes—clearly references Nüwa's great task. The narrator's explanation of why Lao Can chose the character *can* for his pseudonym further confirms the connection to Nüwa's unused stone. According to the narrator, this *can* is derived from the dharma name of the monk Lan Can 懶殘, a character from *Tales of Sweet Enrichment* (*Ganze yao* 甘澤謠, 868), who received his name because he ate others' leftover food (*can* 殘).[6] Thus, *can* in Lao Can's pseudonym also means "leftovers" or "the remains." Bearing a name meaning "smelted iron ore" and a pseudonym meaning "mending the broken / (with) the leftovers," Lao Can is the reinvented vision of that unused smelted stone in the heaven-patching scene from *The Story of the Stone*.[7] The idea of patching up the hole in the heavens with the remains, suggested by the pseudonym Bucan, precisely captures the unused stone's wish to be useful and identifies the stone's untapped potential. By identifying Lao Can, the projection of the novelist himself, with the unused stone in the creation myth in *The Story of the Stone*, Liu E expresses his desperate desire to be used for the salvation of his country.

The pseudonym Bucan, read in reference to the flood taming in the Nüwa myth, expresses Liu E's pride and ambition as a river engineer who tasked himself with controlling the devastating Yellow River and thereby saving his country. Such passion for and courage in shouldering the responsibility for saving China manifests in chapter 1 of *The Travels*. At the beginning of that chapter, Lao Can successfully and proudly heals the sick Shandong gentleman Huang Ruihe 黃瑞和, whose name clearly refers to the Yellow (Huang 黃) River, the lower reaches of which are in Shandong Province. Liu E thus takes up where Cao Xueqin leaves off in the Nüwa myth to create a new sentimental subject, Lao Can, who is eager, and symbolically empowered, to join the grand project of reinventing Chinese civilization through river regulation.

---

6. According to *Tales of Sweet Enrichment*, "Lan Can's original name was Ming Zan. He was a monk from the Hengyue Temple in the early Tianbao era, and he ate others' leftovers. Due to his lazy disposition and his habit of eating leftovers, he received the dharma name 'Lan Can'" 懶殘者，名明瓚，天寶初衡岳寺執役僧也。退食，即收所餘而食，性懶而食殘，故號「懶殘」也 (Yuan 1985, 5).

7. Another example of Liu E's identification with Cao Xueqin, and Lao Can's identification with Jia Baoyu, is the correspondence in how other characters refer to the protagonist. In *The Story of the Stone*, Jia Baoyu is called "second elder brother" (*er gege* 二哥哥) by his cousin Shi Xiangyun 史湘雲; Lao Can is similarly called *er gege* by his cousin Mrs. Shi 石姑娘.

Although Liu E draws primarily on *The Story of the Stone* to convey his national sentiment, he also turns crucially to classics in the poetic tradition to portray a narrative of national salvation. Chapter 12 describes how Lao Can, after seeing an ice jam on the Yellow River, laments his country's misfortune. He recalls lines from the poem "Great East" ("Dadong" 大東) in *The Book of Odes* and is moved to tears. By walking along the riverbank and expressing through poetry his worry for state affairs, Lao Can evokes an image from another poetic anthology: Qu Yuan, the representative poet in *The Songs of the South* (*Chuci* 楚辭), who wandered along the riverbank before killing himself in great despair for his fallen country. Liu E conveys his patriotism in the form of political criticism through the poetic allusion. According to its preface, "'Great East' was composed to protest the political turmoil of its time. The people of the east suffered from hard labor, and the states found themselves in dire financial straits. The official of the Tan state (in the east) thus composed this verse to warn the government" 〈大東〉，刺亂也。東國困於役，而傷於財，譚大夫作是詩以告病焉 (Watson 1971, 28). In this sense, by thinking of the verses from "Great East," Lao Can expresses his worry and sympathy for the country's suffering. Connecting his novel to Chinese poetic classics, Liu E establishes his sentiment for his country within a long tradition.

The allusion to "Great East" also serves as a more specific reference to the Yellow River disasters in Shandong. First, Liu E alludes to the poem immediately after seeing the ice jam on the Yellow River, suggesting an intimate connection between the poem and the river. More importantly, the poem's reference to the Zhou dynasty state of Tan 譚 (?–684 BCE) more specifically connotes the late Qing floods. The state of Tan was believed to have been in the city of Jinan, which became the seat of Shandong Province in the early Ming dynasty (1368–1644). The city was also the seat of Jinan prefecture, one of the areas the Yellow River flooded most severely in the late Qing period. The dire social and financial situations described in the preface of "Great East" aptly capture the immense labor and fiscal challenges in Shandong during Liu E's time. And the allusion to "Great East" in the scene of Lao Can's lament deftly connects his sorrow for the troubled country and the implied sympathy for the victims of the uncontrolled Yellow River.

The Travels, like almost every other work of vernacular fiction on the theme of sentiment since the nineteenth century, owes a major debt to *The Story of the Stone*. Yet unlike other novelists who drew on the eighteenth-century masterpiece solely to address the issue of love (the work's key theme), Liu E drew on the novel to express instead his desire to save his country and his feeling of uselessness in that effort; he expresses not only a sense of responsibility to save the country with his knowledge of hydraulics but also his inability to do so. The author further grounds the association between national sentiment and river regulation in the early Chinese poetic tradition by alluding to *The Book of Odes*. Ultimately, *The Travels* consolidates the idea of national salvation through flood taming by rooting it in the genre-founding works of both the poetic and narrative traditions.

The Analogy of Water, Trauma, and Its Healing

By alluding to literary canons, the novel evokes the national sentiment connected to the Yellow River, yet the connotation between the two is based on a long-established conceptual structure: the analogy between the river's water flow and emotion. This conceptual structure—which Liu E uses throughout his novel to address emotion, including national sentiment, amorous love, and flood trauma—is the heritage of Confucian tradition. As a literatus of broad intellectual interests, Liu E bases his narrative of emotion on both Confucian and Buddhist concepts. The Confucian-Buddhist model of emotion informed Liu E's writing of the story of the flood victim courtesan Cuihuan, which represents his attempt to provide healing through fiction to the trauma of all the Yellow River's flood victims.

The analogy between the Yellow River and emotion has been embedded in the tradition of interpretation of *The Book of Odes* since its earliest stage. Traditionally said to be edited by Confucius, this poetic anthology has long been considered the origin of poetry—the genre Confucianists believed particularly powerful for expressing one's most sincere thoughts and emotions and arousing those of others. The first poem of *The Book of Odes*, "Fair, Fair, Cry the Ospreys" ("Guanju" 關雎), about a gentleman's longing for a lady, is closely related to the Yellow River from its beginning, where the poet evokes the man's amorous emotions with the imagery of ospreys on an island in the Yellow River (Chu 1984, 277). The close relationship between the Yellow River and romantic emotion in "Fair, Fair, Cry the Ospreys" is well captured in *The Analects* (*Lunyu* 論語). There, Confucius regards the poem as "joy, but not excessive; sadness, but not to the point of injury" 樂而不淫，哀而不傷. The word *yin* 淫, which literally means "overflow of water," is extended to mean excessiveness. Specifically, the excessiveness of amorous emotion that causes injury is analogized to the overflow of river water. The analogy between a river's water flow and emotion is operant in the earliest Confucian texts.[8]

The analogy between river and emotion is instrumental to the flood control metaphor in the Confucian discourse of emotion. The use of this metaphor in this context began as early as the Han dynasty (202 BCE–220 CE). *The Exegesis of The Book of Rites* (*Liji jingjie* 禮記經解), composed during the Qin (221–207 BCE)–Han periods, states, "Decorum serves to prevent disorder, just as the dikes serve to prevent flooding" 夫禮，禁亂之所由生，猶坊止水之所自來也 (Ruan 1980, 1610). Dong Zhongshu's 董仲舒 (179–104 BCE) *Luxuriant Gems of the Spring*

---

8. For a discussion of the early development of the Confucian philosophy of emotion, see Cheng 2013; for Confucian philosophy on emotion in general, see Lee 2012.

and Autumn (*Chunqiu fanlu* 春秋繁露) argues, "Those who are fond of sex but do not follow decorum become unrestrained; those who eat and drink but do not follow decorum become contentious. Lack of restraint and contentiousness gives rise to disorder. Now decorum is what embodies emotion and prevents disorder" 好色而無禮則流，飲食而無禮則爭，流爭則亂。夫禮，體情而防亂者也 (Dong 2016, 611–12).[9] The use of the word "prevent" (*fang* 防) to express the restraint of emotion suggests the analogy between emotions and water flow since the word *fang* is etymologically connected to dikes. A similar expression appears in the preface to "Fair, Fair, Cry the Ospreys," also known as the "Great Preface" ("Da xu" 大序) to *The Book of Odes*. For Confucianists, *The Book of Odes* is the model for emotional expression. The "Great Preface," arguably one of the most important statements on the idea of emotion in Confucianism, explicitly explains the essence of this model. It indicates that a poem is supposed to "arise from spontaneous emotion; but stop within the limits of decorum and righteousness" 發乎情，止乎禮義 (Watson 1971, 29),[10] suggesting that decorum should moderate the expression of emotion. Later Confucianists understood this moderation in the "Great Preface" through the metaphor of flood control. For example, the early Ming scholar Luo Lun 羅倫 (1431–1478) discusses emotion by alluding to the "Great Preface," stating, "Human nature and emotions are like water; decorum and righteousness are like dikes. Water stops at dikes and emotions stop at decorum and righteousness so that they don't overflow" 夫性情猶水也，禮義猶防也。水止於防，性情止於禮義，則〔流而不淫〕 (Luo 1987, 2716b). The idea of emotion suggested in *The Book of Odes*' "Great Preface" is understood through the analogy between water flow and emotion and the metaphor of flood control.

The analogy between the river's water flow and emotion provides Liu E with a model to construct the narrative of emotion. Like any scholar well-trained in the Confucian classics, Liu E finds it convenient to allude to the preface to "Fair, Fair, Cry the Ospreys" to address the issue of emotions. Chapter 9 of the novel describes a conversation that took place at the Peach Blossom Mountain about romantic love between Yugu 璵姑, a mysterious and knowledgeable young woman, and Shen Ziping 申子平, a young scholar who seeks a night's lodging after a tiring mountain journey. In a conversation justifying romantic emotions in moderation, Liu E speaks through Yugu to allude to the discussion of emotion and its limits in *The Book of Odes*'s "Great Preface." He comments on how Shen Ziping and Yugu, a grown man and a young girl, behave in harmony with the sage's teaching about "arising from spontaneous emotion but stopping within the limits of decorum and righteousness" despite their feelings for each other (Liu 1990, 101). Liu E's allusion to the "Great Preface" in commenting on a romantic scene illustrates that the analogy between

---

9. Translation slightly adapted.
10. Translation slightly adapted.

water flow and emotion (and the metaphor of flood control) is at work in his discourse of romantic love.

The analogy between emotion and water flow functions not merely in the narrative of romantic love in the Peach Blossom Mountain episode but also in the narrative of national sentiment immediately afterward. In chapter 12, after Lao Can recalls lines from "Great East" and weeps in worry about the crisis of state affairs, we get a similar analogy:

> When he reached this point in his thinking, unconsciously the tears began to trickle down his face. . . . As he walked along, he felt that there was something sticking to his face. He touched it with his hand and felt on each cheek a strip of smooth ice. At first he couldn't understand it. Then he understood and smiled to himself. The tears he had just shed had immediately frozen solid in the cold air. (Liu 1990, 130)
> 想到此地，不覺滴下淚來……一面走著，覺得臉上有樣物件附著似的，用手一摸，原來兩邊著了兩條滴滑的冰。初起不懂什麼緣故，既而想起，自己也就笑了。原來就是方才流的淚，天寒，立刻就凍住了。

Leo Lee (2010) indicates that the description of Lao Can's frozen tears, which he deems one of the novel's most lyrical moments, describes a moment of frozen emotion. Further, this way of writing emotion is unprecedented in the history of Chinese fiction. Lee bases this interpretation on an analogy between frozen tears and frozen emotion, which is reasonable since tears result from strong emotion. But read in the context of the plot, this scene in fact suggests a triple analogy: emotion, tears, and the Yellow River. Crucially, the scene of Lao Can's frozen tears happens immediately after he looks at the frozen Yellow River. Liu E suggests the triple correspondence between the river, national sentiment, and tears. Lao Can's frozen tears are the materialization of the connection between the Yellow River and Liu E's national sentiment.

Liu E's analogy between water flow and emotion also illuminates our understanding of the narrative of another emotion—the courtesan Cuihuan's flood trauma. The novel describes Cuihuan as a sentimental weeper whose memory of the misfortune caused by the 1889 Yellow River flood in Shandong induces tears. With the water flow–emotion analogy in chapter 12, Cuihuan's flood trauma becomes not merely the emotion caused by a Yellow River flood but also itself the recurrent overflow of the river water.[11] Triggered by the damage of flooding, Cuihuan's streaming

---

11. Liu E uses "human nature" (*xing* 性) as an analogy of water flow when discussing flood control in governmental documents. In his *Five Essays on River Management* (*Zhihe wu shuo* 治河五說), which he submitted to Shandong governor Zhang Yao in 1889, Liu adopts an analogy between water and human nature to argue that the channel contraction approach would be "confusing water following its nature with water free of constraint, just like confusing following one's nature with capriciousness and indulgence" 誤以縱水為順水，猶之人以任性為率性也 (Liu 2007, 1:39). This argument apparently draws on Mencius's analogy between water and human nature in his debate with Gaozi.

tears are themselves an uncontrolled torrent of emotion. Once the courtesan bursts into tears, she symbolically produces a flood and thus becomes victimized by the flood of her own unmoderated emotion. By adopting the analogy of water flow and emotion in the narrative of flood trauma, Liu E suggests a mutually defining relationship in which the traumatic emotion caused by floods is, metaphorically, itself devastating floods.

Although the analogical relationship between water flow and emotion is rooted in the Confucian discourse of emotion, Liu E also constructs the narrative of emotion around the idea of Buddhist transmutation. Liu E was familiar with the theories of the Consciousness Only (Sk. Vijñānavāda, Ch. Weishi 唯識) sect, which stresses the transmutation of consciousness (*vijñāna*) to wisdom (*jñāna*), or *zhuanshi chengzhi* 轉識成智.[12] In the novel, the theme of transmuting amorous pain appears in a poem that the enlightened hermit Yellow Dragon composed:

> The sky of love and sea of desire are full of wind and wave,
> Vast and immense is the river of love
> Led into the garden as Water of Virtue,
> It is everywhere planted with the *māndārava* flower. (Liu 1990, 95–96)
>
> 情天欲海足風波，渺渺無邊是愛河。
> 引作園中功德水，一齊都種曼陀羅。

The Buddhist tradition uses the river of love as a metaphor for the love and desire that, as floods, drown their victims (Ding 2012, 2352a). Liu combines this idea of transmuting deadly water with the Confucian notion of moderating the currents of emotions. He does so through the metaphor of water control: the overwhelming river of love is diverted into the Water of Virtue, the holy water from a pond in a Buddhist pure land (Ding 2012, 135b–135c), which nurtures the *māndārava*, the flower of wisdom and enlightenment (Hurvitz 2009). This combination of the Confucian and Buddhist ways of dealing with emotion is unsurprising given that the poem's author, Yellow Dragon, embodies the Three Teachings—Confucianism, Buddhism, and Daoism. Although Yellow Dragon's poem uses the metaphor of water control from the Confucian understanding of emotion, it also evokes a Buddhist conception of emotion focused on transmuting rather than merely moderating floods. In this poem, excessive romantic emotions are analogized to the immense drowning floodwater to be regulated, but in a Buddhist way.

Yellow Dragon's poem, which describes the transmutation of the immense flood and the current of romantic love into the pure water of Buddhist wisdom, foreshadows the narrative of a Buddhist form of flood trauma healing. The poem's metaphor of flood control suggests that relieving the pain of romantic love is metaphorically

---

12. One of the Taigu school's two core approaches for self-cultivation is *zhuanshi chengzhi*, which is directly borrowed from the Buddhist Consciousness Only sect (see Han 2017, 83).

equivalent to controlling trauma-causing floods. Liu E brings this equivalence in Yellow Dragon's poem into the novel's narrative of trauma healing. Lao Can first brings healing to Cuihuan's life, and to that of all flood victims symbolically, by redeeming her from prostitution and taking her as his concubine. In doing so, Lao Can tries to channel Cuihuan's sentiment in a positive direction while comforting her. But a major part of the fictional trauma healing also involves Cuihuan's religious conversion under the guidance of the enlightened Buddhist nun Yiyun 逸雲. Since Cuihuan's flood trauma, as mentioned, is metaphorically equivalent to devastating floods, healing Cuihuan's flood trauma, therefore, is a metaphorical effort of flood taming. Her conversion brings relief by using metaphorical flood regulation to transcend the pain of romantic love. Liu E describes Cuihuan as a tearful, traumatized flood victim and, simultaneously, as a woman weeping in pain after parting from her loving husband, Lao Can. Relief from the suffering of amorous love is the key to Cuihuan's salvation, as suggested by her religious teacher's own experience: Yiyun attained enlightenment by casting off love, foreshadowing the journey upon which her disciple Cuihuan is about to embark. Cuihuan's apprenticeship to Yiyun thus provides a narrative of trauma healing, ending the tears induced by first her emotional attachment to Lao Can and second her misfortune caused by the flood. Cuihuan's conversion to Buddhism symbolizes the effort to bring both relief to flood trauma and end the trauma-causing flood.

While Cuihuan's conversion symbolizes the effort to bring relief, neither the flood trauma nor the flood truly ends on the narrative level until Liu E introduces a scene of irrigation. In chapter 7 of the sequel (serialized in 1907), after the symbolic trauma healing and flood control represented by Cuihuan's conversion, Lao Can visits his brother-in-law Gao Wei 高維 in Huai'an. The narrator introduces this trip with a scene in Gao Wei's Little Wangchuan Garden 小輞川園, a clear reference to the famous Tang poet and devoted Buddhist Wang Wei's 王維 (701–761) Wangchuan Garden 輞川園. As the narrator describes, Gao Wei waters the Chinese roses in his garden by channeling the water from Lake Shao 勺湖, where "the pavilion of Great Compassion [stood] in the middle of the lake, with water on every side" 〔湖〕中有個大悲閣，四面皆水 (Liu 1989, 25). This scene effectively narrativizes the following line from Yellow Dragon's poem: "Led into the garden as Water of Virtue / It is everywhere planted with the *māndārava* flower." The Chinese rose, fed by water from the lake of compassion, alludes to the flower of enlightenment watered by the clean and pure water transformed from the floodwater of love. Gao Wei's Chinese rose is arguably the near Chinese incarnation of *māndārava* because, in Chinese, the transliteration *mantuoluo* 曼陀羅 is used to refer to the camellia, which strongly resembles the Chinese rose in bloom.[13] The irrigation of the Buddhist garden in

---

13. According to *Manual of Aromatic Plants* (*Qunfang pu* 群芳譜), "Camellias, also known as mantuoluo trees, can grow to heights exceeding a zhang, while some may only reach two or three chi. Their

Huai'an is thus not only a pastoral description of a close relative's garden but also a symbol of successful flood trauma healing and flood control.

The analogy between water flow and emotion informed how Liu E crafted the narrative of national salvation, which takes the form of healing from flood trauma. Liu E seeks symbolic compensation for flood damage on the narrative level by arranging the flood victim Cuihuan's conversion to Buddhism. The courtesan is the epitome of the flood victims, and her conversion symbolically relieves the collective trauma caused by the flood and its terrible aftermath. In the story of Cuihuan, Liu E establishes a metaphorical equivalence between flood trauma and painful love. And based on this, he proposes that flood trauma can be transcended by relief from the pain of romantic love. Cuihuan's conversion stands for not merely trauma healing but also symbolic flood taming, which is most manifest in Lao Can's visit to his brother-in-law's garden in Huai'an. The visit marks the end of the novel's narrative of Buddhist healing of the flood trauma. Liu E, the river engineer, was traumatized by his failure to help tame the floods and save lives; Liu E, the novelist, implements a metaphorical flood taming, providing trauma healing to the fictional flood victims.

The Hydraulics of Emotion

That Liu E analogizes flood trauma to flooding itself suggests he believes one must deal with trauma as one deals with a flood. Hydraulics was not merely the scientific knowledge on which Liu E based his river regulation work. Hydraulics—the technology and the controversial issues around it—also played a significant role in the novel's narrative of flood trauma and its healing. Such a narrative of emotion is founded upon both Liu E's understanding of hydraulics and the long history of hydraulics in China.

Liu E's conceptualization of hydraulics addresses the conflicting relationship between the Shandong government and the people residing along the banks of the newly formed river course. The late Qing Shandong government encountered a dilemma in Yellow River management: to demolish the people's dikes built by local residents and implement a unified and more efficient water control method, or to keep the people's dikes and preserve the residential areas and farming sectors between the people's dikes and the government dikes constructed farther from the riverbanks. To resolve this dilemma, Liu E proposed a new embankment design, which he called the oblique dike system (see Introduction and Chapter 2). In his design, the people's dikes are the lynchpin of flood defense. Liu's emphasis on the importance of the people's dikes contrasted with the incumbent Shandong governor

---

leaves resemble tea leaves and can be brewed into a beverage, hence the 'cha [tea]' in their name." 山茶，一名曼陀羅樹，高者丈餘，低者二三尺，……，以葉類茶，又可作飲，故得茶名 (Wang 2001, 693a–693b).

Zhang Yao's river control policy. Zhang adopted what we might call a "river expansion" method, which involved demolishing the people's dikes to expand the width of the river channel and lower the water level during floods. In Liu's view, this approach was exactly what would bring about devastating floods in the long run.

This technical perspective informs how Liu E narrates—through the voice of a courtesan—his own flood trauma, rooted in his experience of the 1889 flood. In chapters 13 and 14, Cuihuan's companion Cuihua, who is also a courtesan, speaks on behalf of Liu E with strong emotion. She recalls the flood victims in the summer of 1889 "crying out for fathers, calling for mothers, weeping for husbands, wailing for children—a continuous sound of lamentation more than five hundred *li* long" 喊爹叫媽的，哭丈夫的，疼兒子的，一條哭聲，五百多里路長 (Liu 1990, 150–51). Cuihua's account of flood victims' experiences might not be the only one of its kind in Ming–Qing vernacular novels. However, it is the most detailed and vivid account. More importantly, unlike other novelists who attribute flooding almost exclusively to natural forces, karma, or corruption in river work, Liu E attributes the deluge and its tragic consequences directly to a technical error. According to Cuihua, the flood was a man-made disaster caused by the abandoning of the people's dikes by Governor Zhuang—a character that recalls Zhang Yao, the incumbent Shandong governor at the time Liu served as a hydraulic adviser in Shandong. While abandoning dikes was (and remains) a standard practice in the channel expansion approach to flood control, Cuihua holds Governor Zhuang accountable for the huge casualties, claiming that his river regulation policies were the "big sword" that killed several hundred thousand people. Although Cuihua modestly claims that she, a commoner, is ignorant of river work, she criticizes the governor's policy using sound knowledge and from a technical perspective atypical for an uneducated commoner. The courtesan's heartbreaking hindsight assessment expresses Liu E's hydraulic viewpoint, his condemnation of misguided river work policies, and his compassionate lament for the flood victims.

Although it would be reasonable for Liu E, a river engineer, to bring his professional view into the novel's description of the flood, its criticism of Governor Zhuang/Zhang Yao's river work policy is not just an objective technical judgment. Instead, the hydraulic criticism in Cuihua's distressed accusation is highly charged with moral emotion. Yet her powerful moral emotion obviously rises from her technical judgment: Governor Zhuang is highly immoral because his misjudgment in the river work led to several hundred thousand deaths. This technology-based morality is even clearer in Liu E's commentary on chapter 13. Speaking in the voice of a commentator, Liu E blames Zhang Yao for the 1889 Shandong flood. He suggests that Zhang, though celebrated for "benevolence and integrity" 慈祥愷悌, is morally wrong because of his poor decisions related to hydraulic engineering. Liu also directly equates his traumatic emotions and Zhang's technical error by identifying the abandonment of the people's dikes in Shandong as one of three heartbreaking events in his life.¹⁴ For Liu, the 1889 flood and subsequent trauma were technology-based moral and emotional issues.

Liu E's hydraulic concerns also inform the narrative of trauma healing in the novel, as represented in Lao Can's visit to Little Wangchuan Garden in Huai'an. Originally from Dantu, Liu E settled southeast of Lake Shao in Huai'an at age twenty-one. While there, he lived in a residence that his brother-in-law Gao Deming 高德明, courtesy name Weizhi 維之, had purchased on behalf of Liu's father (Liu and Liu 2019, 59, 137). Although Liu E was frequently on the road, as he had been since his youth, Huai'an remained his permanent residence. This Huai'an brother-in-law, Gao Weizhi, was the model for the character Gao Wei, Lao Can's brother-in-law, whose house is a transformation of Liu E's own residence. That Lao Can, the literary surrogate of Liu E, visits Huai'an thus symbolizes a homecoming for the river engineer. This symbolic homecoming, which follows the healing of Cuihuan's flood trauma and the metaphorical flood control represented by Cuihuan's conversion, is also highly symbolic for its reference to the river work tradition. The homecoming clearly refers to the legend of Da Yu, the great ancient cultural hero who returned home after successfully subduing the great floods after thirteen long years, paving the way for the creation of the Xia dynasty. That is, Liu E identifies with Da Yu by reviving the legend. This fictional homecoming thus implies the flood has been controlled, the social order restored, and the trauma healed. By referencing the most famous homecoming in Chinese history, Lao Can's visit to Huai'an marks the end of the novel's narrative of flood trauma healing and flood taming.

As the primary imagery in the restaging of Da Yu's homecoming, the irrigation of Chinese roses in Little Wangchuan Garden also resonates with Liu E's view of river engineering. It suggests the idea of utilizing the floodwater beneficially—an idea Liu E incorporated into his design of the oblique dike system, which he claimed to have inherited from the ideas of Pan Jixun and Jin Fu, the most celebrated river engineers in the Ming–Qing periods. According to Liu, unlike other hydraulic designs aimed solely to prevent the Yellow River from overflowing into the floodplain, his design steers disastrous floodwaters into the riparian area and, through silting, turns the waters into a resource for irrigation. The mechanism of Liu E's hydraulic design finds its first literary materialization in the irrigation imagery in Yellow Dragon's verse, which describes the transformation of the floodwater into pure water to grow the flower of enlightenment. This mechanism is again embodied in the imagery of gardening at the end of the narrative of trauma healing. Liu's embankment design deeply shapes the novel's trauma-healing narrative.

Little Wangchuan Garden, if we consider the geographical significance of Huai'an in the history of Yellow River regulation, even more strongly implicates

---

14. "There were three heartbreaking events in his life, and the abandonment of the people's dikes in Shandong was one of them" 生平有三大傷心事，山東廢民埝，是其傷心之一也 (Liu 2013, 262).

hydraulic engineering. Gao Wei's channeling of water from Lake Shao to irrigate his garden easily calls to mind the Yellow River–Huai River regulation projects that happened during the Ming–Qing periods at Lake Hongze 洪澤 in Huai'an, though the latter was much larger in scale. Lake Hongze, where Pan Jixun and Jin Fu implemented the river regulation projects that Liu E claimed to inherit, was the most prominent site of Yellow River regulation in the late imperial period.[15] Lake Hongze's hydraulic history is thus the hidden background for the narrative of trauma healing in *The Travels*. Furthermore, Huai'an is a city historically famous for the Chinese rose and its crucial role in controlling Yellow River floods. Lao Can's visit to the city is thus a visit also to the home of the flower symbolizing Buddhist trauma healing and to the site bearing the historical weight of Yellow River regulation. Liu E interweaves his narrative of flood trauma healing into the history of river engineering in Huai'an. The city is thus the most appropriate place for ending the narrative of healing for Cuihuan's flood trauma.

In the novel, flood trauma expression takes the form of criticism of the deadly hydraulic errors that Liu believed could have been avoided. Yet this criticism does not merely combine Liu's profession in hydraulic engineering and his sympathetic and caring response to those in pain. It also features the expression of flood trauma constituted by hydraulic criticism and a technology-based morality. The built-in hydraulic concern in his expression of flood trauma comes from the analogy between water flow and emotion, or that between floods and flood trauma. It is because Liu considers flood trauma as analogous to floods that he narrates the flood trauma from the perspective of river taming. The embedding of technological concerns in moral emotions echoes the hydraulic concern in the novel's narrative of trauma healing—a vehicle for salvation Liu feels obliged to provide. Liu E completes this trauma healing narrative with the scene in Little Wangchuan Garden, which resonates with his view of river engineering and the history of Yellow River hydraulics. As a river engineer, Liu E embeds his view of hydraulics into the novel's narration of flood trauma and its healing.

Disaster Relief, Media, and National Identity

Although Liu E bases his narrative of flood victims' trauma and its healing on technology, his concern for flooding disasters is social. The salvation of flood victims in the late Qing is essentially the work of disaster relief, which is often a vital driving force in the formation of national identity. Liu E was an active philanthropist, and his narration of Cuihuan's salvation is his participation in forming the discourse of disaster relief and in shaping national identity. While the novel was serialized

---

15. For discussions on the Grand Canal management in Huai'an in the Ming–Qing periods, see Tsai 1998, 376–82; Lin 2006, 93–122; Wang 2008.

in a newspaper over which Liu E had influence, he facilitated this identity-making through editorial layout. To Liu E, promoting his novel and promoting nationhood were the same thing.

For Liu E, disaster relief is a fundamental duty of a national citizen. Beginning in the 1890s, Liu E began to participate in disaster relief projects and became an experienced humanitarian worker. He expresses his understanding of disaster relief in relation to national identity formation nowhere more clearly than in his letter to Lu Shufan 陸樹藩 (1868–1926), leader of the Chinese Relief Society (Zhongguo jiuji shanhui 中國救濟善會).[16] In the letter, Liu states his intention to join the disaster relief for the victims of the Eight-Nation Alliance's invasion:

> Try to think this way: We are all the yellow skin nation, and the descendants of the Three Kings and the Five Emperors. . . . Take for example a large sinking ship with half of the passengers already landing and the other half in water. Shouldn't those who have already landed do their best to rescue those sinking? . . . What is the difference between these examples and today's situation? (Liu 2007, 1:748)
>
> 試思同為黃種，同是三王五帝之裔孫……譬如大舟觸礁而沉，舟人登陸者半，沉溺者半，則登陸者不當盡力拯救沈溺之人乎？……今日之事，何以異此？

By identifying the victims of the war in Beijing as "the yellow skin nation, and the descendants of the Three Kings and the Five Emperors," Liu shows that national identity has driven his engagement in relief efforts. The metaphor of the large sinking ship, which Liu E uses to convey the need for immediate relief, recalls the sinking ship allegory at the novel's beginning, by which he expresses his worry for the Chinese nation in crisis. The shared metaphor in the narratives of disaster relief and national salvation suggests that Liu identifies the rescue of disaster victims as the rescue of China. For Liu E, relief was not merely a humanitarian response to disasters, but also an action motivated by national identity.

Liu E's story of rescuing the flood victim Cuihuan reflects his experience in disaster relief projects, which he saw as a way to save his country and build national identity. In the novel, Lao Can cooperates with his friends in government to fundraise the ransom money needed to rescue Cuihuan from prostitution—reflecting exactly the cooperation between civil and governmental entities often seen in the humanitarian aid work in which Liu participated. Liu E also bases his account of Cuihuan's rescue on real disaster relief management. That Cuihuan eventually

---

16. In 1894, Furun, the governor of Shandong Province, commissioned Liu E to organize flood-relief donation campaigns (Liu and Liu 2019, 287), from which Liu E acquired fundraising experience. In the fall of 1900, Liu E joined the Chinese Relief Society, which was organized by the Zhejing merchant gentry Lu Shufan, for the relief of the invasion of the Eight-Nation Alliance in Beijing. Liu E made a generous donation to the relief and played a leading role in the society's humanitarian work and fundraising (Liu and Liu 2019, 372–88).

finds herself in a convent, practicing Buddhism, also reflects the role that Buddhist institutions assumed in late nineteenth-century disaster relief operations: Buddhist temples often sheltered victims and often with the assistance of humanitarian aid providers (Edgerton-Tarpley 2008, 159–96). Liu E draws on his rich experience as a humanitarian worker in broader disaster relief projects since the 1890s to write the story of the flood victim courtesan Cuihuan's salvation.

Liu E based his depiction of the novel's female victim not only on his experience as a patriotic humanitarian worker but also on media coverage of grassroots disaster relief. Media coverage of such relief played an important role in forming a sense of late Qing collective identity. From the 1870s, popular periodicals and newspapers such as *Shanghai News* (*Shen bao* 申報) were the principal carriers of information regarding grassroots emergency operations (Chen and Liu 2005, 407). Late-Qing intellectuals astutely observed how public media aroused sympathy for disaster victims and helped to promote humanitarian aid from those in unaffected areas.[17] Such public sympathy is most apparent in media coverage of female famine victims. The most common accounts in late nineteenth-century foreign and local coverage of large-scale famines tell of women sold to brothels by their families. The human traffickers' physical abuse of these female victims stands out as a striking theme. Spurred by such reports and calls to liberate the victims, the elite gentry from wealthy coastal districts moved to counter famine and save the nation (Edgerton-Tarpley 2008, 159–96).

The story of Cuihuan draws on this narrative of female and national salvation. Cuihuan's mother sold her to a brothel during the post-flood famine. There, she had to endure physical abuse from the brothel's madam. She therefore represents the female victims often seen in late Qing media coverage of environmental disasters. Lao Can, who redeems Cuihuan from prostitution and later sends her to a Buddhist convent, is the literary representation of the resourceful gentry elites who provided humanitarian aid to women similarly victimized. We can therefore consider the story of Cuihuan's rescue as grounded in late nineteenth-century media coverage.

The story of Cuihuan's conversion, however, is more than an attempt to evoke national sentiment by drawing on media coverage of past flood disasters. Rather, this story directly responds to a flood disaster happening when Liu E wrote the novel. On July 11, 1907, the Yongding River 永定河 breached its dikes, causing flooding in Zhili Province. The breach was finally closed on November 12, 1907 (Zhao et al. 1977, 959–60). During the flood, the *Tianjin Daily News*, where Liu E's novel was serialized, was saturated with news about the disaster and relief efforts. The

---

17. Zheng Guanying 鄭觀應 (1842–1922), one of the most renowned late-Qing reformists, entrepreneurs, and philanthropists, once pointed out that newspapers contributed to disaster relief by making the misery of the flood and drought victims in distant provinces vivid to the eyes of the readers, and that the victims were thus able to survive thanks to the inpouring donations of clothes and funds (Zheng 2013, 124).

Yongding River waters had poured into Tianjin seven times during the preceding century, most recently in 1893 and 1896 (Yao 1991, 64). Although the 1907 flood caused less harm to central Tianjin, the news coverage may have evoked alarming memories for residents only a decade or so removed from their previous sufferings. Liu E began to serialize the story of Cuihuan's conversion between September 30 and October 9, 1907 (Tarumoto 1983, 147), when the *Tianjin Daily News* prominently featured coverage of the flood and disaster relief efforts. His writing thus immediately echoed front-page news.

Liu E's relationship with the *Tianjin Daily News* had an additional important dimension. He was its cofounder (Liu and Liu 2019, 356), and he was very likely involved in the timing of the novel's serialization. Liu had developed a close friendship with the chief editor of the *Tianjin Daily News*, Fang Ruo 方若 (style name Yaoyu 藥雨, 1869–1954), who reserved a room in the newspaper's offices where Liu could stay during his regular visits to Tianjin from Beijing in the summer of 1907. Liu even wrote part of the novel in the *Tianjin Daily News* office (Liu and Liu 2019, 431). Although Fang Ruo was the newspaper's chief editor, Liu E may have been essentially in charge of running the publication (Liu and Liu 2019, 356). He could therefore have had the opportunity and power to make editorial decisions. Considering Liu's involvement in the *Tianjin Daily News*, we can regard the story of Cuihuan's conversion to Buddhism, which bears a strong symbolic meaning of flood trauma healing, as Liu E's attempt to use the media under his influence to participate in forging a narrative of disaster relief.

The story of Cuihuan's conversion, written and serialized during the Yongding River flood, draws a suggestive parallel between that flood in Tianjin and the Yellow River flood in Shandong described in the novel. On the one hand, such a parallel encouraged newspaper readers to identify with Cuihuan, the fictional flood victim in the newspaper's serial novel, letting them sympathize with the real suffering of the Yongding River flood victims. On the other hand, Cuihuan's conversion provided healing for traumatized reader-witnesses of the ongoing flood event within the realm of fiction. *The Travels*, in this sense, participated in forming an emotional event shared by readers of the *Tianjin Daily News*. By associating past disasters with present ones, the serialization of Cuihuan's conversion helped to construct a collective and continuous traumatic memory spanning 1889 through 1907. It also provided a remedy within the fictional realm for the flood trauma shared by the *Tianjin Daily News* reader community. In these ways, the story of Cuihuan's conversion contributed to the forging of a collective identity based on flood trauma and its healing.

The newspaper layout further enhanced Liu E's effort to foster a sense of shared identity. At the time, it was an emerging practice for media editors to manipulate the placement of serial novels and commercial advertisements to simulate the ongoing urban development in the first decade of the twentieth century (Yang 2022). The *Tianjin Daily News* adopted a similar practice: its layout design created an interplay between the novel and flood-related advertisements to promote a narrative of disaster relief. In late August 1907, readers of the *Tianjin Daily News* found *The Travels* printed on the same page alongside reportage of the flood and advertisements for the flood relief fundraisers.[18] These advertisements carried profound nationalistic connotations. One announces that the nationally renowned Shanghai theater Playhouse of Orange Osmanthus (Dangui yuan 丹桂園) is staging a new play to raise funds for the Yongding River flood. It stresses that the fundraiser's initiator had "felt compassion for his compatriots" 義切同胞. Another advertised a magic show fundraiser for disaster relief, featuring the famous magician Zhu Liankui 朱連魁 (Ching Ling Foo, 1854–1922?), whom his contemporaries considered an international spokesperson for the country and who was a figure representing national identity and pride at that time.[19] The newspaper layout juxtaposed these advertisements with installments of the novel, which together worked to shape a sense of national identity arising from the public sympathy for flood victims. While the advertisements for fundraisers echoed Liu E's attempt to shape a collective identity, those for insurance, which prevailed in the newspaper during the flood and were placed adjacent to the novel, spoke to readers' need for safety under the threat of unexpected flood disasters. For example, Arnhold, Karberg & Co. (Ruiji yanghang 瑞記洋行), one of the most famous foreign trading companies in the late Qing, advertised the launch of a combined life insurance and flood insurance policy, targeting transporting businesses based in Tianjin.[20] The newspaper layout generated a space for interaction between the novel, flood reportage, and advertisements for relief operations, life insurance, and flood insurance.

Read in a mutually referencing manner, these diverse elements together form a discourse of national identity constructed in response to the havoc of disasters, the fear of vicissitudes, sympathy toward the community, and healing for the suffering

---

18. The advertisement for the fundraisers on August 18, 1907, featured the Playhouse of Orange Osmanthus's play. The advertisement of the fundraiser on August 31, 1907, featured the magic show performance. The cosigners of the statement in the advertisements of the magic show included celebrities in business, theater, and media in Tianjin. Ning Xingpu 甯星普 (1841–1928) was the associate general manager of the Chamber of Commerce in Tianjin. Liu Ziliang 劉子良 was the leader of the Association of Theater Arts That Transform Social Mores (Yifeng yuehui 移風樂會), a learned society created in Tianjin in 1907 under a government mandate; it had great influence in the theater reform movement in the late Qing (Wong 2017, 385–88). Ying Lianzhi 英斂之 (1867–1928) was the founder and chief editor of the prominent newspaper *L'Impartial* (*Ta kung pao* 大公報). Regarding the development of charity performance and formation of national identity in the late Qing, see Chung 2012, 13–44; Zhu 2018.
19. Better known as Ching Ling Foo, Zhu left for the United States in 1898 to perform traditional Chinese magic tricks, taking American audiences by storm. In 1905, he traveled to London to debunk the imposture of the American magician William Ellsworth Robinson (1861–1918), who claimed to be Chinese. For Foo and Robinson, see Cullen, Hackman, and McNeilly 2007, 222–25; Steinmeyer 2006.
20. Arnhold, Karberg & Co.'s insurance advertisement was placed in the *Tianjin Daily News* on August 23, 1907.

through fiction. Liu E's serialization of the Cuihuan story in the *Tianjin Daily News* in late 1907 contributed to the emotional mobilization of disaster relief in Tianjin. By serializing the story, Liu E attempted to evoke a collective identity associated with shared flood trauma and public sympathy through media, and he sought to provide trauma healing within a fictional context for victims and witnesses of a real, contemporaneous flood event. More importantly, the novel's serial form is part of a collaborative project of national identity building in the media. The newspaper layout formed an integrative sphere for collective traumatic sentiments, engendered through disaster reportage and disaster relief and flood insurance. The novel capitalizes on this sphere: Liu E transforms his fictional remedy for flood trauma into a larger discourse of national identity and merges his emotions for himself, the country, society, and the Chinese race into a unified whole—as the novel's preface evoked.

Liu E's River Elegy

The writing and serialization of *The Travels* between 1903 and 1907 are not just an expression of Liu's sympathy for the suffering of his countrymen. The novel was Liu's attempt to mold disaster relief, trauma healing, and national sentiment into one interdependent discourse. Liu E's writings on emotions in the novel are part of a larger project concerning the construction of Chinese national identity. He endeavored to build a sense of national identity with the aid of public media and grounded that effort in late nineteenth-century flood control technology.

The disasters caused by the Yellow River floods were cataclysmic. Yet those deluges have also been a rich source of literary creation. Containing the floods and steering the river in a safer direction and to the desired destination were among Liu E's main concerns. It is through these concerns that *The Travels* represents the disasters, tears, traumas, and the need for healing brought about by the flooding of the Yellow River in the late nineteenth century. In the novel, the Yellow River becomes a pivotal image that joins together suffering; trauma; love; desire; earlier literary traditions; the national crisis at the time; Liu E's personal life, career, and river engineering accomplishments; and many other complex elements. It is both the reservoir of novelistic creation and the junction where all concepts mentioned above converge. What the novel's narrative aims to represent is how, through Liu's river control philosophy, violent and even destructive emotions can be metaphorically regulated, contained, tamed, and converted into a productive force for shaping national identity.

This understanding urges us to reassess the significance of *The Travels* in the history of Chinese fiction. It is the first novel used as a coping mechanism to deal with collective trauma caused by environmental disasters. Liu E suggests that the grand project of national salvation depends on regulating the Yellow River. He builds an affective structure through which traumatic emotions for floods become productive for nation-building, and hydraulic engineering is a fundamental component of this structure. In this sense, *The Travels* inaugurated a new paradigm in the novelistic expression of affects and emotions in Chinese literature. As the following chapter reveals, this emotional paradigm was not the novel's only revolution: it also marked the beginning of a new kind of landscape writing.

4
Water, Landscape, and the Appearance of a New National Literature

> *The Travels of Lao Can*'s most outstanding contribution to the history of Chinese literature . . . lies in the incredible techniques the author applied in scenic depiction and character portrayal. In the past, fiction writers devoted remarkable effort to the latter, but few showed any creativity in the former. . . . In my opinion, they were largely hindered by inadequate language . . . whenever it comes to scenic description, [traditional novels] were inundated and swarmed with set expressions borrowed from parallel prose or poetry. Old norms die hard, indeed. . . . Writing techniques are what *The Travels of Lao Can* excels in. No matter whether he is describing a human figure or a scene, the author always shuns cliché in favor of innovations specially developed for the occasion. In this regard, the novel has no precedent. . . . Poetic hand-me-downs are usually vague, irrelevant, unfit for describing the unique feature of a specific location or scene. . . . [From this,] we can see the importance of vernacular writing.
>
> —Hu Shih, A Preface to *The Travels*, 1925

With water regulation so central to Liu E's framework for nation-building, the description of the natural landscape became critical to his dual agendas of political reform and the construction of national sentiment. It is therefore unsurprising to find literary innovations in Liu E's landscape writing, and from very early in its critical reception, scholars have recognized *The Travels* as marking an important contribution to the wider literature reforms of the early twentieth century. The year 1903, when the novel was first serialized, witnessed the emergence of reform movements of language and literature that sought to formulate new standards and envision a modern national literature. Liang Qichao initiated the movement in 1902, with Hu Shih and others developing it in the late 1910s. This literary revolution undermined the traditional hierarchy that held classical Chinese in higher regard than vernacular language, leading to the identification of vernacular language with national language and of vernacular literature with national literature.[1]

The literary reformers in the early Republican period, especially Hu Shih, looked to *The Travels* as setting the vernacular literary norms. Thanks to Hu Shih's favor, the novel entered the sights of researchers of modern Chinese literature as early as the 1910s. In 1916, Hu wrote his famous article "Literary Revolutions in Our Nation's History" ("Wuguo lishi shang de wenxue geming" 吾國歷史上的文學革命), which argued that in the past five hundred years, only the novels of Wu Jianren 吳趼人 (1866–1910), Li Boyuan, and Scholar of Hundred Temperings from Hongdu (Liu E's pen name) are worthy of being considered lively, vibrant, "living literature" (2013, 1:11–12). By contrast, his fellow reformer Qian Xuantong 錢玄同 (1887–1939), a linguist and radical literary revolutionary, reacted negatively to Liu E's novel. In the magazine *La Jeunesse* (*Xin qingnian* 新青年), the movement's central stage, Qian disagreed with Hu for overrating *The Travels*. He criticized the novel's prophecy about the fruitless ending of the political revolution in chapters 9 to 11, dismissing it as the "unenlightened output of an old reformist" 老新黨頭腦不甚清晰之見解, and argued that this failing put the novel beneath the works of Wu Jianren and Li Boyuan (Qian 2010, 6). Hu Shih agreed that Liu E's conservative political visions had no place in the new republic (Hu 2013, 1:130; 2:1042). However, Hu rejected that claim as a plausible excuse to overlook the literary value of *The Travels*. In his 1923 article, "Chinese Literature in the Past Fifty Years" 五十年來中國之文學, Hu upheld his favorable view of *The Travels* and recommended it as an exemplary vernacular literary creation suitable for readers of the new nation. Apparently, Hu had realized the literary innovation of *The Travels* in terms of its form of language instead of its political vision.

Hu Shih's preface for the 1925 Yadong Library Press edition of *The Travels* is not only the earliest, most specific literary analysis of Liu's novel but also one of the earliest treatises on late Qing novels—even one of the earliest studies of vernacular novels in general. Hu Shih regarded vernacular Chinese as the sole legitimate form of the modern Chinese language. He identified the novel as a modern literary work and praised its exceptional scenic descriptions as the most desired literary application of the new national language. Although traditional Chinese novels employed plain vernacular prose in general narration, novelists commonly reused and recycled certain well-established expressions—poetic verse, rhymed stock phrases, or parallel prose (*pianwen* 駢文) in classical Chinese—to introduce landscape. Hu Shih's preface argued these set expressions fail to portray landscapes in their particularity. He argued *The Travels* is unprecedented in the history of Chinese fiction for the intricacy of its landscape description and that this intricacy depends on the use of

---

1. Hu puts it clearly: "The core of Chinese literary history *is* the history of vernacular literature" 白話文學史就是中國文學史的中心部分 (1986, 12).

vernacular prose in lieu of hackneyed formulations. According to Hu, Liu's adoption of vernacular language enables him to illustrate the landscapes in all their beauty and in full color, an effect unachievable with classical language (2013, 2:1045–1050). Hu's argument serves his agenda for language and literature reform. It enabled him to incorporate this widely popular novel into his project of national literature building, whose basis was the dichotomy between vernacular and classical language. Hu's judgment lifted *The Travels* to the ranks of exemplary national literature in the early Republican era—it literally established the novel as the outset of modern Chinese literature—while the preface itself raised the curtain on modern Chinese literary research.

Hu Shih's appraisal made the novel canonical. It also set the tone for how the novel has been taught, as part of national language education, for many decades beginning in the 1920s (Li 2016). The passages describing scenery in *The Travels* were furthermore the most frequently selected passages for Republican national language textbooks (*guowen keben* 國文課本) from that same decade.[2] Hu's evaluation of the novel was so influential that it became literary scholars' main target for criticism. In his important 1969 article, C. T. Hsia argues that the popular emphasis on the literary merit of the novel's scenery descriptions obscures its breakthrough in narrative form and technique (2004, 247). Hsia's criticism, though aiming to diminish Hu's influence, in turn, ultimately proves the importance of the reformer's commentary by acknowledging its impact on the novel's reception.

Influential as his reading is, Hu ultimately misrepresents the nature of Liu E's innovation in landscape writing. Hu viewed the set expressions of rhymed verse and parallel prose in traditional novels as contrary to vernacular language. However, traditional novels used parallel prose in both classical and vernacular language to introduce landscape. What distinguishes Liu E's landscape writing, then, is not that he replaces classical language with vernacular language but that he replaces rhymed verse and parallel prose with plain prose. The landscape writing in *The Travels* differs from that in earlier novels not because of linguistic form (the difference between vernacular and classical) but because of generic form (the difference between plain prose and rhymed verse and parallel prose).

Although Hu Shih misjudges the nature of Liu E's landscape writing, his argument is still a useful point of departure to reexamine its significance. As this chapter argues, Hu's observation foregrounds a simple yet easily ignored fact: the landscape writing in *The Travels* marks a turn in how the experience of landscape is expressed. Literary evolution often involves new experiences that require new modes of expression to be properly conveyed. Consequently, this shift in language represents a shift in observation and perception. Liu E's innovation is less to change how landscapes are described but to change how they are experienced—and his experience evidently

---

2. On *guowen keben* in high school education, see also Su 2004; Hu 2007; Zhang 2010.

differed from that of earlier novelists. Landscape is no longer simply a background against which stories take place, as in earlier vernacular fiction, but rather one of the narrative's main subjects, requiring the novelist's full descriptive attention. To Liu, landscape is as or more important than other elements in the novel. It thus deserves equal or more detailed vernacular prose instead of convenient, borrowed set expressions.

This chapter argues that the unprecedented intricacy of Liu E's landscape writing comes from his unique experience as a professional river engineer. The landscape writing in *The Travels* embodies Liu's enchantment with light and his anxiety about the limitations of vision, and it reflects Liu's particular interest in the mechanism of visual perception, all of which are triggered by the technical difficulties he encountered in river work. Yet Liu E's landscape writing is not merely a reflection of his hydraulic concerns. Instead, Liu was highly conscious of making sense of landscape writing in relation to a broader political agenda and the national sentiment embedded in his writing. He attempts to convey his passion and his frustration related to nation-building through a combination of philosophical discourse and his hydraulically informed writing of landscape. *The Travels*, a landmark work of twentieth-century Chinese national literature, thus emerged out of a river engineer's desire to describe China's landscapes in new ways that consequently reinvented landscape narration.

Landscape Writing of Anti-tradition

Like most classically trained literati, Liu E was versed in poetic writing. As an outstanding calligrapher and internationally known collector of antiques and classical Chinese paintings, Liu also possessed rich knowledge of traditional artistic works. These models celebrate the traditional aesthetic ideal of fusing one's feelings with natural scenery (*qing jing jiaorong* 情景交融). However, Liu does not draw on these traditional resources when writing landscapes in *The Travels*. On the contrary, he tries to negate them. For Liu E, natural landscape is not knowable through human aesthetic empathy. Rather, it is something mysterious and difficult to capture.

Landscape writing in the novel begins in chapter 2 with a description of scenery expressing the cultural weight of nature. Liu E's sensitivity to and familiarity with painting informed his writing of one of the most famous scenic descriptions in modern Chinese literature: Lao Can's visit to the beautiful Lake Da'ming 大明湖, a celebrated vista in Ji'nan, the seat of Shandong Province. The scene reflects the influence of the artistic and literary tradition with which Liu was engaged. He describes the fair sight of Thousand Buddha Hill near Lake Da'ming:

> [Lao Can] saw facing him on the Thousand Buddha Hill groups of monastic buildings among the gray-green pines and blue-green cypresses. The trees were crowded

together, some red with a fiery red, others white with the white of snow, some indigo blue, others jade green, a few patches of maple red showing among the rest. It was as though a great painting by the Song artist Zhao Qianli had been made into a screen several tens of *li* long. (Liu 1990, 13–14)

只見對面千佛山上，梵宇僧樓，與那蒼松翠柏，高下相間，紅的火紅，白的雪白，青的靛青，綠的碧綠，更有那一株半株的丹楓夾在裡面，彷彿宋人趙千里的一幅大畫，做了一架數十里長的屏風。

Liu E compares the colorful mountain scene to a landscape painting by the Southern Song (1127–1279) artist Zhao Boju 趙伯駒 (courtesy name Qianli 千里, 1119–1185), famous for blue-green mountain (*qinglü shanshui* 青綠山水) paintings.[3] While Liu E explicitly contextualizes Lao Can's observation of the mountain scene within the Chinese painting aesthetic tradition, he connects Lao Can's appreciation of Lake Da'ming to the poetic tradition. Surprised to see no tourists around the fabulous sightseeing spot, Lao Can turns around and finds a couplet inscribed on the columns of a gate. The verse, composed by the famous Qing poet Liu Fenggao 劉鳳誥 (1761–1830), depicts the beauty of the lake view, which prompts Lao Can to nod in agreement. As Leo Ou-fan Lee points out, the protagonist at this moment looks for company, someone with whom to share the marvelous beauty of the view (2010, 22–25). Lao Can's company is a dead poet, and poetry makes this moment of transtemporal connection possible. Liu E calls forth the Chinese aesthetic and poetic tradition to capture, from the beginning of the novel, his experience of landscapes in the most representative scenery in Shandong.

Liu E's drawing on poetic and artistic traditions in landscape writing is evident throughout the novel. In chapter 8's account of scholar Shen Ziping 申子平's journey in the snowy mountains, the narrator likens the mountainscape (see chapter 2) to a screen painted in the blue-green landscape style:

> He saw a stretch of mountains rising before him like a great screen . . . the rocks were blue against the white snow; the twigs on the trees were brown; and the many pines and cypresses were green in tufts like the moss that painters represent by dots. (Liu 1990, 85–86)
>
> 只見不遠前面就是一片高山，像架屏風似的，迎面豎起⋯⋯。石是青的，雪是白的，樹上枝條是黃的，又有許多松柏是綠的，一叢一叢，如畫上點的苔一樣。

This mountainscape, which Shen Ziping sees through the lens of traditional blue-green landscape painting, is effectively another large-scale screen painted by Zhao

---

3. Tang dynasty (618–907) blue-green mountain paintings stress these mountain colors. This painting style contrasts with literati-style ink painting (*wenren hua* 文人畫), an often-monochrome landscape painting style popular in the Song dynasty. Zhao Boju was an expert in blue-green mountain paintings, into which he incorporated literati-style ink painting techniques.

Boju. Like Lao Can, who encapsulates his aesthetic experience of seeing Thousand Buddha Hill and Lake Da'ming in a couplet, Shen Ziping likewise attempts to capture this painting-like mountainscape with a verse. In writing this mountain landscape of inland Shandong in chapter 8, Liu follows the same aesthetic and literary conventions of the earlier scene at Lake Da'ming in the provincial seat.

Liu E at the same time doubts whether these traditional aesthetic forms can capture the visual experiences. In chapter 2's closing commentary, Liu E (2013, 33) declares that the descriptive passages on Da'ming Lake are something "the author [Liu] can write, but Zhao Qianli would not be able to paint" 作者倒寫得出，吾恐趙千里還畫不出. In chapter 8's description of the mountain scene with Shen Ziping, the narrator interrupts the power of poetry. Just as Shen Ziping is enthralled by the snowy view and tries to create poetic lines to describe it, "He heard a sound, *ke-duo*, and suddenly felt a weakness in his legs. His whole body began to sway and he rolled down into the gully" 只聽殼鐸一聲，覺得腿襠一軟，身子一搖，竟滾下山澗去了 (Liu 1990, 86). This rather comical fall disrupts a lyrical moment of a literatus trying to describe a picturesque landscape through poetry, aborting a moment of traditional literati aesthetics before it begins. *The Travels* appropriates a traditional aesthetic form not to preserve it but, on the contrary, to question its efficacy in capturing visual experiences of nature.

Liu E attempts to capture the visual experience of nature in a way that he believes traditional artistic and literary techniques cannot fully convey. In the latter half of chapter 8, after Shen Ziping's fall, Liu E presents what he considers a new way to describe visual experiences. After being rescued from the gully, Shen Ziping and his servants stumble across a tiger:

> When they had gone thirty or forty steps, they heard in the distance two cries, "*wu, wu.*" The men said, "A tiger!" They went on but strained their ears listening. . . . They saw something bounding along in the moonlight on the western ridge. When it reached the top, there was another roar. No sooner had they seen it crouch to spring than it had already reached the bank of the west stream, where it gave another cry. The men hiding there, cold and frightened, were unable to control their trembling, and kept their eyes fixed on the tiger. When the tiger reached the stream he stood still, his eyes reflecting the moonlight and glowing brightly. . . . He roared in the direction of the men, then crouched again, and bounded toward them. . . . Their souls had long ago fled from their bodies! They waited quite a long while but saw no further signs of the tiger. One of the men up in the tree was the boldest of them all. He came down and cried to the rest, "Come out! The tiger is miles away." The men came out one after another and pulled Ziping, dumb with fright, out of his crevice in the rock wall. After some time he managed to open his mouth and asked, "Are we dead, or are we alive?" The men said, "The tiger has gone." Ziping said, "How did he go? Is no one hurt?" One of the men who had been up in the tree said, "I watched how he came down the west slope of the gully; he darted through the air like a bird and here he was. The place where he landed was

seven or eight *zhang* higher than the top of our tree. After he'd reached that point, another leap and he was on the eastern ridge. He gave one roar and went off to the east." (Liu 1990, 89–90)

走了不過三四十步,聽得遠遠嗚嗚的兩聲。車夫道:「虎叫!虎叫!」一頭走著,一頭留神聽著。⋯⋯只見西邊嶺上月光之下,竄上一個物件來。到了嶺上,又是嗚的一聲。只見把身子往下一探,已經到了西澗邊了,又是嗚的一聲。這裡的人又是冷,又是怕,止不住格格價亂抖,還用眼睛看著那虎。那虎既到西澗,卻立住了腳,眼睛映著月光,灼亮灼亮⋯⋯對著這幾個人,又嗚的一聲,將身子一縮,對著這邊撲過來了⋯⋯。這幾個人早已嚇得魂飛魄散了。大家等了許久,卻不見虎的動靜。還是那樹上的車夫膽大,下來喊眾人道:「出來罷!虎去遠了。」車夫等人次第出來,方才從石壁縫裡把子平拉出,已經嚇得呆了。過了半天,方能開口說話,問道:「我們是死的是活的哪?」車夫道:「虎過去了。」子平道:「虎怎樣過去的?一個人沒有傷麼?」那在樹上的車夫道:「我看他從澗西沿過來的時候,只是一穿,彷彿像鳥兒似的,已經到了這邊了。他落腳的地方,比我們這樹梢還高著七八丈呢。落下來之後,又是一縱,已經到了這東嶺上邊,嗚的一聲向東去了。

Liu E comments on this passage in the closing commentary.[4] He first compares his writing of the tiger with the tiger paintings of the famous Ming literati painter Tang Yin 唐寅 (1470–1524, courtesy name Ziwei). He declares Tang Yin's tigers dead because his paintings fail to render the animal's vital dynamic flow.[5] This echoes Liu E's assertion that Zhao Boju would be incapable of painting the Da'ming Lake scenery as well as Liu writes about it. Liu E proceeds to compare his writing of the tiger with the widely celebrated Ming heroic romance *The Water Margin* (*Shuihu zhuan* 水滸傳), attributed to Shi Nai'an and well known for the iconic "Wu Song fights the tiger" 武松打虎 scene. Liu E thinks that although *The Water Margin* renders the tiger vividly, it still loses luster beside his writing, which captures the untraceable divine tiger. Liu E clearly states the unprecedented achievement of his description of Shen Ziping's encounter with the tiger in comparison to the tradition of art and literature.

Shen Ziping's encounter with the tiger is essentially an allegory of visual perception. An encounter with a tiger in the mountains is an important trope in traditional Chinese novels. In major late imperial novels like *The Water Margin*, *The Scholars* (*Rulin waishi* 儒林外史, 1749), and *Flowers in the Mirror* (*Jinghua yuan* 鏡花緣, 1817), tigers are killed by a hero or some beast or are scared off and flee.

---

4. The comment says, "Tang Ziwei did not paint a tiger as well as Shi Nai'an described it. Tang Ziwei painted a tiger that is dead, while Shi Nai'an described a living one. Shi Nai'an did not describe a tiger as well as the Scholar of Hundred Temperings [Liu E's pen name] described it. Shi Nai'an described ordinary tigers, while Scholar of Hundred Temperings describes a divine tiger" 唐子畏畫虎,不及施耐庵說虎。唐子畏畫的是死虎,施耐庵說的是活虎。施耐庵說虎,不及百鍊生說虎。施耐庵說的是凡虎,百鍊生說的是神虎 (Liu 2013, 146–47).

5. No authenticated painting by Tang Yin depicts a tiger. However, tiger paintings attributed to him appear in the art market every now and then, even today.

In these stories, the encounter with a tiger symbolizes the character's conquest of internal fear. However, the tiger that Shen Ziping encounters is a new species in the history of Chinese fiction. The character in the episode has a limited perspective on the beast, and this tiger is impossible to trace. The tiger's roar fills Shen Ziping and his servants with dread, but they cannot track down its physical presence. Unlike in earlier novels, the crisis here ends not with the tiger being killed or taking flight but with it leaving by itself virtually unseen. This scene in *The Travels* does not provide readers with a conventional allegorical meaning of bravery. Here, it entwines feelings of fear with visual elusiveness. Liu E's description of an elusive and untraceable tiger wandering freely in the moonlight introduces a new visual experience. The tiger signifies an untraceable natural world, and the encounter with the unseen tiger allegorizes the effort to visualize nature as fundamentally unperceivable.

In chapter 8, Liu E questions traditional art forms' ability to capture—like a tiger—the natural environment and attempts to describe unpredictable and uncapturable nature. Liu E's writing does not express the attainment of unity between humans and nature, a key principle of traditional philosophical and aesthetic views on nature. Instead, nature is so enigmatic and unpredictable that it cannot be expressed within traditional literary and artistic frameworks. In his writing of natural landscapes, Liu E attempts to convey the challenges of expressing nature understood and experienced in this way.

Telescoping the Yellow River

We should understand Liu E's expression of the difficulties in capturing natural landscapes through the relationship between his landscape writing and his experience in river work. For Liu, no natural landscape is more significant and impressive than the Yellow River, which he spent all his energy and time understanding during his prime, in his thirties. Liu was commissioned in 1889 to lead a delineating survey and mapping of the Yellow River reaches in the provinces of Henan, Zhili, and Shandong. His experience of surveying, mapping, and governing the Yellow River defined how he understood and perceived natural landscapes more generally.

In his task of measurement, a major concern for Liu E was the limits of human visual capacity. Liu E lists the instability of perception as one of the ten greatest difficulties of measuring the Yellow River in an official work report. He writes, "The view changes with one's position, and [the moments to capture the precise shape of the river] are transient. One uses all five senses together to secure [the precision of the measurement]" 移步換形，稍縱即逝，五官并用，庶免遺忘 (Liu 2007, 1:25).[6]

---

6. The phrase "view changing with position" is used by the Qing scholar Dai Mingshi 戴名世 (1653–1713) in his essay, "A Travelogue to Mount Yandang" ("Yandang ji" 雁蕩記), where it means that the mountainscape changes as the viewer moves (see Dai 1986, 276).

The phrase "the view changes with one's position" was originally used to describe the aesthetic experience in traditional Chinese landscape painting. It suggests one can experience a single scene in multiple ways. However, Liu turns the aesthetic term into an expression of frustration over the visual faculty's inability to capture transient changes in detail. He points out that measurement depends on extraordinary eyesight but also that eyesight is deeply limited when capturing motion. As Liu E explains, imperfections in the eye's curvature produce deviations in measurement, and atmospheric refraction and the Earth's curvature cause metrological uncertainties; the consequent minor discrepancies almost always lead to huge errors. The eye's observation is thus fundamentally flawed. His solution is to incorporate accurate measurement techniques and to use optical apparatus and math to correct human error (1:35). Liu E highlights both how river measurement's demand for precision challenges the limits of the visual sense and how optical apparatuses are crucial to precisely investigating the river.

Embedded in the novel's Yellow River landscapes is Liu E's perspective as a river map delineator, which he was developing during his Shandong river work. The passage most obviously related to Liu E's profession is the description in chapter 12, which portrays the ice jam on the Yellow River's Qihe County reach in Shandong. Liu E was very familiar with this river reach as he had meticulously registered the river's route within Qihe County when he was a river map delineator.[7] The ice jam is a tour de force of descriptive precision:

> When Lao Can had washed his face and arranged his baggage, he locked his room and walked out to the dike to see what was happening. The Yellow River came from the southwest and, making a bend here, went due east. The bed of the river was not very wide, the two banks being not more than two *li* apart. Lao Can saw piled up before him layers of packed ice which rose seven or eight inches above the surface. He wandered up the river a couple of hundred paces. The ice from above kept coming down block after block, until at this point it was caught by the ice in front, couldn't move, and came to a standstill. More ice came and pressed it with a rustling sound, chi-chi, until the ice behind, pressed harder by the flowing water, simply jumped on top of the ice in front. Pressed down in this way, the ice in front was gradually submerged. The surface of the water was not more than a hundred *zhang* wide. In the middle the main stream was not more than about twenty or thirty *zhang*, and on both sides was smooth water. This smooth water had long before been frozen over completely and the surface of the ice was smooth but had been covered with dust by the wind so that it looked like a sandy desert. The main stream in the middle, however, continued to roar on with noise and power, pushing

---

7. The Qihe County reach in Shandong Province was one of the most comprehensively examined, such as in Liu E's "Riverway of the Yellow River in the Three Provinces II" ("San sheng Huanghe hedao er" 三省黃河河道二) and "The Constructing Work of Embankments along the North Bank of the Yellow River" ("San sheng Huanghe bei'an tigong biao" 三省黃河北岸堤工表). See Liu 2007, 1:7, 11.

the packed ice so that it jumped away on both sides, until the ice on the smooth water was crushed by the pieces from the main stream and driven five or six feet up on the shore. Many broken pieces of ice were stood on end by the pressure, forming a low screen. Lao Can watched it for about an hour, until the packed ice was wedged solid.[8] (Liu 1990, 130–31)

> 老殘洗完了臉，把行李鋪好，把房門鎖上，也出來步到河堤上看，見那黃河從西南上下來，到此卻正是〔河〕的灣子，過此便向正東去了。河面不甚寬，兩岸相距不到二里。若以此刻河水而論，也不過百把丈寬的光景。只是面前的冰插的重重疊疊的，高出水面有七八寸厚。再望上游走了一二百步，只見那上流的冰還一塊一塊的漫漫價來，到此地被前頭的攔住，走不動，就站住了。那後來的冰趕上他，只擠得嗤嗤價響。後冰被這溜水逼的緊了，就竄到前冰上頭去。前冰被壓就漸漸低下去了。看那河身不過百十丈寬。當中大溜約莫不過二三十丈。兩邊俱是平水。這平水之上早已有冰結滿。冰面卻是平的，被吹來的塵土蓋住，卻像沙灘一般。中間的一道大溜卻仍然奔騰澎湃，有聲有勢，將那走不過去的冰擠的兩邊亂竄。那兩邊平水上的冰被當中亂冰擠破了，往岸上跑。那冰能擠到岸上有五六尺遠。許多碎冰被擠的站起來，像個小插屏似的。看了有點把鐘工夫，這一截子的冰又擠死不動了。

The observations on the ice jam stylistically mimic a technical report concerned with measurement, highlighting the channel curvature, channel width, and bankfull width.[9] Notably, despite the detailed and analytic depictions of the landscape, the speaker, Lao Can, does not emphasize a unified vision of the landscape typical of traditional travelogues. The description is broken into pieces with the precise, methodological vision of an engineer. Lao Can notices that "the two banks [were] not more than two *li* 里 [approx. 960 m] apart" and that "the surface of the water was not more than a hundred *zhang* 丈 [approx. 300 m] wide." He walks upstream to observe the ice jam at a distance of no more than one or two hundred *bu* 步 (approx. 160 m).[10] The area observed in this account falls within one square *li* (approx. 480 m2), the smallest unit of measurement in Liu E's river map delineation.[11] Liu's perspective

---

8. Translation has been modestly adjusted.
9. Bankfull width refers to the distance between the banks when the water level rises to the top of its banks.
10. Traditional units of length include the *chi* 尺, *bu*, *zhang*, and *li*. The length of the units and the ratios between them has varied over time. One *bu* has consisted of either five or six *chi*; one *zhang* has consisted of ten *chi*; one *li* has consisted of 300 or 360 *bu*. In the Qing dynasty, one *chi* was equivalent to 0.30–0.33 m (see Schinz 1996, 428).
11. Liu E explains the precision of his river map as follows: "This map is made at one *li* per *fang* [a square on a map divided into a grid for accurate reference], which is unprecedented. The river is tortuous, with several twists and turns within one *li*, and the dams and the dikes are only few *zhang* in width and length. If we draw it at two *li* per *fang*, then the river, which turns every dozen *zhang*, and the dams and dikes, which are a few *zhang* in length and width, cannot be presented within a *fang*" 此圖每方一里，尤為前此所無。蓋河形曲折，一里數變，坝身堤面，丈尺無多。如以二里為一方，則數十丈一曲之河，與長數丈之坝、寬數丈之堤，皆不能繪入方內 (Liu 2007, 1:34).

as a river map delineator frames the novel's description of the Yellow River ice jam, which is marked by engineering precision.[12]

The precise units of measurement in the ice jam scene suggest the operation of optical instruments. The narration starts from the two banks, then moves to the river's mainstream at the center of the channel, then to the piled-up pack of ice above the water's surface. It then turns to the ice flowing downstream, moves back to the packed ice crushed by the floating ice pushed on top of it, and shifts from the mainstream to the frozen surface of the smooth water near the river shore. After these quick shifts in visual focus, the narrator's gaze turns back to the river's mainstream, refocuses on the ice at its center, goes to the ice driven from the mainstream to the smooth water area near the shore, and finally moves to the small pieces of ice pushed five or six feet up the shore by the bigger ice pieces driven from the mainstream. This constantly moving vision, shifting back and forth, zooming in and out, mimics the effect of adjusting the focus of an optical instrument such as a telescope. Furthermore, the narrator delivers an illusion of immediate visual experience similar to the experience of a telescope user.[13] While the narration provides an impression of panoramic Yellow River landscapes, it simultaneously describes the most intricate activities of the water and ice. The narrator invites readers to participate in the visualization of every detail of the vast landscape. The distance between the spectator-narrator and the landscape seems nonexistent, such that the ever-mutable landscape totally occupies, fills, overwhelms, and even engulfs the spectator's senses. Here, Liu E uses language not so much to record the natural scenery as to simulate the vision made possible by an engineer's optical instrument with adjustable focus.

Liu's professional training as a river map delineator shaped his descriptions of the Yellow River landscape in the novel. The landscape, requiring painstaking and repetitious observational labor to capture, is far more complicated and patternless than poetic phrases and parallel prose can express. Liu's telescopic language bespeaks his need to overcome the limits of human vision in his work surveying and mapping the river with the aid of optical instruments. His description of the Yellow River landscape ushered in a moment when landscape writing outgrew set poetic and parallelistic diction and vernacular language, which had already been widely

---

12. The ice jam on the Yellow River described in chapter 12 is actually a magnified version of the crushing ice in the stream in chapter 8, where "small pieces of ice striking against the large sheet of ice as they were carried forward by the current" 水流帶著小冰，與那大冰相撞擊的聲音 (Liu 1990, 85). We can also see Liu E's incorporation of his technical perspective of river mapping into the writing of water landscapes in this passage. The detailed view of the greatly expanded landscape implies an omniscient narrator with rich experience and knowledge of river and mountain topology, which only an expert river mapping delineator such as Liu E could possess.
13. This "illusion of presence" produced by monoculars has already been played on and developed to the fullest in Li Yu's 李漁 (1611–1680) short story "Xiayi lou" 夏宜樓 (A tower for the summer heat) (see Shang 2016, 117–18).

used in chaptered novels, then aptly undertook the role of expressing such survey and mapping experiences.

Visuality and National Sentimentality in Landscape Writing

To Liu E, river work was more than a profession. Driven by national sentiment, Liu identified his engagement in Yellow River regulation as a significant part of his technical efforts to save the nation. That is, his river engineering efforts were both technical and sentimental. His interest in optics, which arose from his anxiety about the limits of human visual capacity in managing the instability and unpredictability of the untamed Yellow River, related not merely to the issue of visuality but also to that of national sentimentality. Liu E's landscape writing presents an integrated concern for visuality and national sentimentality in its fullest form.

Light refraction is the focus of the two most famous landscape descriptions, the passages related to Lake Da'ming and the springs in Ji'nan. In chapter 2, the narrator describes Lake Da'ming as a mirror, whose reflection of Thousand Buddha Hill is clearer and more beautiful than the hill itself. Through comparison, the narrator points out the illusory nature of a visual experience in which a reflection is more reliable and appealing than the original. The narrator proceeds to describe a white bloom of reeds that resembles a rose-colored velvet carpet because of the reflection of "the vaporous beams of the setting sun" 帶水氣的斜陽. The sunbeams that come in at an oblique angle, together with the water vapor that forms the medium of light refraction, present a fascinating sight. This description reveals the conditions and process by which a visual experience is formed. Liu E exhibits the same interest in light refraction when describing the Golden Thread Spring in chapter 3. Legend has it that there is a golden thread in the spring, but Lao Can cannot figure out how to see it. Only with a local gentleman's guidance does he learn that an observer must stand in a specific position and bend over at a specific angle to see a golden thread on the water's surface, created by two springs of matching strength, which when flowing against each other force up between them a current that catches the sunlight. Lao Can's discovery of the mechanics of observation here shows Liu E's sensitivity to hydrodynamics, originating in his river engineering knowledge and experience. Liu's landscape writing emphasizes the interrelationship between water, angle, light, and the creation of illusion.

Although the lake and the springs are separate sightseeing spots, Liu described them against the hidden context of an interconnected water system. Lake Da'ming was fed by a drainage system connected to the springs in Ji'nan, whose water discharged through the lake to a canal connected to the Yellow River. As the narrator suggests in explaining the history of the river port town Luokou 雒口 in chapter 4, the water system in Ji'nan is considered part of the Yellow River water system:

Water, Landscape, and the Appearance of a New National Literature 101

> Formerly, before the Yellow River took the bed of Daqing River, the streams from the seventy-two springs in the city entered that river here and it was a very flourishing place. But ever since the Yellow River took the bed of the Daqing River, although there is still some coming and going of cargo boats, the traffic is not more than ten or twenty percent of what it was formerly, a big difference. (Liu 1990, 44)
>
> 當初黃河未併大清河的時候，凡城裡的七十二泉泉水，皆從此地入河，本是個極繁盛的所在。自從黃河併了，雖仍有貨船來往，究竟不過十分之一二，差得遠了。

The narrator sees Luokou's glorious history as linked to the convergence of the seventy-two springs of Ji'nan and laments the town's decline, which began with the Daqing River's capture by the Yellow River, a consequence of the latter's historically significant course shift in 1855.[14] The narration of Luokou's decline implies that Ji'nan's spring drainage system should be understood in relation to the history of the Yellow River's regulation. Liu E, through the narrator's voice, suggests that Lake Da'ming and the springs in Ji'nan—whose depiction focuses on the effects of light refraction—are hydraulically connected to the broader Yellow River water system and its history. The themes of flooding and governance of the Yellow River underlie the description of water landscapes in the novel's beginning chapters. The landscape writing features the interplay between light and water and Liu E's concern for river work.

Liu E's emphasis on the mechanics of light and visual effect in landscape writing reflects far more than his hydraulic professional concern. It also reflects the strong national sentiment he expresses powerfully and publicly from the outset of the story. The famous sinking ship allegory in the novel's first chapter tells how, in a dream, Lao Can and his friends try to save a passenger ship from sinking in the raging sea. The scene conveys Liu E's anxiety about the internal and external dangers China faces and justifies his effort to aid its dire political situation. Although it is widely considered Liu's self-defense for his controversial attempts to participate in national industrial projects,[15] this allegory expresses strong national sentiment amid motifs of light and visuality. The narrator first pays attention to how Lao Can and his friends fascinate themselves with illusions of mirages. The narrator then explores the mechanics of atmospheric refraction in a lengthy discussion on why, even though daytime and nighttime are equally long in autumn, the day seems longer, arriving early. Liu E embeds his interest in the complicated mechanics of light at the beginning of the novel, where he sets the tone for his national salvation narrative.

---

14. For a comprehensive study of the history of Ji'nan's water system and its relationship to the Yellow River, see Yang 2017.
15. See Chapter 2 for the discussion of Liu E's controversial participation in the national industrial projects.

The relationship between landscape writing and the narrative of national salvation, conveyed implicitly at the beginning of the novel, manifests fully in chapter 12, hinging on Lao Can's responses to the vista. The chapter contains the description of the mountain view that Lao Can sees on his way back to the inn from the riverbank—Hu Shih lauds it as the most extraordinary landscape writing in the novel. While Hu attributed the excellence of the scenery writing to Liu E's exquisite observation, the description reflects, rather, the limited capacity of human vision to perceive changes in light. This passage is narrated from Lao Can's limited perspective:

> He raised his head and looked up at the hills to the south. The snow-white line reflected the light of the moon; it was extraordinarily beautiful. The mountain ranges rose tier on tier, but they could not be clearly distinguished. A few white clouds lay in the folds of the hills so that you could hardly tell cloud from hill unless you looked intently. The clouds were white, and the hills were white; the clouds were luminous, and the hills were luminous too. Yet because the moon was above the clouds and the clouds beneath the moon, the clouds were luminous with a light which had penetrated from behind. This was not true, however, of the hills; the light there flowed directly from the moon and was then reflected by the snow, so that the light was of two kinds. But only the nearer parts were like this. The hills stretched away to the east farther and farther until gradually the sky was white, the hills were white, and the clouds were white, and nothing could be distinguished from anything else. (Liu 1990, 131–32)
>
> 抬起頭來看那南面的山,一條雪白,映著月光分外好看。一層一層的山嶺,卻不大分辨得出。又有幾片白雲夾在裡面,所以看不出是雲是山。及至定神看去,方纔看出那是雲那是山來。雖然雲也是白的,山也是白的,雲也有亮光,山也有亮光,只因為月在雲上,雲在月下,所以雲的亮光是從背面透過來的。那山卻不然,山上的亮光是由月光照到山上,被那山上的雪反射過來,所以光是兩樣子的。然只就稍近的地方如此,那山往東去,越望越遠,漸漸的天也是白的,山也是白的,雲也是白的,就分辨不出甚麼來了。

Lao Can's experience of the vista begins with the beauty of the "snow-white line," an indistinguishable and luminous band of moonlit hills and white clouds. However, he does not dwell long on this aesthetic aspect of the reflected moonlight. Once he "looks intently," he realizes that the white mountain and white clouds differ in brightness and hue and that this difference stems from their relative location to the moon. The single "snow-white line" thus results from a momentary trick of the eyes. The moment Lao Can "looks intently" is not only about discerning the differences of light but also exploring the creation of illusions; and the contours of the mountain and clouds change with the way Lao Can looks at them. In other words, as the novel discloses the cause of illusions, it rewrites the landscape in a new way. The narrator also describes Lao Can's poetic response to the snowy scene, connecting the protagonist's observation of the mountainscape with Liu E's national sentiment. While looking at the snowy mountains, Lao Can thinks of Xie Lingyun's 謝靈運 (385–433)

poem "The Year's End" ("Suimu" 歲暮), which expresses the poet's lament for lost time and his failure to achieve what was expected for the year. Liu E further defines Lao Can's melancholy mood as a feeling of powerlessness in the face of national crisis: immediately after the reference to "The Year's End," Lao Can thinks of the poem "Great East" from the *Book of Odes*, written to protest political turmoil (see Chapter 3 of this book). The snowy white moonlit mountainscape evokes Lao Can's worry for his troubled nation and his incapability to help. Liu E's national sentiment is coded as the landscape writing that addresses his anxiety regarding the limitations of visuality and his interest in the mechanics of visual effects stemming from his experience as a river engineer.

Landscape writing in *The Travels* focuses on the mechanism of visual experience. It involves not just *what* but *how* one sees. The novel's landscape writing originates from Liu E's anxiety over the limitations of human visual perception—which stemmed from his experience surveying and mapping the Yellow River—and a keen interest in optical knowledge derived from that anxiety. Liu E's attention to the mechanics of visual effects in his landscape writing is closely associated not only with his flood control expertise but also with his national sentiment. He describes not so much natural landscapes as national landscapes.

Philosophies, Light, and Visions of China

For late-Qing intellectuals troubled by China's peril, the nation's unknown future was their core concern. Consequently, they showed interest in precognition, or supernormal knowledge of future events.[16] Precognition had never been strange to traditional Chinese literati. The *Doctrine of the Mean* (*Zhongyong* 中庸, fourth century BCE), one of the *Four Books* (*Sishu* 四書, compiled 1190) in Confucianism, considers precognition an ability acquired through moral cultivation, as in the expression "the way of utmost sincerity entails foreknowledge" 至誠之道，可以前知.[17] This Confucianism-based interest in foreknowledge, combined with the late Qing interest in vision-enhancing technology, formed an important part of contemporaneous intellectuals' vision of the nation's future.[18] The association between foreknowledge, moral cultivation, and visuality, however, was not a late Qing invention but rather the heritage of Chinese philosophical tradition. Early Confucianism

---

16. For a discussion of how early twentieth-century Chinese intellectuals understood extrasensory perception, see Huang 2014, 121–96. For a history of extrasensory perception studies, see May and Marwaha 2015.
17. The way of translating "cheng" 誠 in this context has been controversial. Traditionally, "cheng" is translated as "sincerity." For a discussion of "cheng" being translated as "creativity" rather than "sincerity," see Ames and Hall 2001, 31–32. Here I follow the traditional translation.
18. For a discussion of the relationship between foreknowledge and *zhicheng*, see Wang 1914, 11–12; 1915, 5–6; for a discussion of the associations between foreknowledge and the introduction of visual technology in early twentieth-century China, see Hsu 2015, 138–43.

had considered human visual capacity as directly related to moral cultivation. Sages, with their perfect morality and understanding of the ultimate principle of the universe, were believed to have limitless visual capacity and access to foreknowledge.[19] Late-Qing intellectuals' vision for China was a modern transformation of an early Confucian tradition.

Liu E envisions China in a similar but more complicated sense. In chapter 1 of volume 1, Lao Can sees the sinking ship awaiting rescue, an allegory of China in crisis, through a telescope. It suggests a link between vision-enhancing technology and political foreknowledge. The first chapter of the novel's second volume—a sequel published in 1907—starts with a discussion of precognition in relation to moral cultivation, which is a familiar way of addressing the issue in the Confucian tradition. Although the novel bases its understanding of precognition on their common themes of visuality and morality, we should understand Liu E's approach to political precognition in a more personal context. As a follower of the Taigu school, a religious school with syncretic doctrines combining the Three Teachings—Confucianism, Daoism, and Buddhism[20]—Liu E understood the practice of moral cultivation differently than traditional Confucianists did. In addition, for Liu, the issue of visuality involves not merely visual capacity but, as mentioned, a strong interest in optics and the mechanics of visual experience. A true understanding of the novel's imagination of the nation's future is grounded in Liu E's unique approach to philosophy and visuality.

Liu E addresses the anxiety for the nation's future via philosophical dialogues in two episodes, each at the structural center of a volume of the novel. The two episodes—a conversation in the Peach Blossom Mountain (Taohua shan 桃花山) and a trip to Mount Tai to watch the sunrise—represents Liu's attempt to incorporate his interest in visuality and Taigu school philosophy into a broader political imagination of China. Imbued with highly political implications, Liu builds the two episodes around the ultimate origins of light emanating from the moon and sun. His fascination with light, rooted in his profession as a river engineer, manifests not merely in natural landscape writing but is embodied in the novel's political imagination of the nation.

Chapters 10 and 11 of the first volume, which narrate a conversation between the scholar Shen Ziping, the prophet Yellow Dragon, and the philosopher Yugu

---

19. Wang Chong (1962, 114) 王充 of the Han dynasty criticized his contemporary Confucianists as follows: "The literati, discoursing on Sages, are of the opinion that they know thousands of years of the past, and ten thousand future generations. Merely by the keenness of their sight, and the subtlety of their hearing, they are able to give the proper names to new things, which they know spontaneously, without learning, and understand, without inquiring, wherefore the term Sage is equivalent with supernatural" 儒者論聖人，以為前知千歲，後知萬世，有獨見之明，獨聽之聰，事來則名，不學自知，不問自曉，故稱聖，則神矣. Translation slightly adapted.
20. For a history of Taigu philosophy and practice, see Han 2017.

in the Peach Blossom Mountain, express Liu E's understanding of philosophy in relation to his political imagination. The conversation at the structural center of the twenty-chapter first volume debates whether there is a real difference between upward and downward in the future developments of state affairs. The debate is carried out from two philosophical standpoints. One is Song Neo-Confucianism, of which Shen Ziping is a pedantic adherent. It emphasizes the dichotomy between the virtue of the heavenly principle and the vice of human desires (see Chapter 2). The other, represented by Yellow Dragon and Yugu, is Liu E's favored Taigu school. Liu E, as many scholars indicate, uses the debate to address his vision for Chinese politics from a Taigu perspective (Hsia 2004, 248–49, 263; Wang X. 1993a, 1993b, 2000). Stressing the complementarity of the Three Teachings, the Taigu school followers drew on Confucianism, Buddhism, and religious Daoism to suit their needs. For the conversation in the Peach Blossom Mountain, Liu E draws on Buddhism to criticize Neo-Confucianism. Shen Ziping, following the Neo-Confucian conceptual framework marked by dichotomic opposition, holds that the difference between upward and downward movement, like that between human desires and the heavenly principle, should be firmly defined. Yellow Dragon and Yugu challenge Shen Ziping's view with the Buddhist negation of dualism in the concept of emptiness,[21] arguing instead that the difference between upward and downward exists only in appearance, not essence. The debate about the future of China's state affairs is one of Neo-Confucianism and Buddhism.

The conversation in the Peach Blossom Mountain shows how Liu E identifies Buddhism as a propelling force for Chinese political history. Whereas Neo-Confucianism had dominated political discourse since the fourteenth century, it was not until the late nineteenth century that Buddhism began to claim significance in the political domain. Buddhism attracted almost all renowned late-Qing Westernizing faction members and constitutional reformers. The political reform movement drew largely on Buddhism to address the problems caused by Neo-Confucianism's long-term dominance in the political domain and the cultural challenges from the West (Wang 1985, 38; Zhang 1988, 30–31; Ge 1998, 44; Yang 2004a, 2004b). As a supporter of the Westernizing faction, Liu E followed this trend and incorporated the dialogue between Neo-Confucianism and Buddhism into the novel. Liu saw Chinese state affairs as far more complex than Neo-Confucianism's dichotomous framework could address and even considered China's dire political straits as a repercussion of it. The Peach Blossom Mountain debate ends with the Buddhist view prevailing, suggesting that adopting a Buddhist negation of dualism is the only way to avoid falling prey to a dichotomous and disastrous political framework.

---

21. For a detailed discussion of the Two Truths (*erdi yi* 二諦義) concept in Chinese Buddhism and its deconstruction of dualism, see Shih 2004.

Liu E constructs the debate over Neo-Confucianism and Buddhism with the concern for visuality. The three interlocutors compare the vicissitudes of the nation's future development to lunar phases, with the speakers offering different astronomic understandings of the moon. The detailed discussion of the moon's phase changes reflects both Liu E's passion for astronomy and late Qing newspapers' increased coverage of the observation of celestial bodies. In such media coverage, astronomical telescopes were invariably the focus.[22] Considering this, the telescope as an optical instrument is an implicit but important context to the Peach Blossom Mountain debate. More importantly, the three debaters' recognition of the moon's phase changes as a visual effect represents Liu E's enthusiasm for the mechanics of light and visual effects. Shen Ziping, arguing that a clear distinction exists in the ups and downs of state affairs, points to the fact the moon has permanently bright and dark hemispheres because of the sunlight's reflection. In contrast, Yellow Dragon and Yugu suggest that the state's upward and downward swings are like the waxing and waning of the moon: they are transient illusions observed by the human eye from Earth. To Yellow Dragon and Yugu, the moon is a metaphor for transcending the dichotomous thinking that Shen Ziping advocates. The debate about China's future in the Peach Blossom Mountain integrates Liu E's concerns for philosophy, visuality, and the nation's destiny.

The moon phase allegory can be traced to the early development of the Neo-Confucian and Buddhist philosophical traditions. Zhu Xi, one of the most important founders of the Song Neo-Confucianism, argued for the doctrine of "one principle with many manifestations" (*li yi fen shu* 理一分殊), meaning all phenomena are the diverse manifestations of the universe's single ultimate principle, or the Way. Zhu Xi's most famous explanation of the doctrine uses the moon as a metaphor. Yet Zhu Xi was not the first to employ this metaphor to explain the Way. As early as the Tang dynasty, Buddhism employed it to explain the concept of emptiness. In other words, Buddhism and Neo-Confucianism share the imagery of the moon, which both use to illustrate their doctrines.[23] The use of the moon phase allegory in the Peach Blossom Mountain debate illustrates how Liu E transforms a traditional philosophical metaphor into an allegory of light and visual effect to envision a new China.

While Liu E uses the moon phase metaphor for state affairs, he adopts sunlight as a metaphor to address his anxiety about China's political future. The sun, the

---

22. The observation of the moon and Mars was the focus of scientific news coverage around the turn of the twentieth century. As one report puts it, "As science makes progress, it is possible that there will be transportation between Earth and other planets. Since observation of celestial bodies relies on telescopes, the progress in telescope technology represents the progress in the study of celestial bodies" 世界科學日見進步，地球與星球將來或有交通一日。唯星球觀察純依望遠鏡作用，故望遠鏡之進步即研究星球之進步也 (Baozi 1913, 5).
23. For a discussion of the relationship between Tang Buddhism and Neo-Confucianism, especially the use of the moon metaphor, see Zhang and Chen 2019.

earth's most important light source, has always symbolized the emperor in Chinese political tradition.[24] *The Travels* extends the symbolism from the emperor himself to China's political prospects. This symbolic meaning is implied as early as the novel's first chapter, where Lao Can and his friends fail to see the sunrise because clouds mask the sun. Immediately afterward, they see a sinking ship—an allegory for China's political crisis. The message is clear: the sun that Lao Can misses symbolizes the promising future of Chinese politics, the opposite of crisis. Chapter 5 of the second volume—the midpoint of the nine-chapter sequel—picks up this theme of political disappointment. In that chapter, Lao Can and his friend De Huisheng 德慧生, in the company of the enlightened Buddhist nun Yiyun, ascend Mount Tai for their second sunrise watch:

> De Huisheng and Lao Can followed on foot and before long they came to the Sunrise Pavilion to wait for the coming up of the sun. "Look there," said Yiyun, pointing at the distance. "You see there is a streak of light on the horizon like a thread of gold; people say that line is the water of the great sea." Before they had exchanged a few words, half of the sun's disc had come above the earth. Unfortunately, there was a stretch of dark clouds lying close to the horizon, so that soon after the sun appeared, it disappeared again behind the dark cloud, and by the time it emerged again, the bottom of the sun's disc had already left the horizon, and the streak of gold had vanished. (Liu 1936, 74)

> 慧生、老殘步行，不遠便到了日觀峰亭子等日出。看那東邊天腳下已通紅，一片朝霞，越過越明，見那地下冒出一個紫紅色的太陽牙子出來。逸雲指道：「儜瞧那地邊上有一條明的跟一條金絲一樣的，相傳那就是海水。」只說了兩句話，那太陽已半輪出地了。只可恨地皮上面，有條黑雲像帶子一樣橫著。那太陽才出地，又鑽進黑帶子裡去，再從黑帶子裡出來，輪腳已離了地，那一條金線也看不見了。

---

24. This rhetorical practice of comparing a country's prospects to the sun dates to the Jin dynasty in the fifth century. See *Shishuo xinyu* 世說新語 (A new account of the tales of the world) and its record of a conversation between the young Emperor Ming (Sima Shao, r. 323–325) and his father, Emperor Yuan (Sima Rui, r. 317–322). There was a man present who had come from Chang'an. Emperor Yuan was asking him news of Luoyang, sobbing all the while and letting his tears flow. Emperor Ming asked, "Why does it make you cry?" Emperor Yuan then told him the whole story of the eastward crossing of the Yangtze River (307–12) and took the occasion to ask Emperor Ming, "In your opinion, how far away is Chang'an compared with the sun?" He replied, "The sun is farther away. Since I never heard of anyone coming here from the sun, we can know it for certain." Emperor Yuan marveled at him. The next day he assembled all the ministers for a banquet to report this remark, and once more he asked the same question. This time Emperor Ming replied, "The sun is nearer." Emperor Yuan turned pale [and asked abruptly], "But why did you change from what you said yesterday?" He replied, "By just lifting your eyes you can see the sun, but [even if you lift your eyes] you can't see Chang'an" (Liu 1976, 298). 晉明帝數歲，坐元帝膝上。有人從長安來，元帝問洛下消息，潸然流涕。明帝問何以致泣？具以東渡意告之。因問明帝：「汝意謂長安何如日遠？」答曰：「日遠。不聞人從日邊來，居然可知。」元帝異之。明日集群臣宴會，告以此意，更重問之。乃答曰：「日近。」元帝失色，曰：「爾何故異昨日之言邪？」答曰：「舉目見日，不見長安。」

The fleeting nature of the sunrise and black clouds render the whole viewing experience unfulfilling: a streak of sunlight emerges, and clouds immediately obscure it. Despite Yiyun's attempt to point to the sun and verbally locate it, Lao Can witnesses just a fleeting thread of gold. This is another of the many examples of anxiety over visual limitation in the novel. More importantly, that the sun remains elusive to Lao Can delivers a clear message: China has missed the chance to resolve its crisis, and the opportunity is beyond retrieval. Liu E uses a scene about light and visual limitation to convey his concern for China's pessimistic future.

Aside from being a political allegory, sunrise-watching in chapter 25 also delivers a clear message about moral enlightenment. Lao Can and De Huisheng's journey to Mount Tai, which features enlightenment brought by the beautiful and wise nun Yiyun, easily reminds us of the theme of "encountering the goddess" in the hero's journey from the perspective of comparative mythology study (Chang 1996). However, the central vignette of the journey to Mount Tai suggests a reading in a context more relevant to Chinese intellectual history. The scene where Yiyun tries to point out the rising sun to Lao Can on Mount Tai easily calls to mind a famous story from Wang Chong's 王充 (27–97 CE) *Discourses Weighed in the Balance* (*Lunheng* 論衡). It recounts Confucius and his favorite student Yan Yuan 顏淵 at the top of Mount Tai gazing into the distance. Confucius sees a white horse tied to a post outside the palace gate of Wu and points it out to Yan Yuan, asking him whether he perceives anything. Yan Yuan wrongly identifies it as suspended silk. Realizing Yan Yuan has failed to perceive the object, Confucius stops him from continuing to look. After descending Mount Tai, Yan Yuan soon dies of sickness. According to the story, the student, whose spirit did not equal that of Confucius, died because he overstrained his strength (Wang 1962, 242). The vignette of the sunrise watching in chapter 25 is a moral allegory that connects the level of moral cultivation with visual capacity.

The sunrise-watching vignette in chapter 25, a reinvented version of Wang Chong's original story, conveys a strong moral implication.[25] Yiyun replaces Confucius, and Lao Can becomes Yan Yuan. Liu E rewrites the scene of Confucius showing Yan Yuan the white horse at Chang Gate, depicting it as Yiyun pointing out the sunrise for Lao Can. Just as Yan Yuan died after descending Mount Tai, Lao Can passes away in a dream soon after he descends Mount Tai. By referencing one of the most famous stories about moral cultivation in the Confucian tradition, Liu E imbues this episode with a strong Confucian moral meaning.[26] He endows the

---

25. Liu E is highly intrigued by this story. In the "ten difficulties" of Yellow River measurement he proposed in 1890, Liu E uses the idiom "White Horse at the Chang Gate is easily mistaken as white silk" 白馬昌門，易成匹練 derived from this story to illustrate measuring errors that could ensue from visual limitation (2007, 1:35).
26. The highly moral connotation of this episode is even evidenced by Lao Can's companion in the sunrise-watching event, De Huisheng, the allegory of Lao Can's morality and wisdom.

sun, which is the object of Lao Can's gaze, with particular moral weight. Just as the Chinese political tradition compares the emperor to the sun, Confucius, who is called the "uncrowned king" (*suwang* 素王) for his kingly virtue, is also compared to the sun.[27] Lao Can's ascent of Mount Tai, following in Confucius's footsteps, and his gazing at the sun symbolize his pursuit of Confucius's moral height; his failure to capture the moment of sunrise represents, then, the novelist's frustrated moral cultivation. The protagonist's sunrise-watching journey symbolizes the pursuit of Confucian political ideals in addition to moral practice. Lao Can's frustration in watching the sunrise shows a pessimistic view toward both China's political prospects and the possibility of moral perfection.

Although Liu E loads the Mount Tai sunrise scene with strong Confucian political and moral implications, it cannot be fully grasped from a Confucian perspective. Notably, the character who points out the sunrise for Lao Can is not a Confucianist but a Buddhist nun. And the sun symbolizes not only Confucian political and moral ideals but also Buddhist teaching. In his poem, Liu E states his deep understanding of and immersion in Flower Garland (Huayan 華嚴) Buddhism and Pure Land (Jingtu 淨土) Buddhism.[28] These were two of the most influential Buddhist branches in China, and both use the sun as an important metaphor for their teachings.[29] This Buddhist meaning allows a very different reading of the sunrise-watching episode. Although Lao Can fails to spot the sun even with Yiyun's guidance, the following episode compensates for this frustration metaphorically. In chapter 6, Lao Can lets his concubine Cuihuan apprentice herself to Yiyun, expecting her, after attaining enlightenment, to redeem Lao Can when he is in need. In other words, Cuihuan embarks on a journey of Buddhist cultivation for Lao Can. This vicarious journey is evidently fruitful. After his death, Lao Can is permitted to enter the Pure Land because of the meritorious karma reaped through his affinity with bodhisattvas,

---

27. The comparison of Confucius to the sun and the moon can be seen as early as the "Zizhang" 子張 chapter in *The Analects* 19:24, where Zigong 子貢 says, "The worthiness of other people is like a hill or mound, in that one can still climb to the top of it. Confucius is like the sun and the moon—it is impossible to surmount him. Even if a person wished to cut himself off from their radiance, what harm could he do to the sun and the moon" 他人之賢者，丘陵也，猶可踰也；仲尼，日月也，無得而踰焉。人雖欲自絕，其何傷於日月乎 (Slingerland 2003, 229–30). Later Confucian scholars inherited this metaphor. Northern Song poet Tang Geng 唐庚 (1070–1120) in his *Tang Zixi wen lu* 唐子西文錄 says, "On the wall of an inn on the road of Shu, there is a couplet, 'Had Heaven not sent Confucius to the world, all ages would have been a long night'" 蜀道館舍壁間題一聯云：天不生仲尼，萬古如長夜 (1995, 405–6). Later, Zhu Xi (1994, 2350) cited this couplet in *Zhuzi yulei* 朱子語類. The Yuan (1271–1368) scholar Tao Zongyi 陶宗儀 (1988, 384) also mentioned Tang's encounter with this couplet in his *Shuofu* 說郛.
28. Liu E wrote a poem three months before his death, which contained the following line: "At the age of fifty-three, I have come to understand Huayan Buddhism. Converted to Pure Land Buddhism, I bow to worship every single day" 勘破華嚴五十三，皈依淨土日和南 (Liu and Liu 2019, 735).
29. Vairocana, the main Buddha revered in Huayan Buddhism, connotes the luminous sun. On the relationship of Pure Land Buddhism and sun worship, see Yinshun 1984, 21–22.

that is, the enlightened nun Yiyun and her disciple Cuihuan. The sunrise-watching event thus symbolizes both the disillusionment with Confucian moral and political pursuits and the opportunity to attain Buddhist enlightenment. Seen this way, the episode of sunrise watching represents a leap from Confucianism to Buddhism.

Liu E's profession as a river engineer inspires his interest in light, and his writing of the moon and sun—two light sources at the center of the first and second volumes, respectively—is the utmost embodiment of this interest. Both have multiple, layered symbolic meanings. Liu E combines his interest in light with his view of the vicissitudes of Chinese state affairs, opening a discursive space for Confucianism, Buddhism, and Western astronomy. Liu E's political imagination and envisioning of China's future, presented as an exploration of scenes involving the moon and sun, are established on a foundation of knowledge about optics, astronomy, philosophy, and importantly though implicitly, river engineering at the turn of the twentieth century.

How Seeing Happens

The revolutionary way Liu E writes about landscape is not just a shift from classical to vernacular, but also a shift from one vernacular to another. Although cognizant of classical literary aesthetics that fuse feeling and nature, Liu E questioned the efficacy of such methods and instead created a mode of portrayal unlike anything that had preceded it. This linguistic innovation stems primarily from a novel experience of the environment—an experience, I argue, that was the result of Liu E's professional work as a river engineer. Surveying, mapping, and governing the flow of water made him see the world differently and so describe it differently. His writing consequently incorporated the language of measurement and mathematics, optics and illusion, and its overriding characteristic was a sense of deep struggle to visualize an essentially unknowable and unperceivable nature. This concentration on the anxious experience of perception rather than perception itself resulted in a fresh way to understand the relationship between humans, the natural landscape, and the nation.

The Travels concerns itself not with the harmonious relationship between the subject and the object—one between a tourist and a scenic spot or between a hermit and the space where he finds tranquility—as was common in traditional landscape writing and painting. As a river map delineator, Liu E faced not pleasant, picturesque views of natural scenes but the ferocious, capricious Yellow River whose regulation held the key to the country's fate. One of the greatest challenges in his role was the instability of perception and the inability of the eye to accurately capture movement. Accordingly, the novel's landscape writing concerns itself with human sight's incompetence to accurately perceive its surroundings and with the mechanics of visual experience. The scenic views are either blurred and amorphous beyond recognition or fleeting and elusive, and the gap between visual experience and reality seems forever unresolvable. This gap appears in the form of optical illusions: what is perceived by the human eye is merely the product of light refraction, and its ensuing errors in perception are taken in by the easily deceived eye. The novel narrates not so much what is seen but how seeing happens.

Furthermore, the integration of national sentiment into the novel depends on Liu E's ability to express these anxieties about perception in his landscape writing. Grounded in his hydraulics-informed framework for understanding the nation-state, his anxiety about the perception of water becomes in *The Travels* an anxiety about China's future. The connecting piece in this association is, of course, the Yellow River—the waterway symbolizing the birth of Chinese civilization and the sorrow of the nation. Such an urge to capture the unpredictable Yellow River and overwhelming national sentiment goes beyond what can be conveyed by set poetic verse and parallel prose, the conventions employed by past vernacular novels. Liu E's answer to this problem is to embed the mechanics of light and optical illusion within his description to establish a link between vision-enhancing technology and political foreknowledge. This comes to a head most powerfully in the philosophical debate between the Neo-Confucian and Buddhist understanding of political history and state affairs. Liu E has his characters couch this debate in a metaphor of the moon phases, with the participants discussing light and visual effect as metaphors for state affairs. Elsewhere, sunlight becomes a metaphor for ideal government—a way to envision and address concerns for China's future.

In the 1920s, Hu Shih lauded Liu E's vernacular prose in *The Travels*'s landscape writing in an attempt to incorporate the extremely popular novel into his project of national literature building. However, Hu also admitted that the novel's conservative political visions had no place in the new nation. To the literary reformers of the early Republican era, Liu E's national imagination, compared to the novel's literary techniques, appears disappointingly out of date. With the founding of the Republic, Liu's political visions were left behind and branded as "premodern." For this reason, researchers of late Qing novels have tended to discuss the novel's landscape writing and national imagination separately. Yet the "premodern" label of the novel's national imagination is more a product of historical hindsight than a fact. As a supporter of the Westernizing faction, Liu E had developed his own plans for building a modern state and his own visions for rejuvenating the nation. As this chapter demonstrates, *The Travels*'s landscape writing and national imagination are not two independent issues but are inseparable. And the novel's celebrated innovation in landscape writing technique is, in fact, the representation of Liu E's literary imagination of the modern Chinese nation.

5
Toward China's Rejuvenation
The Taigu School and Yellow River Regulation

> I've heard that in the stone studios of celestial mountains, there hide heavenly scrolls with green incantations inscribed on golden slips. Mortals read it but cannot understand it or follow it. This chapter is the same. Mortals read it but cannot understand it or follow it.[1]
>
> —Liu E, comment for *The Travels*, chapter 11

Just as the early Republican literary revolution dismissed Liu E's political vision in favor of his literary innovation, so too have scholars failed to fully appreciate another central theme in *The Travels*: Taigu philosophy. Liu E was a lifelong adherent of the secret religious cult, and as this chapter will explore, its teachings informed the conceptual core of his nation-building alongside his concern for river regulation. The failure to fully understand the significance of this theme surfaces most evidently in the treatment of the novel's most puzzling episode, the gathering of a hermit-prophet, a female philosopher, and a Confucian scholar in chapters 8 to 11. Scholars have frequently regarded this part of the novel as an anomaly, irrelevant to the main plot or its major themes and innovations. This misunderstanding and dismissal began early in the novel's reception history—in December 1903 at the hands of Liu E's editor, Li Boyuan.

Li Boyuan was editor-in-chief of *Illustrated Fiction* (*Xiuxiang xiaoshuo* 繡像小說) in which *The Travels* had been serialized since 1903. In December 1903, he made an editorial decision that led to the termination of the novel's serialization. Li made major changes to chapters 10 and 11, and Liu E immediately stopped providing manuscripts. The novel ceased to appear in print, and it was not until 1905 that Liu E, invited by his friend Fang Ruo, editor-in-chief of the *Tianjin Daily News*, decided to serialize the novel again. Liu's decision to terminate the novel's serialization was

---

1. The comment is based on Xiangjun Feng's translation (2023, 203), with minor adaption.

motivated by the fact that Li had changed an element that was unique and, to Liu E's mind, core to the novel.

The two chapters that Li changed are part of what has been considered the novel's most mysterious episode. Chapters 8 to 11 recount the experiences of the young scholar Shen Ziping in the Peach Blossom Mountain, where he has journeyed to seek out Lao Can's friend and the martial art master Liu Renfu's help in dealing with crime in Chengwu County, Shandong. On his way up the mountain, Shen spends a night with the recluses Yellow Dragon and Yugu. The mysteriousness of the four chapters comes not only from the divine tiger (*shenhu* 神虎) that Shen encounters while traveling to the mountain or the enigmatic identity of Yellow Dragon and Yugu. It also comes from the two strange figures' performance of "Melody of Sea Waters and Heavenly Winds" ("Haishui tianfeng zhi qu" 海水天風之曲), a *qin* musical piece, which the recluses claim had never been circulated as a score (chapter 10), and from Yellow Dragon's prophecy about China's national crisis and cultural invigoration (chapter 11).

When *The Travels* was reserialized in 1905, Liu E added a comment to chapter 11 (see chapter epigraph), announcing this mysterious chapter's profound significance. Li Boyuan's most drastic changes were to this chapter, and Liu's comment should be read as a direct counter to the edits. To Liu E, Li Boyuan's tampering with the novel was outrageous. In addition to deleting significant parts of chapters 10 and 11, Li had changed Shen Ziping's experience in the Peach Blossom Mountain into nothing more than a dream that Shen has after fainting from his frightful encounter with the tiger. Li added the following comment to explain the edited scene: "[The author] suddenly closes the story with a dream to warn readers against buying into fairy tales and unfounded stories. This is the message that the author tries painstakingly to deliver" 忽然以一夢了之，使世人毋惑於神仙之事，及一切不經之說，此是作者一片苦心 (Li 2006, 524). Failing to comprehend Liu E's intention, Li Boyuan corrupted what Liu E considered a highly significant episode, framed it inappropriately as a fairy tale and, moreover, ascribed the narrative result of his aggressive editing to the author himself. It is, then, no surprise at all that Liu terminated the novel's serialization in *Illustrated Fiction*.

His objection to Li Boyuan's claim that chapters 8 to 11 constitute "unfounded stories" notwithstanding, Liu admits these four chapters, filled with otherworldly encounters rather than earthly suffering and pain, are difficult for readers to understand. C. T. Hsia (2004) gives one of the most insightful readings of them. He argues the yearning for a more inclusive political discourse, represented by the musical performance in chapter 10, and the expectation for China's cultural reinvigoration following national crises, revealed by Yellow Dragon's prophecy in chapter 11, marks the most striking features of *The Travels* as the first political novel in China. Chapters 10 and 11, situated at the structural center of the novel's first volume, are the core of its political imagination and therefore key to understanding its significance.

This political imagination is grounded in Liu E's two main lifelong concerns: the moral teachings of the Taigu school and methods for regulating the Yellow River. Critics have long noted the relationship of Shen Ziping's Peach Blossom Mountain visit to the teachings of the Taigu school, the religious sect promoting a syncretic teaching of Confucianism, Buddhism, and religious Daoism (the Three Teachings), of which Liu E was a devoted disciple. The influence of the Taigu teaching on Liu E's framing of these two central chapters is easily observable. However, what scholars have failed to notice, and that this chapter will argue for, is that Liu E also draws heavily upon his framework of Yellow River regulation to integrate the philosophy of the Taigu school into his broader political vision and nation-building agenda. Just as Liu E weaves together biological nationalism, political governance, discourses of emotion, and innovative literary techniques within his hydraulic framework, so too does he ensure his two major concerns—the inheritance of the Taigu teaching and his specific approach to Yellow River regulation—converge and overlap, serving as the overarching narrative climax to the story of Lao Can's travels. In this way, far from being an anomaly worthy of excision or exclusion from the critical discourse, chapters 10 and 11 form the core of the novel's political imagination.

The Taigu School: Its Rise, Crisis, and Revival

The Taigu school is a religious sect of academic nature founded by Zhou Taigu 周太谷 (1762?–1832) in the 1820s in Yangzhou. Centered on mystical Confucian teachings and Buddhist and Daoist practices of self-cultivation, the Taigu school was an important affiliation for Liu E, who was a third-generation disciple. Offering both moral and spiritual cultivation, the school attracted a strong following and, consequently, continual persecution by authorities. Although the school lasted into the Republican period and disbanded only with the founding of the People's Republic of China, spanning five generations,[2] a particularly violent act of persecution in 1866 caused an existential crisis. The transmission of the teaching thus became a core anxiety for its followers throughout the late Qing period, and the resulting crisis of succession, along with disagreement about the teaching, was a chief preoccupation for Liu E that he took up in his novel.

In the Ming and Qing dynasties, the authorities made the Cheng-Zhu school of Neo-Confucianism the orthodoxy, but to propagate Confucianism, minor Confucian sects with popular appeal, religious characteristics, and communal organizations started to appear. The Taigu school was a product of this trend. Different from "popular Confucianism" (*minjian rujiao* 民間儒教) advocated by local gentries, which was based on Confucian dogma, the Taigu school borrowed

---

2. Scholarly investigations show that the Taigu school still has a small number of active followers to this day (see Zhou 2010).

substantially from Buddhism and Daoism, straying from the Confucian mainstream and developing into a highly hybrid folk religion. The school centered on Confucian mysticism, stemming mainly from Western Han new-text Confucian classic studies and apocryphal texts, or *chenwei* 讖緯 (Han 2017, 92). The school's leading figures, such as Zhou Taigu and his disciples Zhang Jizhong 張積中 (1806–1866) and Li Guangxin 李光炘 (1808–1885), all employed apocryphal readings to explain Confucian classics. The school's self-cultivation methodology employed two major techniques—"mind-respiration coordination" (*xinxi xiangyi* 心息相依) and "transmutation of consciousness to wisdom," both originally Buddhist and Daoist practices. The Taigu school considered social practice equally important to spiritual cultivation and encouraged its adherents to value moral pursuits over life. The school's spiritual leaders and central authority, like Zhou Taigu, Zhang Jizhong, and Li Guangxin, were revered as saints by their followers, who shared common ideals in the moral and spiritual pursuits they advocated and a strong sense of belonging and mutual reciprocity. These characteristics make the Taigu school a typical folk religious organization.

The Taigu school flourished despite severe religious persecution inflicted by the Qing regime. Zhou Taigu, the school's founder, started to preach his thought in Yangzhou around 1821. By approaching audiences from various social strata in a flexible, diversified way, he successfully attracted a large following. The Qing authorities had always guarded against popular religious activities and condemned as heresies all religions except the mainstream Buddhist and Daoist factions. Zhou's increasing popularity in Yangzhou predictably provoked the government. In 1832, Zhou was arrested and died in prison.[3] After the death of Zhou Taigu, Li Guangxin and Zhang Jizhong continued their work, the former in Yangzhou and the latter in Shandong.

The Taigu school peaked in northern China under Zhang Jizhong's leadership in the mid-nineteenth century, with more than twenty thousand followers from all walks of life. Yet within a decade, its fortunes shifted dramatically. In 1857, Zhang founded a fortress-like settlement in the Yellow Cliff Mountain, creating a self-sufficient religious, political, and economic community, with its own military defense force.[4] With its growing power and influence over many followers, Zhang's northern

---

3. For discussion on Zhou Taigu's death, see Zhou 2014, 67–68.
4. Zhang Jizhong's preaching was mysterious. He placed great emphasis on grand ceremonial worship in his teaching. His figures of worship include both Confucian sages and Daoist deities, giving a strong religious hue to his sect. Based on the mountain, Zhang built a self-sustaining military fortress. Property ownership was prohibited, and Zhang allocated all resources. A full-function administration was established. Various public facilities were built to tend to the community's daily needs, like diet and medical care. An internal market was created for the members to trade with each other. Thus, a self-sufficient community emerged. Zhang also bought weapons, organized military training, and built defense works. For details on Zhang's construction and operation of the Yellow Cliff Mountain fortress, see Zhou 2014, 81–93.

sect drew the local government's suspicion.⁵ In 1866, after Zhang Jizhong refused to surrender to provincial military forces, Shandong governor Yan Jingming 閻敬銘 (1817–1892) ordered an attack on Yellow Cliff Mountain. Around two hundred people, including Zhang Jizhong, his family, and his close followers, committed self-immolation; thousands of other followers were killed by soldiers, and countless died jumping off the cliff (Zhou 2014, 93–102). Thus, the Taigu school's history in the first half of the nineteenth century began with the tragic martyring of its founder and ended with the most brutal religious persecution in Chinese history.

The 1866 massacre on Yellow Cliff Mountain led to the near extinction of the northern sect and marked a watershed in the school's history. Moreover, it also changed the destiny of Li Guangxin and his southern sect. After the incident, the Qing government labeled and monitored the Taigu school as a society associated with popular uprisings against the government; in some cases, it was even considered a revolutionist group.⁶ Northern sect survivors scattered, and their activities went underground. To avoid punishment, Li fled to the countryside and preached in secret. He also restricted the admission of new followers: only those with a friend's recommendation or a disciple's introduction could join the school. Although an undeniably brutal blow, the Yellow Cliff Mountain tragedy also brought an immense collective sense and solidarity to the school's already close-knit community. The community turned further away from mainstream society and became increasingly an underground religious organization. In other words, the Yellow Cliff Mountain incident transformed the Taigu school from a nonmainstream religion into an illegal secret religious society. The collective memories of trauma reshaped the followers' self-identity and the school's operation.⁷

Liu E found in the school his spiritual home during this difficult time. In 1876, aged twenty, Liu E went to Yangzhou to meet with Li Guangxin. As Harold Shadick suggests, Liu E, who had been so forward and unruly, apparently "experienced what

---

5. In 1856–1866, responding to the Nian and Taiping uprisings, various autonomous fortresses sprang up in the mountainous depths of northern China. Each fortress was an extremely closed society, an independent kingdom. The castellan oversaw the financial and judicial affairs. Militarily, these fortresses constituted great hazards to local governments (Perry 1980). With the Taiping War raging, these hilltop fortresses appealed to many as a haven from the storm. Among them, the Yellow Cliff Mountain fortress was the most influential. To the local authorities, the most upsetting aspect of this fortress was its strong religious hue. Since the Han dynasty, local uprisings were often instigated by religions. Therefore, it was quite natural for the local authorities to suspect Zhang Jizhong of conspiring against the state. More than once, they ordered Zhang to travel to the provincial capital Ji'nan to declare his loyalty to the local government, but Zhang had no interest in interacting with the authorities. Authorities interpreted his indifference as traitorous.
6. The Taigu school was brought up in a letter from Wang Daxie 汪大燮 (1859–1929), who was then the Chinese ambassador to Britain, to Wang Kangnian 汪康年 (1860–1911), secretary of the Grand Secretariat. He even called Taiguists such as Qiao Shu'nan 喬樹枏 (1849–1917), Mao Qingfan 毛慶潘 (1846–1924), and Liu E "revolutionists." See Liu and Liu 2019, 663.
7. For the southern sect's history after the Yellow Cliff Mountain incident, see Han 2017, chap. 2.

might very well be called a religious conversion" and "developed a sense of social responsibility and was filled with the spirit of sympathy and pity for men" (Liu 1990, xxii–xxiii). Liu E, though having the chance to meet Li Guangxin only three times before Li's death in 1885, became an adherent follower of the school. Liu E found in the Taigu school an inclusive philosophy that accommodates apparently mutually exclusive positions and thus helps to meet the unprecedented challenges of the complex and turbulent political climate in which he found himself. The Taigu school provided him with tools to pursue his life goal, and the Taigu teaching was the intellectual resource and driving force in his attempt to save the nation through his industrial and commercial activities.

The turn of the twentieth century witnessed a revival of the Taigu school. After Li Guangxin's death, his senior disciple Huang Baonian 黃葆年 (1845–1924) rose to lead the southern sect. On June 1, 1902, Taigu followers gathered at the famous Yu Yuan 愚園 (Garden of the Slow-Witted) in Shanghai. The Yu Yuan gathering was highly significant for the Taiguists. The garden recalled the heyday of the school represented by Li Guangxin, who had in 1882 moved to Yu Yuan Road, where the garden was located and where he remained until his death. The gathering in this highly symbolic garden was the southern sect's first grand event since Li's death and the first meeting of the two sects since 1896 (Wang 1990). The future of the Taigu school and its teaching was decided there: the followers of both sects agreed to reunify, and Huang Baonian was named the leader of the newly reunified school. The Yu Yuan gathering at the beginning of the twentieth century thus marked the revival of the Taigu school after its tragic decline.

Whereas the Yu Yuan gathering symbolized a revival for Taigu followers, it marked the beginning of Liu E's difficult relationship with the school. Although Liu saw himself as a faithful follower and even an important disciple, his fellow Taiguists regarded him as unqualified and even a negative example. Their antipathy toward Liu stemmed from his controversial business and industrial engagements, for which he suffered long-term impugning. In 1895, Liu moved on from river work to industry and commerce. To fund coal mining and railway projects that would strengthen the national economy, he advocated borrowing from abroad. The proposal backfired; both the authorities and social groups scorned him for being a servile, self-interested dog running to foreigners, receiving kickbacks, and selling out the country. The Taigu school, headed at this time by Huang Baonian, also harshly denounced him. After the Yu Yuan gathering in 1902, Huang accused Liu of apostasy for engaging in industrial and commercial ventures to finance and satiate his personal pleasure and, furthermore, of plotting to supersede Huang as the school's leader (Liu 1993; Wang X. 2000). Liu E countered that their deceased master Li Guangxin had considered Liu, together with Huang, as the two disciples to succeed as co-leaders of the Taigu school. Confident as the school's self-identified successor, Liu E further argued that he used a different but complementary way to bring the Taiguist core teaching to fruition. His engagement in industrial projects, he asserted, was a means to "nurture all under heaven" (*yang tianxia* 養天下) and therefore of equal moral value to Huang's devotion to "educate all under heaven" (*jiao tianxia* 教天下) through preaching and lecturing (Liu 2007, 1:754). Huang Baonian was unpersuaded by Liu's self-defense.[8] The school's denouncement of Liu continued even after his death. Liu's official break with the Taigu school's authority thus resulted from his ambition to share the helm.

Despite accusations otherwise, Liu insisted his claim was well grounded. In 1902, Liu wrote a letter to Huang, reminding him that Li Guangxin had once told both men that "in the future world, two Si-year-borns will take the lead to preach" 將來天下，二巳傳道 (Liu 2007, 1:754). According to Liu, Li meant Huang Baonian, born in the year of Yi-si 乙巳 (1845), and himself, born in the year of Ding-si 丁巳 (1857). Yet as Wang Xuejun (1990, 2000) points out, Li had actually referred to Huang Baonian and Jiang Wentian 蔣文田 (1845–1909), leader of the northern sect after the Yellow Cliff incident and a disciple of Li Guangxin, who was the same age as Huang. Yet Liu E has reason to count himself one of the "two Si-year-borns." In terms of affinity, Liu E had much to share with his master, Li Guangxin. Li opposed the Cheng-Zhu school and revered the school of mind. He led a libertine life, enjoying the company of courtesans, and penned several prostitute-themed amorous verses. When preaching, Li employed apocryphal readings to explain the classics. *The Travels* frequently ridicules Cheng-Zhu school adherents. He took pleasure in the companionship of courtesans and composed numerous romantic poems centered on them, following in his master's footsteps. And the political prophesy of Yellow Dragon exhibits strong apocryphal characteristics. Compared with the self-disciplined Huang Baonian—who more closely followed the Cheng-Zhu school, opposed apocryphal prophecy, and strove to rid the Taigu school of its mystic elements—Liu was undoubtedly closer in thinking and conduct to their master.[9] As such, it was natural for Liu to believe himself a more rightful successor to Li Guangxin than Huang Baonian.

The Sound of Music

The history of the Taigu school and Liu E's concern about leadership succession are the background to a striking scene within the episode of Shen Ziping's Peach

---

8. Even after Liu's death in 1909, Huang's critique remained unchanged. In "Ji Liu Tieyun wen" 祭劉鐵雲文, Huang Baonian praised Liu E for his gallantry, integrity, and erudition but also said Liu's conviction and his death at the borderlands were due to his inability to find peace in poverty (see Fang 1997, 561). Huang Baonian also warned his students against Liu E's bad example: "Liu Tieyun was so deluded as to hope to pursue both familial well-being and the learning of the Way. Now that he has failed to attain the Way, look at what's become of his family! You all must quickly wake from such dreams" 劉鐵雲誤於成家、學道兩事雙全。現在道既未成，家又何如？汝等不可不趕緊醒夢也 (Fang 1997, 19).
9. For Huang Baonian's significant role in transforming the Taigu school, see Han 2017.

Blossom Mountain journey. In this scene in chapter 10, the recluses Yellow Dragon and Yugu play "Melody of Sea Waters and Heavenly Winds." Described as a polyphonic musical piece, the tune is "unlike anything else in the world, and the way of playing is in the traditional mountain style not known to outsiders" 不但此曲為塵世所無，即此彈法亦山中古調，非外人所知 (Liu 1990, 108). Some scholars read this piece as Liu E's evangelical expression since the polyphonic structure could connote the Taigu philosophy's diverse teachings. Others read it as his self-defense against Huang Baonian's accusation of apostasy, considering that the multiple musical lines may suggest the equal validity of Liu E's and Huang Baonian's different approaches to attaining the Way (Liu 1993; Wang 1993b). However, this musical piece also relates to a broader issue regarding the history of the Taigu school: the crisis in the transmission of the school's teaching during the late Qing. For Liu E, "Melody of Sea Waters and Heavenly Winds" was his fictional attempt to cope with this anxiety.

In Chinese literati culture, music appreciation has played a crucial role in expressing the idea of—and the hope to find—mutual understanding between likeminded individuals, often articulated as *zhiyin* 知音 (literally, one who understands the music). The story in *Liezi* 列子 of the mythical *qin* 琴 player Boya 伯牙 exemplifies this idea of perfect understanding. Boya's friend Ziqi 子期 understands what Boya intends to express through his playing. Early conceptions of *zhiyin* addressed music as the medium of genuine communication and the ability to understand the musician's true intention.[10] Subsequently, this story was transformed into one about the complementarity of Confucianism and Daoism. In a later version by the late-Ming novelist Feng Menglong 馮夢龍 (1574–1646), Boya is presented as a high official and Ziqi as a hermit. In this scenario, *zhiyin* represents the mutual understanding between a Confucian scholar seeking to confer benefits on the people and a Daoist scholar looking for peace by leading a reclusive life. The music-playing scene in chapter 10, in which the reclusive Yellow Dragon and Yugu perform for the Confucian scholar Shen Ziping, obviously adapts Feng Menglong's version of the Boya-Ziqi story. This scene addresses the idea of music as a medium that facilitates mutual understanding between people with different views, such as Liu E and Huang Baonian.

The musical performance in Liu's novel also alludes to another story about Boya to signify a different but equally important theme of literati culture—the transmission and inheritance of knowledge. The title of the piece played by Yellow Dragon and Yugu suggests a direct allusion to this Boya story in which he learns to play the

---

10. The idea of *zhiyin* later developed into one of the most significant themes in Chinese literary tradition—the mutual understanding between poets and readers—in addition to the more general theme of mutual understanding between friends. On *zhiyin* in late imperial Chinese musical culture, see Wu 2020, 42–88. On *zhiyin* and its relationship to conceptions of friendship in early China, see Henry 1987. See Huang 1994 for a discussion of *zhiyin* in the literary tradition.

qin. In the story, Boya's master, Chenglian 成連, takes him to Mount Penglai 蓬萊, an island of immortals in the East Sea, to help Boya to overcome his difficulties in learning the *qin*. There, after listening to the roaring sea waters and heavenly winds, Boya experiences a movement of feeling (*yiqing* 移情) that results in spiritual transcendence and achieves a breakthrough in his *qin* playing. This story addresses the correspondence between humans and nature that can create a sudden awakening in learning. The story implies this awakening represents a successful transmission of ancient knowledge guided by the teacher. With a title that directly alludes to this story of Boya, the musical piece that Yellow Dragon and Yugu play for Shen Ziping ("Melody of Sea Waters and Heavenly Winds") signifies this conception of how a learner awakens to and inherits knowledge.

Taigu followers often referenced the Boya story of "the movement of feelings" to address the succession of their school. The Boya story was highly significant in building community during the school's succession crises, especially in their writings about the 1902 Yu Yuan gathering.[11] In particular, the *qin* performance of Jiang Wentian, leader of the northern sect until the school's reunification, became a central subject of their writings on inheritance. Li Taijie 李泰階 (1871–1927), grandson of Li Guangxin, compared Jiang's *qin* performance to Boya's after inheriting his master's skills: "He played the music of Chenglian with heavenly winds at the end of the East Sea" 一鼓成連曲，天風東海頭 (Liu and Liu 2019, 481).[12] Through this reference linking Jiang to Boya, Li Taijie confirmed Jiang as the heir to Li Guangxin's teachings. The allusion to Boya was used similarly to describe southern sect leader Huang Baonian. At the gathering, Mao Qingfan asked Huang to lecture on Taigu learning to "resound the sound of sea tides again to rouse a deaf person [like him]" 請宣海潮之音，震我聾瞶 (Liu 2007, 1:575). Mao's comparison of Huang's lecture to "the sound of sea tides" alludes to the sound of sea waters that moves Boya's feelings. Although the Boya story has been a common allusion in literati writings of musical scenes throughout history, the Taiguists' allusion to Boya is more than a literary convention. It was a shared practice among the Taiguists to analogize the inheritance and transmission of the school's teaching to Boya's music learning. And by comparing Jiang's *qin* performance and Huang's lecture to Boya's *qin* playing, the Taiguists inferred the two leaders' inheritance of the Taigu learning from their late mentor Li Guangxin.

Through the allusion to Boya's learning, the novel presents a story of conversion—a story about how Shen Ziping, a Neo-Confucian scholar, abandons his

---

11. After the gathering, the famous artist Zhu Naifang 諸乃方 (1812–1908), who was also a Taiguist, created *Painting of the Yu Yuan Gathering* (*Yu yuan yaji tu* 愚園雅集圖) to commemorate the event. Liu E wrote a preface for the painting while others contributed poems.
12. Similarly, Liu E in his preface to the painting of the event compares Jiang's *qin* performance to Boya's playing of "Melody of Water Lily" ("Shuixian cao" 水仙操), the piece that Boya is said to play following his "moving of feelings" (Liu and Liu 2019, 480).

philosophical beliefs and turns to Taigu teaching. Liu E foreshadows the conversion in a scene where Shen, on his way to Yugu's room for the music appreciation, "heard the sound of heaven falling and earth crumbling, and felt a shaking and quaking underfoot. He was so frightened that his souls fled from his body fearing the mountain would topple over" 聽得天崩地塌價一聲，腳下震震搖動，嚇得魂不附體，怕是山倒下來 (Liu 1990, 106). The frightening noise, as Yellow Dragon explains, was a mass of packed ice and snow rolling down the mountainside. The collapse is not only physical but also symbolic—of Shen's Neo-Confucian belief system. After the psychological avalanche, Shen has the same experience of awakening as Boya: listening to the sea waters and heavenly winds suggested by the title of the musical piece, Shen is moved, and he achieves transcendental enlightenment. Through this, he is symbolically converted into a Taigu disciple. This mysterious episode of Shen Ziping's appreciation of a musical performance expresses Liu E's concern for the transmission of Taigu teachings.

To picture their utopia, Taigu followers used another literary allusion: Tao Qian's 陶潛 (365–427) "Story of the Peach Blossom Source" ("Taohua yuan ji" 桃花源記, 421). It is a parable about the inaccessibility of utopia. It describes how a fisherman, haphazardly sailing into a river in a forest of blossoming peach trees, finds a self-sufficient village. Isolated from the outside world, the village is inhabited by descendants of the original villagers, who had found refuge there from the political unrest of the Qin dynasty (221–207 BCE). As the fisherman leaves, the villagers inform him that revealing his experience to the outside world would not be worthwhile. He nevertheless tries to mark the route on his way out and reveal the existence of the village to the local authority, yet his repeated attempts to find the utopia again fail. Arguably the most favored allusion throughout Chinese literary history in writings about the pursuit of peace and serenity, "Story of the Peach Blossom Source" is a significant allusion for Taiguists. They regarded it as one of the three spiritual stages they aspire to reach (Liu, Zhu, and Liu 1987, 81; Liu 1931). Writing about the Yu Yuan gathering, Jiang Wentian uses this allusion to describe the pleasures of the event: "A wayfarer returns to the Chestnut Village; many old friends gather in Peach Blossom Source" 栗里有歸客，桃源多故人 (Fang 1997, 87). Jiang refers to the Yu Yuan Garden by alluding to both Tao Qian's hometown, Chestnut Village, and the utopia of Taiguists, the Peach Blossom Source; he furthermore conceives of the Yu Yuan gathering attendees as people who at last return to their utopia. Jiang's reference to Peach Blossom Source helped create an image of the Yu Yuan gathering as the realization of a spiritual stage for Taiguists.

Jiang Wentian's writing about Yu Yuan Garden inspired Liu E's setting for the music-playing episode. Peach Blossom Mountain, which is isolated from a socially and politically tumultuous China, borrows directly from Jiang's verse analogizing Yu Yuan Garden to The Peach Blossom Source and the Taigu followers to returnees to utopia. The setting for the music-playing scene on a remote mountain was apparently inspired by another poem by Jiang, which describes the Yu Yuan gathering with the line, "The master and disciples gather in Haishang" 春風海上聚 (Fang 1997, 87). Haishang 海上, literally "in the sea," clearly points toward the East Sea, where Boya was enlightened, and toward Shanghai 上海, which is nicknamed Haishang and where Yu Yuan is located. Liu E adopts Jiang's associative wordplay, modeling his Peach Blossom Mountain on the tranquil garden situated amid the hustle and bustle of Shanghai, which is itself an analogy to Penglai Mountain, isolated amid the raging waves of the East Sea. Accordingly, Liu E transforms Jiang's *qin* performance in the Yu Yuan into Yugu and Yellow Dragon's performance of "Melody of Sea Waters and Heavenly Winds" in the Peach Blossom Mountain. By inventively adapting Jiang Wentian's writings on the Yu Yuan gathering, Liu E turns the gathering into the fictional scene of music playing.

The music-playing scene in chapter 10 represents more than the inclusive and syncretic nature of the Taigu teaching or Liu E's self-defense against Huang Baonian's accusation of apostasy. By adopting the allusions to music and utopia that Taigu followers used for the Yu Yuan gathering in his description of the Peach Blossom Mountain gathering, Liu E transposes the real gathering into a fictional one. "Melody of Sea Waters and Heavenly Winds" is significant for how it encapsulates the Taigu school at a crucial historical moment of revival and articulates Liu E's vehement call for handing down the school's legacy.

Putting Fictional Music to Print

"Melody of Sea Waters and Heavenly Winds" in *The Travels* symbolizes the inheritance of the Taigu school for a reason more personal to Liu E than the metaphorical significance for Taigu followers of learning the *qin*. The instrument had been a significant part of Liu's life since childhood, when his musically knowledgeable mother inspired him to play the *qin*. As an adult, Liu E traveled to study with several *qin* teachers; one was Zhang Ruishan 張瑞珊, a successor of the Guangling 廣陵 *qin* school and teacher to Empress Dowager Cixi. Liu E was also interested in collecting ancient *qin* and rare scores of *qin* music. In 1907, Liu E reprinted the score of the legendary *qin* piece "Guangling Melody" ("Guangling san" 廣陵散) and wrote a preface for it.[13] Although purportedly about "Guangling Melody," his discussion in every way points to "Melody of Sea Waters and Heavenly Winds" and the Taigu school's history of political oppression.

Reprinting the "Guangling Melody" score was deeply significant for Liu E and his concern for the Taigu school's future, constituting a key part of his efforts to

---

13. The "Guangling Melody" score was printed with the score of a piece by Liu E's *qin* teacher Zhang Ruishan, under the title *The Score of the Eleven Strings Studio* (*Shiyi xian guan qinpu* 十一弦館琴譜). Liu E wrote three prefaces for the printed score, on the piece's provenance and history, his experience of performing the piece, and its political connotations.

promote the school's revival through the fictional musical piece in the novel. In his preface to the score, Liu E links "Guangling Melody" and "Melody of Sea Waters and Heavenly Winds." Describing his transcendental experience playing "Guangling Melody," Liu states, "The insiders said, 'It's not worth telling outsiders'" 此中人語云：不足為外人道也. This line, taken from Tao Qian's "Story of the Peach Blossom Source," suggests his experience was unintelligible and inaccessible to those without access to his score and the learning.[14] This account readily calls to mind "Melody of Sea Waters and Heavenly Winds," which is performed, circulated, and understood only in the Peach Blossom Mountain. This connection, via Tao Qian, suggests the reprinted score of "Guangling Melody" symbolized the fictional musical piece's circulation in the real world and in material form. Furthermore, to Liu E, the inheritance of "Guangling Melody" is just like the inheritance of the Way. He makes this analogy explicit in the same preface: "The *qin* works in the same manner as the Way. *Cantong qi* and *Wuzhen pian* are both books about how to attain the Way. But without the guidance of a mentor, they are useless. The art of the *qin* is passed down through music scores, but dependence solely on scores does not grant one access to the greatness of the music. Without a mentor, they are useless" 琴之為物也，同乎道。《參同契》、《悟真篇》傳道之書也。不遇明師指授，猶廢書也。琴學賴譜以傳，專恃譜又不足以盡琴之妙，不經師授，亦廢書也 (Liu 2007, 2:625). With this direct analogy, Liu E's comments on the transmission of the art of *qin* point toward the transmission of the Taigu teaching. The reprint of the "Guangling Melody" score, therefore, is symbolic of propagating the Taigu teaching: it promoted the circulation of the Taigu teaching in musical form.

By building the connection between the printed music score and the novel's music, Liu E imbues both pieces with political weight, derived in both cases from allusion to Tao Qian's "Story of the Peach Blossom Source." This story is a deeply political parable about people escaping from tyranny to utopia. Its most powerful

---

14. Liu E (2007, 2:628–29) describes his experience of playing *Guangling Melody* as follows: "The three's spirits meld with the tune, as if we were on the top of the best scenery under heaven at Qujiang. The moon hangs high, and chilly billows surge. Worldly tumults are cut off from all directions, and the piping of heaven flows everywhere. Is it the player or the *qin*? Feelings or scenery? There is no way to tell . . . Tao Jingjie [Tao Qian] said, 'The insiders said, 'It's not worth telling outsiders'" 三人精神與音韻相融化，如在曲江天下第一江山山頂。明月高懸，寒濤怒湧，塵囂四絕，天籟橫流。人耶，琴耶。情耶，景耶，俱不得而知之矣……陶靖節之言曰：「此中人語云：不足為外人道也」. "The best scenery under heaven" refers to Beigu Mountain 北固山. Located in Zhenjiang 鎮江, where Liu E came from, the mountain sits right across the Yangtze River from Yangzhou (anciently known as Guangling). Although it is perfectly appropriate for Liu to imagine himself playing "Guangling Melody" on top of Beigu Mountain, with Guangling in sight on the other side of the Yangtze, this description, for Liu E, is more than just cleverly fitting imagery. This description, like that of the musical performance in the novel, echoes the legend of Boya's learning of *qin*: the imagined experience of performing "Guangling Melody" on Beigu Mountain, overseeing the torrents of the Yangtze, mirrors the scene of Boya performing "Water Lily" on Penglai Mountain amid the roiling East Sea.

political significance lies in the inaccessibility of its utopian world, expressed by the line, "The insiders said, 'It's not worth telling outsiders,'" that Liu E quotes to summarize his experience of playing music. The depiction of this utopia as inaccessible is Tao's veiled criticism of the tumultuous political situation of his time. Liu E also brings this implication of the Peach Blossom Source into his novel. The political implication of this allusion manifests in the episode where Shen Ziping, during an intermission of Yellow Dragon and Yugu's musical performance, peruses a collection of verses on political criticism titled *The Sayings of the Insiders* (*Cizhongren yu* 此中人語)—the same words the villagers used to request the fisherman not to disclose the utopia to the outside world in "Story of Peach Blossom Source." That Shen peruses the collection during the performance's intermission also suggests the music's political implication. By summing up his experience of playing "Guangling Melody" with an allusion to the "insiders said" line from the Peach Blossom Source parable, Liu E endows the printed musical piece and the fictional musical piece to which it refers with hidden political significance.

The political implication in the "Guangling Melody" preface is delivered obliquely yet very powerfully. A legendary musical piece, the melody relates to a period of great political turbulence in Chinese history. According to a famous legend, Ji Kang 嵇康 (223–263), a late-Wei (220–266) philosopher, musician, and political figure, received the piece from a ghost. Before being executed by his political enemy Sima Zhao 司馬昭 (211–265), a military general who controlled Wei, Ji is believed to have played "Guangling Melody" at the execution ground and lamented that the music would die with him. In his preface to the reprinted score, Liu E provides another version of the story, arguing that the music has survived political persecution and bears significant political implications.[15] Liu E also argues for Ji's authorship: he holds that Ji, saddened by the impending demise of the Wei dynasty caused by Sima Zhao, composed "Guangling Melody," using musical mimicry of fierce tidal waves to symbolize the political tumults. Liu further claims that Sima Zhao persecuted Ji out of anger over the political implication of "Guangling Melody" and that the musicians who later learned the piece attributed it to a spirit to obscure its sensitive political message. Liu E provides his own interpretation of the story, portraying "Guangling Melody" as a symbol of political resistance in disguise.

Liu E conceived "Guangling Melody" as a symbol of political resistance out of an urge to right a wrong in the Taigu school's tragic history. In 1906, a year before

---

15. In the preface (Liu 2007, 2:630–31), Liu E cites Tang musician Han Gao 韓皋 (746–824) to argue "Guangling Melody" has strong political connotations. Han Gao maintained that "Guangling Melody" was composed by Ji Kang before Wei's collapse and that he so named the music to mourn the Yangzhou governors who were killed for their attempts to revolt against the Sima family. To evade the political pressure that might result from these musical gestures of subtle dissent, Ji Kang, Han Gao argued, claimed that the music was passed on by a spirit. For Han Gao's thoughts on "Guangling Melody," see Li et al. 1961, 1540.

the "Guangling Melody" score was printed, the Taiguist Qiao Shu'nan, an imperial censor and a friend of Liu E, pleaded with Empress Dowager Cixi in a memorial to redress the Yellow Cliff incident, a deep trauma for Taigu followers, and clear the school's name. Qiao's plea was unsuccessful, and the school's political stigma persisted. Liu E's reprinting of "Guangling Melody" and promotion of its circulation were very likely a response to Qiao's failed effort: a subtle, indirect protest of the court's refusal to right the injustice against the Yellow Cliff victims. More importantly, since Liu E saw "Guangling Melody" as the printed version of the fictional "Melody of Sea Waters and Heavenly Winds" symbolizing the Taigu teaching, reprinting and circulating the score represented a symbolic, public transmission of the politically sensitive Taigu teaching. By reprinting "Guangling Melody," Liu E set the record straight on the Yellow Cliff incident: the ruling power was accused of persecution, and the school was cleared of the imputation of rebellion.

For Liu E, the "Guangling Melody" allegorizes the legacy of the Taigu school and its political persecution. Yet the title of the musical piece also incarnates his ideal form of the Taigu school. Guangling is the ancient name of Yangzhou, while Yangzhou was Zhou Taigu's first preaching site, the sacred land where the Taigu teaching first flourished. This city was where the young Liu E first met Li Guangxin and gained admittance into the Taigu school as Li's immediate disciple. Hence, it testified to his initial affinity for the school's teaching and his legitimacy as a Taiguist. However, Huang Baonian tested these when he assumed leadership of the school. Unlike Li Guangxin and other leaders of the first two generations, Huang adhered to the Cheng-Zhu school. He shunned apocryphal texts. And he disapproved of followers' proactive involvement in politics and social affairs. After Huang took over, the Taigu school transformed from a highly mystical hybrid religious society into an essentially intellectual Confucian sect (Han 2017). Liu E, who proclaimed himself the true bearer of Li's legacy, naturally found Huang's leadership distasteful. Thus, Yangzhou became for Liu E a symbol of the Taigu teaching before Huang changed the school's course and of the time he spent in the city at an innocent age before his ideological conflict with Huang. I refer to Liu's early experience as a Taiguist, which he recalled with great nostalgia and loss, as his "Yangzhou moment." That moment later became a moral and spiritual haven for Liu.

Reprinting the "Guangling Melody" score inspired Liu E to develop his consideration of the Taigu school in the novel's second volume, written only two months afterward. Introducing Yangzhou as a homecoming destination in the second volume appears deliberate, with Liu E intending to construct a narrative of spiritual transcendence centered on the Taigu teaching. In the second volume, Lao Can returns with his friend De Huisheng to their hometown in southern China. On the way, they stop to visit Mount Tai and befriend a Buddhist nun Yiyun, who shares with them her extraordinary struggle for spiritual freedom. Here, we must pay special attention to the character De Huisheng, who is an allegory of Lao Can's moral self.[16] As Lao Can's (and thus also Liu E's) moral self, Huisheng is already bestowed with a symbolic link to the Taigu school—Liu E's primary source of spiritual force. The opening chapter of the second volume (chapter 21) further reveals that Lao Can and Huisheng both come from Yangzhou, while in the first volume, this city is not even mentioned.[17] Their Yangzhou citizenship, which echoes Liu's "Yangzhou moment," is most likely a whim inspired by the newly published "Guangling Melody."

Huisheng's Yangzhou citizenship sheds light on the author's purpose in writing the Mount Tai visit. Initially intending to join a sightseeing tour, Huisheng instead ends up hearing the extraordinary story of Yiyun. The narrative pattern reminds us of Shen Ziping's journey to the Peach Blossom Mountain in chapters 8 to 11. On his way to recruit Liu Renfu, Ziping unexpectedly meets Yellow Dragon and Yugu and spends an awe-inspiring night listening to their discourse, debate, and prophecy. However, despite his significant role as Lao Can's moral self, Huisheng seems to participate little in the Mount Tai visit. In his journey to the Peach Blossom Mountain, Shen Ziping acts as Lao Can's alter ego (an underdeveloped, lackluster version) on a mission to receive enlightenment from the Taigu teaching (Hsia 2004).[18] By contrast, Lao Can personally undertakes the Mount Tai journey, making Huisheng's presence redundant until after the visit. At the end of chapter 26, deciding to visit relatives in Huai'an, Lao Can parts with Huisheng, leaving him to continue the homecoming journey alone. In chapter 8, Lao Can entrusts the enlightenment mission to the Peach Blossom Mountain to Shen Ziping; in chapter 26, he chooses to let Huisheng complete the post-enlightenment return to the "Yangzhou moment." Thus, Lao Can can head to the city where the author in reality resided, and his moral self returns to the author's spiritual haven, Yangzhou. Finding havens for his physical and spiritual selves is an important theme of the second volume.

Aside from the spiritual homecoming theme, Huisheng's return to Yangzhou also marks Liu's second attempt to rectify his relationship with Huang Baonian

---

16. De Huisheng first appears in chapter 1 together with Wen Zhangbo 文章伯, another friend of Lao Can. From their names, we can fathom that they represent Lao Can's morals and literary works—the two most important commitments of a traditional Chinese literatus. The name "De Huisheng" refers to both morality (*de* 德) and wisdom (*hui* 慧), signifying one who is both moral and wise. The name "Wen Zhangbo" is even clearer, denoting a person with knowledge and literary skills (*wenzhang* 文章).

17. The first volume more than once mentions Lao Can's place of origin. In chapter 3, the narrator recounts Lao Can sends silver taels to his hometown Xuzhou; in chapter 6, Lao Can signs his poem with the signature "Tie Ying of Xuzhou in Jiangnan" 江南徐州鐵英.

18. Character splitting was a common technique in Qing literati novels. Examples of such alter ego pairs include Leng Yubing 冷於冰 (meaning "cold as ice") and Wen Ruyu 溫如玉 ("warm as jade") from the Qianlong-era novel, *Tracks of Immortals on the Green Field* (*Luye xianzong* 綠野仙蹤), as well as Zhen Baoyu 甄寶玉 (homophone for "real precious jade") and Jia Baoyu 賈寶玉 ("fake precious jade") from *The Story of the Stone*. The same literary device is clearly employed here in *The Travels*.

after the Peach Blossom Mountain allegory. As scholars have observed, the fictional polyphonic music piece in chapter 10 may suggest the equal validity of Liu E's and Huang Baonian's different approaches to attaining the Way (Wang 1993b). However, the mutual inclusiveness stressed by this musical piece at best claims the possibility of conflict resolution; it does not provide a true narrative resolution. The conflict goes unresolved until the novel's second volume, where Liu E provides a spiritual and moral homecoming for his literary surrogate Lao Can. Huisheng's return to Yangzhou symbolizes Liu E's return to his most cherished "Yangzhou moment." As mentioned, the moment also signifies Liu E's initiation in the Taigu school, his direct inheritance of the Taigu teaching, and a point in time before his ideological split with Huang Baonian. This fictional spiritual return serves little purpose in resolving Liu's actual conflict with Huang, but it undoubtedly represents a symbolic escape from the predicament: retreating to a time before the rifts had happened. The possibility of this resolution arises first when "Melody of Sea Waters and Heavenly Winds" is played in the Peach Blossom Mountain, but it is narratively realized only in Yangzhou.

To Liu E, reprinting "Guangling Melody" was an event with significant symbolic meaning for the succession of the Taigu school. After the Yellow Cliff incident in 1866, Taigu disciples had to shoulder the school's oppressed history, while a sense of duty to pass down the great Way prompted them to covertly conduct their preaching mission. Their teachings circulated orally or through manuscripts but never in print. This history explains why in the novel Liu E describes "Melody of Sea Waters and Heavenly Winds," signifying the Taigu teaching, as an ancient mountain tune that has never been transcribed to a score. To Liu E, the fictional *qin* music in the novel is not only a token of Taigu school succession but also a reference to the historical trauma suffered because of ruthless political oppression. Liu considered "Guangling Melody," a musical piece he believed strongly implied political resistance, as an alternate form of "Melody of Sea Waters and Heavenly Winds" from the novel. Reprinting the "Guangling Melody" score, then, was his effort to symbolically turn the fictional musical piece into a material form within the real world. Such effort was a gesture that allowed the Taigu teaching, suppressed because of the court's political persecution and Taiguists' self-censorship, to symbolically circulate and survive in public in camouflage. "Guangling Melody" not only echoed the music in the novel's first volume but also, in turn, inspired the narrative in its second volume, where the conflict between Liu E and Huang Baonian is finally released. With the mediation of "Guangling Melody," the major concerns expressed through the scene of music playing—the inheritance of the Taigu school's teaching, resistance against political pressure, and reconciliation between Liu and Huang—are fully considered and resolved.

Where the Taigu School and Yellow River Governance Converge

As a polyphonic musical piece with numerous melodic lines performed by multiple players on different instruments, "Melody of Sea Waters and Heavenly Winds" is a symbol with multiple meanings. In addition to the inheritance of the Taigu school, it also refers to another of Liu E's lifelong concerns: the inheritance of Yellow River regulation methods. Placed at the structural center of the first volume, "Melody of Sea Waters and Heavenly Winds," is where his two major concerns converge.

Just as Liu E viewed himself as the keeper of the Taigu school's flame, he also proudly considered himself the contemporary successor to Da Yu. Liu E claimed to have inherited the method of taming the Yellow River that Da Yu had invented, which had been selectively transmitted to only a few people throughout history, via the river engineers Wang Jing 王景 (30–85 CE), Pan Jixun, and Jin Fu. According to Liu, the method employed the principle of divide (*bo* 播) and unite (*tong* 同).[19] In chapter 3 of his novel, Liu E writes himself into this flood control genealogy in a conversation between his literary surrogate Lao Can and the Shandong governor about river work. Lao Can suggests the key to flood control is no more complicated than dividing and uniting, a technique rediscovered by Wang Jing after reading an account of Da Yu's river work in "Tribute of Yu." That Wang Jing came up with the method in "Tribute of Yu," however, is historically unfounded and another instance of Lao Can's idiosyncratic interpretation of hydraulic history. This interpretation, trickily, discloses less about Wang Jing than about the novelist himself. In a treatise on river regulation, Liu E writes, "I read 'Tribute of Yu' (in *The Documents of Antiquity* [*Shangshu* 尚書]) and found that, while it refers to the regulation [of all rivers] using the word *direct* (*dao* 導), it further uses the words *divide* and *unite* in the case of the Yellow River" 伏讀〈禹貢〉⋯⋯皆以一「導」字貫之。惟河⋯⋯又復曰「播」、曰「同」 (Liu 2007, 1:39). As this line indicates, it was Liu E himself who learned the importance of the two magical words *divide* and *unite* in taming the Yellow River after reading "Tribute of Yu." The fictional river engineer's eureka moment, misleadingly attributed by Lao Can to Wang Jing, belongs to Liu E, the ventriloquist. Lao Can, or in effect, Liu E, does not just claim succession to Wang Jing's intellectual legacy. He goes further: by assuming direct inheritance from Da Yu, he also claims to be the incarnation of the master hydraulician Wang Jing himself.

This inheritance theme is also represented in the gathering in the Peach Blossom Mountain, where Shen Ziping and Yugu have a furtive conversation about romantic love. It has long been noted that Shen Ziping's nighttime visit to Mount Peach Blossom shared the theme of "encountering with immortals in the mountains" with

---

19. To tame the fierce waters of Yellow River's middle reach, Liu E explains, Da Yu divided the waters into nine streams, then united the nine streams into one to facilitate water flow in the lower reach, where the flow rate is low and sedimentation prevails. For Liu E's discussion of the divide-and-unite strategy and his comment on Pan Jixun's and Jin Fu's river work, see Liu 2007, 1:39.

early Chinese rhapsody and classical tales in the Six Dynasties and Tang dynasties (Chang 2001). The episode of Mount Peach Blossom, however, is more closely related to the earlier legend of Da Yu. Shen Ziping, the visitor to the mountain, is associated with the tradition of Yellow River regulation through his relationship with Lao Can: traveling to the Peach Blossom Mountain instead of Lao Can, Shen Ziping functions, according to C. T. Hsia (2004), as Lao Can's literary alter ego. As Lao Can's splitting character, we can arguably view Shen Ziping as another incarnation of Da Yu's successor, as Lao Can identifies himself. The character Yugu also points to the origin of China's flood control tradition. Yugu is believed to have been modeled after Li Suxin 李素心, the niece of Li Guangxin, nicknamed Yugu 璵姑 (Wang 1993b). Liu E adopts Li's nickname to create the character, to whom he curiously gives a rarer family name, Tu 塗. With this family name, the character of Yugu is invested with the historical and mythical weight of Da Yu's river taming. The family name Tu descends from the ancient Tushan 塗山 clan, from which Da Yu's wife hailed in the river-taming myth. In the myth, Da Yu met the maiden of the Tushan clan at Mount Tu and married her when he was quelling the great floods. By giving the family name Tu to Yugu, Liu E suggests Yugu's connection to Da Yu's wife, who in some records is called Nüwa 女媧 (Sima 1982, 81). This is the same name as the heaven-mending and flood-controlling goddess. Liu E uses multiple historical references to suggest Yugu's identity as a descendant of the flood control hero and heroine. The gathering in the Peach Blossom Mountain references not only the gathering of Taigu followers at Yu Yuan but also the legend of Da Yu's river taming.

Like Shen Ziping and Yugu, Yellow Dragon, the other figure in the Peach Blossom Mountain gathering, is also associated with the flood control tradition. Scholars have attempted to link Yellow Dragon to Huang Baonian or Li Guangxin (Liu 1985, 395; Sheng 1983, 10). Yet contextualizing this character within the flood control myth gives deeper insight into the narrative significance of Yellow Dragon. Aside from the name "Yellow Dragon" obviously hinting at the Yellow River, yellow dragons play a crucial role in the legends of Da Yu's flood taming. In one, a yellow dragon helps Da Yu overcome the difficulties he encountered while digging a ditch. In another, Da Yu's father, Gun 鯀, was reincarnated as a yellow dragon after Sage-King Shun 舜 killed him for failing to tame the floods. After Gun's death, his son Da Yu took over his unfinished mission, and Gun in metamorphosed form advised him in river work.[20] As the legends indicate, the yellow dragon was not only Da Yu's father but also his predecessor and adviser in river taming. Liu E incorporates this relationship into his character of Yellow Dragon, who advises Shen Ziping with his wisdom as the yellow dragon did to Da Yu. Like Shen Ziping and Yugu, the character of Yellow Dragon derives directly from the legend of Da Yu's flood taming.

---

20. For the Da Yu legend and Gun's metamorphosis, see Zhao 1989; Yuan 2006, chap. 7.

The gathering of the three characters in the Peach Blossom Mountain bears Liu E's sense of vocation toward both the Taigu school and Yellow River management, the two realms with which Liu E was most concerned in his life. The music-playing event, in which Yugu and Yellow Dragon perform and Shen Ziping listens, not only references the inheritance of the Taigu school, as discussed, but also represents the interweaving and combination of Liu E's two lifelong core concerns. While the two themes are linked in the chapters at the novel's center, their connection is disclosed from its very outset. The first chapter comprises two allegories addressing the themes of river work and the Taigu teaching. The first is Lao Can's treatment of the patient Huang Ruihe, which refers to Liu E's governance of the Yellow River. The second is Lao Can's rescue of a sinking passenger ship, where Lao Can claims that "the winds of heaven and the waters of the sea are sufficient to move my feelings" 天風海水能移我情 (Liu 1990, 6). This refers to the inheritance of the Taigu school, the vocation of which motivated Liu E's industrial ventures to "nurture all under heaven." Tied together at the novel's start, the two allegories perfectly echo Liu's commitment to bring together his vocation of Yellow River management and succession to the Taigu teaching. At both the novel's opening and midpoint, Liu E tries to fuse his two major concerns.

Throughout his life, Liu E had been most devoted to and taken great pride in the inheritance of the Taigu teaching and Yellow River regulation. He references both in the gathering of Yellow Dragon, Yugu, and Shen Ziping to signify the revival of the Taigu teaching and the legend of Da Yu's river taming. The gathering in the Peach Blossom Mountain is in the structural center of the novel's first volume where Liu E's concerns for the Taigu school and river regulation converge. The thematic combination symbolized by "Melody of Sea Waters and Heavenly Winds" makes one thing clear: the Taigu School and Yellow River governance are not two separate themes but mutually define each other.

The River and the Apocrypha

For late-Qing intellectuals anxious about threats to China, the nation's future lay at the heart of their concern. The most explicit expression in Liu E's novel of such concern is the prophecy about China's future in chapter 11. In this chapter, Yellow Dragon, through calendric calculation, explains late nineteenth-century Chinese history and prophesies the trajectory of Chinese politics in the early twentieth century. Drawing on apocryphal texts, or *chenwei*, Yellow Dragon's political prophecy relates to the Taigu school, which had a strong interest in the apocryphal tradition. Yet we can fully understand the apocryphal tradition associated with the novel's political imagination only in the context of Yellow River governance. The prophecy in chapter 11 not only reflects Taigu thought but also shows how the Yellow River serves as an ecological context for the novel's imagination of Chinese politics.

The tradition of *chenwei*, or political prophecy in the form of apocryphal commentaries on the Confucian classics, has deeply shaped political imagination in China. The term *chenwei* is a compound of *chen* 讖 and *wei* 緯, the apocryphal texts popular during the Han dynasty. *Chen* refers to a riddle or riddle-like expression that foretells good fortune or ill luck, usually in the form of verses known as *chenshi* 讖詩. *Wei* refers to a form of political divination derived from the exegesis of the classics, astronomical and calendric calculation (*tuili* 推曆), and observation of atmospheric or meteorological conditions (*zhanhou* 占候).[21] These praxes of divination were based primarily on theories about the interaction between heaven and humankind (*tianren ganying* 天人感應) and the doctrine of the cycle of five elements (*wuxing zhongshi shuo* 五行終始說).[22] The study of *wei* began in the Han dynasty and was long the core of political theories until Song and Ming Neo-Confucianism superseded it. Although apocrypha ceased to occupy a dominant position in political theories after the twelfth century, they remained profoundly influential in popular imaginings of political and historical change, expressed in the form of poetry and especially in times of sociopolitical turmoil.

In the tradition of apocrypha, the *hetu* (the Yellow River Chart), one of the earliest auspicious diagrams documented in Chinese writings, had played a particularly crucial role in establishing an association between political divination and the Yellow River. Described as a jade ritual object in *The Documents of Antiquity*,[23] the earliest of the Confucian classics, *hetu* acquired meaning as an auspicious sign for the rise of sage-kings in *Book of Changes* and *The Analects* and became the symbol of the mandate of heaven (*tianming* 天命), the divine source of authority to rule all under heaven.[24] After the Former Han (202 BCE–8 CE), apocryphal texts of the *hetu* legend began to include the idea of prophecy and river taming. Literature from this period also saw the emergence of narratives recounting that the ancient cultural hero Fuxi 伏羲 created the eight trigrams used for divination according to the *hetu* after receiving them from a dragon horse at the Yellow River. In this narrative, the *hetu* is associated with the Yellow River and the prophecy of the state's future. Later apocryphal texts built a further connection between the *hetu* and Da Yu's flood taming. "Mantic Observations" ("Zhonghou" 中候) in *The Documents of Antiquity*, a famous *wei* text written during the Xin dynasty (9–23 CE), describes *hetu* as

---

21. For a discussion of the practice of *zhanhou*, see Kory 2019.
22. For the doctrine of the five-element cycle, see Loewe 1994, chaps. 2 and 6; Schwartz 1985, chap. 9.
23. The *hetu* was first mentioned in the "Testamentary Charge" ("Guming" 顧命) chapter.
24. The *hetu* had come to be frequently mentioned in conjunction with *luoshu* 洛書, the "Luo Script." In late Former Han (202 BCE–8 CE), *hetu* and *luoshu* began to be called the "green words" (*lüzi* 綠字) and the "red texts" (*chiwen* 赤文), although both the green words and the red texts were later more frequently used to refer to apocrypha books in general. Since the Song dynasty, the *hetu* and *luoshu* have referred to two cosmological diagrams introduced by the philosopher Shao Yong 邵雍 (1012–1077), who claimed that the diagrams are the very *hetu* and *luoshu* mentioned in ancient archives.

a mythical object granted by the lord of the river (*hebo* 河伯) to Da Yu; the text claims the *hetu* emerged as early as the time of the legendary sage-king Yao堯 and has texts with written prophecies on dynastic succession until the Han. According to the story in *Mantic Observations*, Da Yu used the *hetu* to contain the floods and eventually founded the Xia dynasty. In this account, the *hetu* is endowed with the magical capacity to foretell historical events and reveal the secret to controlling floods. Political prophecy and Yellow River governance had been connected since the end of the Former Han dynasty through one of the most important symbols in the apocryphal tradition.

The apocryphal tradition manifests in the political imagination of *The Travels*. Apocryphal texts had long been familiar to Liu E because the Taigu school, as mentioned, had been strongly interested in the apocryphal tradition since its founding. In his novel, Liu embeds apocryphal elements, such as prediction in poetic form and divination based on calendric calculation, in scenes where political prophecies are given. The poem collection *The Sayings of the Insiders*, which Shen Ziping peruses in the Peach Blossom Mountain, contains prophetic verses typical of apocryphal poems, rendering predictions on future political incidents. Yellow Dragon's prophecy, based on transitions in the calendar, that China would be beset by the Boxer Uprising and then reinvigorated after a failed revolution, are also strikingly similar to apocryphal texts that provide political prophecy based on calendric calculation. The predictions made in the poem collection and by Yellow Dragon are furthermore typical of apocrypha because hindsight is the basis for their highly accurate foretelling. While the novel, written in 1903, is set in 1891 (see Chapter 3), the verses in *The Sayings of the Insiders* all refer to historical events between 1894 and 1900, such as the Boxer Uprising and the Eight-Nation Alliance. That is, the prophetic verses are Liu E's postdiction, or prophesying after the fact, a common practice in prophecy-making in China for over two thousand years. Liu E's prophetic claims in his book were so convincing that late Qing and early Republican readers read the novel as apocrypha. One early Republican edition even faked the date of the preface before the predicted events to falsely present the novel as a real book of prophecy.[25] In this sense, chapters 10 and 11 are apocryphal texts in the guise of a vernacular novel.

Yellow Dragon's prophecy in chapter 11, the novel's most crucial political prediction, is not only an apocryphal text by itself but also a strong reference to the relationship between the apocryphal tradition and Yellow River regulation. The closing commentary of chapter 11 (see chapter epigraph) addresses this connection specifically when Liu E compares the prophecy to apocrypha associated with the Da Yu legend. The line "heavenly scrolls with green incantation inscribed on golden slips" (*lüwen jinjian tianshu* 綠文金簡天書)—an obvious reference to "green words," a

---

25. For *The Travels* being read as an apocrypha text in the early Republican era, see Feng 2023; Jiang 2018.

term for apocryphal texts—alludes to the story of Da Yu's flood taming in the *Spring and Autumn Annals of Wu and Yue* (*Wuyue chunqiu* 吳越春秋), a Later Han (25–220 CE) historical chronicle. According to the story, Da Yu was divinely granted a heavenly scroll while in a stone studio atop Weiwan Mountain 委宛山; by using this scroll, he could successfully contain the floods (see He 2021, 150–51). This story is obviously a variation of one in the apocryphal text "Mantic Observations" in *The Documents of Antiquity*, which tells how Da Yu obtained the *hetu* from the lord of the river and thus could tame the floods. By comparing chapter 11, or more precisely, Yellow Dragon's prophecy, to the *hetu*, Liu E's commentary suggests that Shen Ziping, who learns about the hermit's prophecy while in the Peach Blossom Mountain, is analogous to Da Yu, who was granted the heavenly scroll on Weiwan Mountain. Liu E has, most explicitly, revealed the context underlying the chapter's ostensible theme of apocrypha: Yellow River flooding and its governance.

While apocrypha are the basis for Yellow Dragon's prophecy, which informs the novel's political imagination, *The Travels* shows contradictory attitudes toward apocryphal practice. The second volume throws its value into question, especially in a conversation between Lao Can and De Huisheng on the acquisition of foreknowledge (*qian zhi* 前知) at the beginning of chapter 21. Quoting Yellow Dragon, Lao Can explains that "minor gimmicks of divination" (*shushu xiaodao* 術數小道) are not the basis of foreknowledge. Rather, the basis is moral cultivation attained by "emptying one's mind and quieting *qi*" (*xuxin jingqi* 虛心靜氣). Lao Can's dismissal of divination here, however, is clearly antithetical to the novel's approving description of Yellow Dragon's prophesying in chapter 11. Based on five element theory and calendric calculation, the prophecy entails exactly the apocryphal practice Yellow Dragon denounces to Lao Can. By presenting Yellow Dragon as holding contradictory understandings of apocrypha, the novel illustrates the character's ambiguity.

Yellow Dragon's ambiguous attitude toward apocrypha reflects Liu E's ambivalence in his professional activities related to the Yellow River. Liu E's discussion about the Yellow River course map, whose production he oversaw in 1889 and 1890, perfectly demonstrates this ambiguity.[26] The paronomastic discussion, which

---

26. "We can roughly infer that the name [of the apocryphal texts with the word *hetu* in their titles] comes from what is said in *Book of Changes*, 'The *tu* emerged from the Yellow River, and the sages observed it,' and also in *Lu lun* [*The Analects*], 'Since the *hetu* does not come out from the Yellow River, the task of my life is done!' As these classics show, the oldest of all *tu* (drawing) is the *hetu*. A sage dynasty like this is when the great Way is manifested, and apocrypha should be abandoned. What ought to be done now is to promote the supreme Way taught in the *hetu* and *luoshu* and dismiss prophetic apocrypha popular in ages of decadence. I make this *hetu* (river map) in a practical and realistic manner. Compared to how Song Jing predicts floods by calendric calculation and yet falsely claims that he read the prophecy from a jade tablet passed down from Da Yu, my intention is totally different" 尋繹數言略知本《易》稱「河出圖,聖人則之」,《魯論》稱「河不出圖,吾已矣」。夫經典昭垂,圖之最古者,莫《河圖》若也。聖朝苞符大啟,而祥瑞不言,炳軒必之圖書,斥哀平之符讖。河圖之作,主於實事求是。較之宋景以曆紀推言水災,為稱洞視玉版者,意迥殊焉 (Liu 2007, 1:34).

appears in his explanatory notes to the river map, hinges on the polysemy of *hetu*, meaning (1) a river map used in river work, (2) the auspicious omen that first appeared in the Confucian classics, and (3) the cosmological diagram explaining the principle of the universe represented by the hexagrams in *Book of Changes*—the meaning *hetu* acquired after the Song dynasty and accepted as its standard interpretation thereafter. Liu E manipulates the triple meanings of *hetu* to justify his river map's significance. By associating his river map with the first appearance of *hetu* in the Confucian classics and the cosmological meaning *hetu* acquired after the Song, Liu argues in his explanatory notes that his *hetu* (river map) has the weight of antiquity and metaphysics as endorsed by orthodox Confucianism. His river map, Liu indicates, is therefore different from the apocryphal texts that falsely claimed their legitimacy merely by borrowing the word *hetu* for their titles. Yet Liu's attempt to justify the value of his river map contains contradictions. The *hetu* mentioned in *Book of Changes* and *The Analects*, an auspicious sign for the rise of the sage-kings, is mythical rather than metaphysical. Moreover, the relationship between *hetu* and river work, as mentioned, was established nowhere other than in the Han apocrypha. Even though Liu E attempts to relate his river map to orthodox Confucianism in contrast to the apocryphal tradition, he nonetheless draws on the polysemy of *hetu* to supply his river map with an ancient origin that belonged to the apocryphal tradition he denounced.

Liu E's ambivalent positioning of his river map manifests most radically in his discourse about his submission of the map to the authority. The Yellow River map, which the director of the Yellow River Conservancy Wu Dacheng commissioned, was to be submitted to Emperor Guangxu 光緒 (r. 1875–1908) for reference. Liu E, in his explanatory note to the emperor, claims that he submits the map to help the emperor, who embodied the Way and thus needed no auspicious omens to support his rule, to realize the Way revealed by the *hetu*. Liu E's claim, obviously an ingratiating statement, relies on the idea that the river map, bearing an association with *hetu* the cosmological diagram, represents the Way of the universe; thus, it does not relate to the apocryphal tradition or mythical legend. However, Liu's presentation of his river map to the sage emperor recalls descriptions of *hetu*'s appearance in *Book of Changes* and *The Analects*—as an auspicious sign for the rise of the sage-kings. In this sense, Liu's submission of his *hetu* to Emperor Guangxu fulfills the augury for the rise of the sage emperor. Despite Liu's attempt to differentiate his river map from apocrypha and their auspicious omens, he turns his river map into another auspicious omen. In positioning his river map, Liu E struggled and failed to divorce his *hetu* from the apocryphal tradition.

The apocryphal tradition and Yellow River regulation define the novel's political imagination. Prominent features of the apocryphal texts mark Yellow Dragon's prophecy of China's future, which is based on calendric calculation. By evoking the long-established relationship between the apocryphal tradition and river work, Liu

E also suggests Da Yu's legendary river taming as a hidden but important context for Yellow Dragon's prophecy. While the novel's political imagination is embedded in both apocryphal and hydraulic traditions—which were highly intertwined in Chinese mythology—Liu E tended to distinguish the two traditions in his river work. Fully aware of the danger of mixing up the river map submitted to the emperor and the apocryphal text, Liu struggled to divorce his river map from the apocryphal tradition with which it was deeply associated. Such contradiction in the novelist finds expression in the novel's inconsistent attitude toward apocryphal practice.

Prophecies Made of Floods, Mathematics, and Mechanics

Although Yellow Dragon's prophecy pertains to China's political future, the perspective from which the prophecy is made comes from China's ecological past. As the primary context for Yellow Dragon's prophecy (and one of Liu E's primary concerns), the Yellow River is the inexhaustible resource on which Liu E draws to frame his blueprint of national reinvention in chapter 11—one that maps China's tortuous route from destruction to rejuvenation. Yellow Dragon's prophecy compares the devastating Yellow River floods, which nevertheless also fertilize crops with rich soil and nutrients, to disastrous political events that facilitate the progress of civilizations. With this analogy, Liu E suggests all changes and variations during this progress are calculable, just as the movement of fluids is with the aid of mathematics and hydraulic engineering—subjects in which he, a river engineer, was an expert.

Yellow Dragon's prophecy about China's upheaval—the Boxer Uprising and revolution—and reinvigoration echoes a concern about environmental collapse that had been expressed in China since the late eighteenth century. Discussing the impacts of the disastrous political events, Yellow Dragon uses the pattern of seasonal cycles to explain why they were bound to occur. By comparing autumn and winter, which "kill" the life fostered in spring and summer to avoid overgrowth, Yellow Dragon perceives the Boxer Uprising and revolution as part of nature's mechanism for maintaining equilibrium. The way Yellow Dragon views environmental destruction shows the influence of a popular theory of environmental crisis developed by the late eighteenth-century statesman and political theorist Hong Liangji 洪亮吉 (1746–1809). Hong viewed floods and drought as how heaven tempered the environmental pressure caused by rapid population growth since the mid-eighteenth century. Yellow Dragon's explanation for the necessity of the destructive power of the Boxer Uprising and revolution is the inheritance of a mid-Qing environmental approach to population issues.

Although Liu E suggests destructive power is necessary to achieve ecological balance, he also emphasizes in the discourse of China's reinvention that destruction enables growth. He conceptualizes this idea again in terms of the seasonal cycle. Explaining his prophecy's philosophical grounding, Yellow Dragon suggests autumn and winter's killing power allows heaven to return and show his love for life again in the following spring and summer; destruction in nature paves the way for new life. This positive significance of destructive forces comes to the fore in the rhetoric Yellow Dragon adopts in his political prophecy. In predicting China's future between 1904 and 1924, Yellow Dragon employs plant imagery to describe the progress of Chinese civilization:

> These two rebellious parties will both brew disaster, but together they will open up a new era. . . . The words of Wei the Daoist in his *Cantongqi*, "In the beginning of the year, the shoots sprout forth," refer to the year of Jiachen [1904]. Chen is subject to the element of earth [in five element theory]. Since everything grows from earth, after Jiachen there will be a sprouting of cultural shoots, like "a tree seedling bursting through the husk of a seed," like a bamboo shoot splitting its way through its sheath. All that the eye can see is tree seed and bamboo sheath, but the real living buds are concealed within. During the next ten years, sheath and husk will gradually break, and by Jiayin [1914] new life will be fully developed. Yin is subject to element of wood and is a symbol of the calyx [that protects the flower during development]. After Jiayin will be a time of cultural fluorescence, but although brilliant to look upon, it still will not equal the development of other countries. Jiazi [1924] will be a time of a real independent cultural harvest. (Liu 1990, 119–20)
>
> 此二亂黨，皆所以釀劫運，亦皆所以開文明也。……魏真人《參同契》所說，「元年乃芽滋」，指甲辰而言。辰屬上，萬物生於土，故甲辰以後為文明芽滋之世，如木之坏甲，如筍之解籜。其實滿目所見者，皆木甲竹籜也，而真苞已隱藏其中矣。十年之間，籜甲漸解，至甲寅而齊。寅屬木，為花萼之象。甲寅以後為文明華敷之世，雖燦爛可觀，尚不足與他國齊趨並駕。直至甲子，為文明結實之世，可以自立矣。

Yellow Dragon compares Chinese civilization's development to a plant's sprouting, growth, blossoming, and fruition. He takes the Boxer Uprising and revolution as the destructive forces, like floods, that drive civilizational revival.[27] Yellow Dragon implicitly suggests in his plant imagery, therefore, that the Boxer Uprising and revolution, which foment disaster but also birth a new era, are like frequent floods—they cause damage and toll but also replenish the soil and benefit the harvest. Yellow Dragon's rhetoric of political prophecy and explanations for the principle of natural

---

27. As discussed in the Introduction, Yellow Dragon draws a direct link between revolutionists and devastating floods. Although Yellow Dragon does not explicitly connect it to the floods, the Boxer Uprising was historically closely related to the Yellow River floods. We can also infer the suggested relationship between the Boxer Uprising and floods from Liu E's description of the martial arts master Liu Renfu: in the commentary to the novel, Liu E describes his way of body control as an antidote to the uncontrolled proliferation of the Boxer Uprising (see discussion in Chapter 1). In chapter 7 of the novel, Lao Can's scheme to invite Liu Renfu to help deal with local bandits is in fact derived from Liu E's approach to river regulation. The Boxer Uprising, therefore, is imagined in the novel as devastating floods like revolutionists.

equilibrium show that the Yellow River serves as the imagery on which Liu E draws for imagining China's reinvention.

Yellow Dragon's prediction of China's future not only adopts the imagery of the Yellow River floods but also grounds itself epistemologically in river regulation. His political prophecy is based on the derivation of the hexagrams in *Book of Changes*, the canon of Chinese philosophy, which, as he suggests, is arithmetical in essence. While the political prophecy's arithmetical emphasis concerns Liu E's personal interest in mathematics,[28] that interest stemmed from the practical need for engineering measurement in his profession. In one of his treatises on flood control methods, Liu E cites the Han mathematical work *The Mathematical Classic of the Zhou Gnomon* (*Zhoubi suanjing* 周髀算經), pointing out that the study of mathematics initially came into being because of Da Yu's need when wrestling with the flood.[29] Traditional Chinese mathematics and river management were considered closely interrelated in the epistemological sense. "The Origins of Numbers and Their Principles" ("Shuli benyuan" 數理本源), an essay on the development of mathematical concepts in China published by the central government in the early eighteenth century, attributes the arithmetical rules to the *hetu* and *luoshu* from the legend of Da Yu's river taming.[30] *Explanation of The Mathematical Classic of the Zhou Gnomon* (*Zhoubi jingjie* 周髀經解), an explanatory book to *The Mathematical Classic of the Zhou Gnomon*, specifically pinpoints the genesis of mathematics to when Da Yu tried to measure land elevation (Yunzhi et al. [1723] 1987, 11). As Yellow Dragon highlights the arithmetical aspect of *Book of Changes* in describing the winding course of Chinese affairs, he defines his political prophecy in the context of water control, philosophy, and mathematics. Yellow Dragon's prophecy refers to both China's political future and the historical origins of the practical knowledge used to tame the Yellow River.

The political imagination expressed in Yellow Dragon's discussion on divination is deeply associated with the epistemology of Yellow River regulation relating to celestial mechanics. Yellow Dragon considers all changes of affairs, including politics, as representing the dynamics of interaction between contrary forces. However, instead of formless opposing cosmic forces, as in the yin-yang concept

---

28. Liu E was versed in trigonometry and spherical geometry and wrote two books on mathematics.
29. Liu E (2007, 1:41) writes in his *Five Essays on River Management* (*Zhihe wu shuo* 治河五說), "*The Mathematical Classic of the Zhou Gnomon* says, 'It was to serve Yu's need to reign over all under heaven that math came into being.' Han dynasty [mathematician] Zhao Junqing annotated, 'Yu containing the flood is where the Principles of Hook and Thigh emerged'" 《周髀算經》云：故禹之所以治天下者，此數之所由生也。漢趙君卿注云：『禹治洪水，乃勾股之所由生也』. The principle of hook and thigh explains the concept of what is known as the Pythagorean theorem today. For discussion on the translation of *gougu* 勾股, see Raphals 2002, 41–42.
30. The very beginning of *Imperially Composed Essence of Numbers and Their Principles* (*Yuzhi Shuli jingyun* 御製數理精蘊, 1723), a mathematical compendium compiled under Emperor Kangxi's direction, explains the foundations of Chinese mathematical conceptions as derived from *hetu* and *luoshu*. See Yunzhi et al. 1987, 4–7.

as traditionally defined, Yellow Dragon identifies the celestial objects in the solar system as the origin of the forces: "The planets that travel around the sun all depend upon the sun as their controlling power... Since there is contact between this power of attraction wherever it reaches and the responsive power of these places reached, many kinds of changes are produced—more than can be told" 環繞太陽之行星皆憑這個太陽為主動力……又因這感動力所及之處與那本地的應動力相交，生出種種變相，莫可紀述 (Liu 1990, 122). Yellow Dragon suggests the sun is the central force, which he calls the Force Supreme, governing all the interactions between the planetary forces. According to Yellow Dragon, the universe's entire course of affairs, including events such as the Boxer Uprising and revolution, are changes brought about by the interactive powers between the sun and the planets.[31] The calculations made through the derivation of the hexagrams to predict and explain all the changes, therefore, are nothing other than the dynamics or the forces between the sun and the planets. Yellow Dragon's prophecy of China's future, in this sense, is based on celestial mechanics.

The novel's political imagination, partly informed by mechanical concepts, draws upon Liu E's technical design for an embankment system. The Force Supreme, which Yellow Dragon believes presides over all changes in the universe, is unignorably like the oblique dike system Liu E proposed in the early 1890s when in charge of river work in Shandong. Designed using detailed calculations of fluid mechanics, the oblique dike system controls the floods by channeling water currents toward collision or convergence. In Liu E's design, the counterbalancing water pressure on the two sides of the dike achieves a mechanical balance that prevents dike bursts. This system, emphasizing overall water flow control and ecological equilibrium, functions nearly identically to the Force Supreme, which, according to Yellow Dragon, commands all changes and equilibrates life and death. Moreover, the oblique dike system's ability to convert flood water into a productive resource is consonant with Yellow Dragon's understanding of the positive side of annihilating forces. That is, the Force Supreme, which Yellow Dragon hails as the ultimate law of the universe, is the literary variation of the oblique dike, a system that can reconcile, moderate, and convert conflicting forces. Within this analogy between Force Supreme and the oblique dike, all changes in the universe, just like the changing flow of water, fall within mechanics. Like Liu E's tackling of the Yellow River floods, Yellow Dragon's prediction and exposition of the changing state of affairs is a matter of mechanical

---

31. Yellow Dragon's explanation of Force Supreme bears the hue of late Qing studies on *Book of Changes*. His drawing on the intersection of the lines (*yao* 爻) in *Book of Changes* to explain the relationship between the sun and the planets is not a novel invention of Liu E but inherited from late-Qing thinker Tan Sitong 譚嗣同 (1865–1898). Tan used *Book of Changes* to describe the motion of celestial bodies as early as the 1890s, explaining the terrestrial structure and the changes on Earth through the order of the six lines (1981, 125–26). The way Yellow Dragon maps the intersection of the lines onto the solar-planetary relationship is derived from Tan Sitong's theory.

calculation. Fluid mechanics in hydraulic engineering, in this sense, is where Liu E grounds his political imagination.

The political imagination in Yellow Dragon's prophecy, inspired by the late eighteenth-century idea of ecological equilibrium, focuses on the productive aspect of nature's destructive forces. Liu E draws upon the imagery of the Yellow River floods, which embodies both destructive and productive qualities, to imagine the reinvention of China. Such imagination borrows both the imagery of the floods and the language used in the branches of knowledge—mathematics and mechanics—to which river engineering was considered to have given birth. Epistemologically informed by these fields, the novel's political imagination shares with Liu E's hydraulic design the same mode of dealing with force dynamics. Hydraulic engineering is the core idea around which Liu E develops his imagination of China's future.

A Taigu Taming

Chapters 10 and 11, seemingly distinct from the rest of *The Travels*, in fact provide its overarching framework. Echoing the first chapter, these two chapters at the structural center of the twenty-chapter first volume focus on issues related to the Taigu school and Yellow River regulation, Liu E's two major concerns.

The overarching framework is manifested primarily through the multiple symbolic layers of "Melody of Sea Waters and Heavenly Wind." The musical piece expresses not just the Taigu school's syncretic teaching or Liu E's defense against the accusation of apostasy from his fellow Taigu followers. It also represents Liu E's strong sense of duty toward succeeding to the leadership of the school and carrying out its doctrines in the face of political pressure. Described as a polyphony, the musical piece, moreover, signifies the combination of and the interplay between the Taigu teaching and the tradition of river regulation, which Liu E demonstrates further through Yellow Dragon's political prophecy in chapter 11. On the one hand, Yellow Dragon's prediction of Chinese politics reflects the Taigu school's relationship to the apocryphal tradition. On the other hand, it reflects the history and epistemology of flood control with which the apocryphal tradition had been closely associated.

Chapters 10 and 11 are also central to Liu E's imagination of a nation-building agenda for securing China's future. The two chapters together constitute an all-inclusive thematic core, suggesting Taigu teaching and Yellow River regulation as the forces that can propel China's reinvention. To realize this national-cultural mission, the novelist has an ideal candidate already in mind. By traveling to the Peach Blossom Mountain, Shen Ziping, acting as the double for Lao Can, becomes a convert to the Taigu school and is symbolic of the ancient hero of river taming. By creating a character acting as the inheritor of the Taigu teaching and the secret of taming the Yellow River, Liu E imagines himself as a national cultural hero who could be expected to save all under heaven.

Conclusion

Just as the Yellow River management's origin in the myth of Da Yu over four thousand years ago symbolized the earliest Chinese conceptualization of state-building and civilization renewal, it also remained at the heart of Liu E's nation-building efforts in *The Travels*. Throughout Chinese history, no period other than the late Qing—the eve of the dynastic era's collapse—has seen its intellectuals so eager to seek inspiration from the symbolic myth to address the imminent civilization crisis, and Liu E's novel is one of the most important literary expressions of this trend. As this book has argued, the Yellow River floods in nineteenth-century Shandong fundamentally shaped Liu E's life and are the key to understanding his greatest written work.

From a river engineer's perspective, Liu E conceptualized the relationship between the individual Chinese citizen's body and the nation very differently from the mainstream late Qing discourse of nation-building inspired by nineteenth-century Western sociological theories. Based on his hydraulic expertise, the author imagined a complexly analogical and intertwined relationship between the river, the body, and the state that he employed to express his agenda for revitalizing the country. Specifically, through an exploration of local governance, the author proposes a broader governance model that encourages more civilian participation and less state intervention. Meanwhile, by fictionalizing his observations on flood events, Liu E transforms the post-disaster traumas caused by the Yellow River floodings into a key resource for developing the novel's discourse of national emotion. The visually straining experiences Liu E had during his Yellow River survey and mapping tasks contributed to the innovative landscape writing that inspired leading critics to recommend it as an exemplary novel for national literature construction in the early Republican era. By encoding Yellow River floodings and river engineering into the structural core of the novel, Liu successfully connects his political commitment, which springs from traditional Chinese philosophies, to Yellow River engineering and establishes the Yellow River as the core drive for the novel's nation-building narrative. In this way, *The Travels* becomes the landmark work of early twentieth-century literary nation-building—imagining nationhood in literature and making national literature.

Environmental collapse, this book has argued, was the true catalyst for the literary invention of *The Travels*. Its breakthroughs in the narrative, landscape writing, and approach to political issues all impacted post-1910s modern novels, as other scholars have noted. This book is the first to identify the true source of Liu E's literary innovation: the nineteenth-century Yellow River floodings. The perspective of *The Travels* is not local but national. Environmental and scientific explorations have been important subjects for modern writers in the West (Raine 2014)—the decisive influence of mineral resource rushes in the nineteenth and early twentieth centuries on the narrative form of English literature is an illuminating example (Miller 2021). By the early twentieth century, the fascination with the environment and science and technology was no longer a Western phenomenon. Liu E, like many of his Western counterparts, showed a keen interest in the technology of natural resources exploitation, especially hydraulics and mineral extraction technology. It was his intense desire to exploit natural resources to empower the country that motivated him to pen the epoch-making *The Travels*. Acknowledging this fact enables us to interpret the novel from an ecocritical perspective.

In approaching *The Travels* from such a perspective, we cannot avoid reexamining the development of the concept of "youth" in early twentieth-century writings. Beginning with Liang Qichao's "On Young China" (Shaonian Zhongguo shuo 少年中國說, 1900), "youth" became one of the most important explorations of the nation. Unlike Liang Qichao's imagination of China's rejuvenation, which appealed to a "marriage" with the West, Wu Woyao's 吳沃堯 (1866–1910) science fiction novel *The New Story of the Stone* (Xin shitou ji 新石頭記, 1905–1908) opened up another way of imagining China's rejuvenation through the character of Old Youth (Lao shaonian 老少年), which represents China's ability to draw the power of rejuvenation from its ancient traditions without relying on the West (Song 2016). In late Qing literature, however, Wu Woyao's Old Youth is not the only figure created to symbolize the ability of Chinese civilization to renew itself. The Yellow River, the core symbol of *The Travels*, embodies the ancient power of rejuvenation sought after in early twentieth-century political discourse. Written two years before *The New Story of the Stone*, *The Travels* offers another perspective on China's self-rejuvenation. Its protagonist, Lao Can, is associated with the ancient power of rejuvenation, which is both a source of destruction and rebirth. Lao Can, a river engineer and doctor, not only regulates the Yellow River but also possesses the skill of "miaoshou huichun" 妙手回春 (literally, "wonder hands bring the dying back to life"). This ability symbolizes his capacity to revitalize and restore what has been lost, using China's ancient traditions to empower the nation. From an ecological standpoint, *The Travels* establishes a prototypical symbol of China's self-rejuvenation, contributing to the nation-building discourse in the late Qing and beyond.

Also passed down from *The Travels* to later novels was the portrayal of the association between the exploitation of the environment and Chinese nation-building. Wu Woyao's *The New Story of the Stone* can serve as a useful point of comparison to better understand the significant influence of *The Travels* on later literary works, particularly in terms of their portrayal of this relationship. Like *The Travels*, Wu's novel implies the role of environmental technology in nation-building by referring to the prologue from the eighteenth-century classic novel *The Story of the Stone*, which retells the myth of Nüwa melting five-color stones to patch up the heavens in disrepair (symbolizing the dysfunctional political order). In a similar vein, while *The Travels*, based on Liu E's innovative hydraulic technological conception, envisions reinvigorating the Chinese nation by taming the Yellow River into productive power, *The New Story of the Stone* imagines an ideal nation-state built by harnessing natural resources with advanced technology. *The Travels* established the theme of the environment and the state that later eco-literature attempts to address.

Ecocritical studies of Chinese literature typically present a narrative centered on scientific progress and the conquest of nature from the late Qing to the present day, with a return to nature and the pursuit of ecological balance as interludes.[1] The narrative often describes two opposing tendencies regarding nature in thought and literature. However, *The Travels* breaks from this framework. Liu E, unique among late Qing thinkers, promoted scientific, rational exploitation and utilization of the natural world while also emphasizing respect for its principles and irresistible mythic power as the main theme of the episodes at the novel's structural center. He believed that national prosperity and civilizational progress depended on complying with the law of nature and that a return to nature could go hand in hand with exploiting nature. *The Travels*, the most significant work of late Qing fiction, serves as a great reminder for us to reexamine the basic presupposition of China's eco-literary history.

An ecocritical perspective also lends this study a place in the ongoing debate on environmental history. By exploring Liu E's engagements in river work and industrial projects, this study has echoed the emphasis on nonhuman agency in recent scholarship on environmental history. From the 1970s until the 1990s, environmental historians considered problems like how humans should comprehend, utilize, and transform the natural world. Since the 1990s, the focus has shifted to the role of the environment in shaping modern society, including its impacts on politics, society,

---

1. As scholars already note, late Qing thinkers like Zhang Binglin 章炳麟 (1869–1936) were aware of and warned against the sobering environmental consequences of widely launched industrialization and nation-strengthening activities (coal mining in particular). As remedies, they recommended traditional Chinese philosophies (Roddy 2019).

culture, and daily life. The new scholarly trend stresses that historical and social transitions stem from the interplay of multiple nonhuman agencies, especially environmental change and scientific progress.[2] Accordingly, this book has analyzed how the changes on the Yellow River and progress in river engineering have interplayed to shape Liu E's political imagination and how that political imagination set off a chain of xenophobic political events that led to the tragic end of his life. The analysis sheds light on the intricate interlinking of the environment, science and technology, political storms, and nationalist events. In addition, it also introduces a new environmental approach to the interdisciplinary study of early twentieth-century China's local governance, nation-building, and foreign relations.

This study also opens a dialogue with current disaster research. Recent disaster studies have abandoned the previous research model that focuses exclusively on the human response to natural calamities. Instead, they have begun to focus on the interactions among catastrophe, culture, and economy. Mark Carey (2010), in his study on the Andes avalanches due to glacier melt, observes that the catastrophes have reshaped the Peruvian perception of the natural environment. Meanwhile, he also notes that the locals' reactions to the frequent occurrence of avalanches, highly influenced by environmental scientists, is in fact expert biased. Scientists and experts not only play a role in disaster relief and reconstruction; their views also have cultural and psychological impacts. We can observe a similar phenomenon in Liu E's fictionalization of his Yellow River engineering experience. The transformation of visual perception marked by the innovative landscape writing in *The Travels* is an immediate product of his witnessing the Yellow River floodings. Drawing on his hydraulic expertise, Liu started serializing the novel in a local newspaper to shape the flood-stricken people's perception of flood control and their sense of national identity. The role he played is like that of the experts Carey observes. In effect, Liu has exemplified how water disasters shape a witness's perception and how an expert transforms the experience into technical expertise to launch a nation-building campaign.

Calamities, as Carey's study shows, can have some positive outcomes. In a certain way, they may create new opportunities for the local economy. For example, Peru's avalanches have become a tourist attraction, which Carey describes as disaster economics. That is, disasters are also productive. Liu E's engagement in the Western Affairs Movement was also triggered by a "productive disaster." To raise funds for Shanxi's coal mining and railway construction projects, Liu proposed the

---

2. Donald Worster in a 1990 paper tracked the pre-1990s development trends of environmental history. Two years later, William Cronon (1992) criticized Worster and others for overemphasizing agroecology and the mainstream community's Caucasian views. After another two decades, Linda Nash (2013) took it upon herself to summarize the progress and breakthroughs in environmental history since the 1990s, highlighting the cultural turn shaped by the interworking with ecological and environmental disciplines, especially the science and technology studies made by Bruno Latour and others.

build-operate-transfer financing model and advocated for active private sector participation and less state intervention. The governance model reflects the impact of his flood control experience and expertise on his thinking regarding political governance. Although the proposal was eventually shelved under pressure, it is undeniable that the experience and expertise Liu gained from flood control and river engineering produced a (fruitless) chance for modernizing Shanxi. Thus, we may expand the beneficiaries of Carey's disaster economics from areas that are stricken to areas that are not.

By inquiring into *The Travels* as a work of literary nation-building on a personal level, this book highlights the power of the Yellow River and its far-reaching influence on late Qing fiction, the environment, and the development of Chinese nationalism. The study shows how *The Travels* captures the force of the Yellow River, which profoundly shaped not merely the nation's physical, social, and political landscape but also Liu E's career, misfortune, and blueprint for national rejuvenation. In doing so, it sheds light on the dynamics between environmental change, human adaptive response, literary production, and nation-building. The analysis showcases how Yellow River floods and river engineering contributed to the creation of a classic novel often regarded as *the* book of the twentieth century, and it reveals the relationship between the emergence of modern Chinese literature and the environmental crisis—a devastating flood on the Yellow River—that unfolded decades before the fall of the Qing dynasty.

Works Cited

Ames, Roger T., and David L. Hall. 2001. *Focusing the Familiar: A Translation and Philosophical Interpretation of the "Zhongyong"*. Honolulu: University of Hawai'i Press.
Andrews, Bridie. 2014. *The Making of Modern Chinese Medicine, 1850–1960*. Contemporary Chinese Studies. Vancouver: University of British Columbia Press.
Baozi 保茲. 1913. "Wangyuanjing yu xingqiu" 望遠鏡與星球 [Telescope and planets]. *Jiaoyujie* 教育界 [Education] 2 (1): 5.
Berry, Michael. 2008. *A History of Pain: Trauma in Modern Chinese Literature and Film*. New York: Columbia University Press.
Braester, Yomi. 2003. *Witness against History: Literature, Film, and Public Discourse in Twentieth-Century China*. Stanford: Stanford University Press.
Cai Keyuan 蔡可園, ed. 1978. *Qing dai qi bai mingren zhuan* 清代七百名人傳 [Biographies of seven hundred eminent figures of the Qing dynasty]. Taipei: Guangwen shuju.
Cammann, Schuyler. 1960. "The Evolution of Magic Squares in China." *Journal of the American Oriental Society* 80 (2): 116–24.
Cammann, Schuyler. 1962. "Old Chinese Magic Squares." *Sinologica* 7: 14–53.
Cao Xueqin 曹雪芹. 1973. *Story of the Stone*. Translated by David Hawkes. New York: Penguin.
Carey, Mark. 2010. *In the Shadow of Melting Glaciers: Climate Change and Andean Society*. New York: Oxford University Press.
Chang Shu-hsiang 張淑香. 1996. "Xiehou nüshen: Jie *Lao Can youji er bian* yiyun shuofa" 邂逅女神：解《老殘遊記二編》逸雲說法 [Encountering the goddess: On Yiyun's preaching in *The Sequel to The Travels of Lao Can*]. In *Yuwen, qingxing, yili: Zhongguo wenxue de duo cengmian tantao guoji xueshu huiyi lunwen ji* 語文、情性、義理：中國文學的多層面探討國際學術會議論文集 [Language, affection, and philosophy: A multifaceted survey in Chinese literature, a proceeding of international conference], edited by Ko Ch'ing-ming 柯慶明, 437–66. Taipei: Department of Chinese Literature, National Taiwan University.
Chang Shu-hsiang 張淑香. 2001. "Shanzhong chuanqi: Lao Can youji de mixing xuxie" 山中傳奇：《老殘遊記》的女性敘寫 [The legend in the mountains: The writing of femininity in *The Travels of Lao Can*]. In *Shibian yu weixin: Wanming yu wanqing de wenxue yishu* 世變與維新：晚明與晚清的文學藝術 [Change and renovation: Literature in late Ming and late Qing], edited by Hu Siao-chen 胡曉真, 389–427. Taipei: Preparatory Office of the Institute of Chinese Literature and Philosophy, Academia Sinica.

Chen Hsi-Yuan 陳熙遠. 2018. "Yiwei yu jianghu yu miaotang zhijian—Ming Qing zhiji baobiao hangji kao" 依違於江湖與廟堂之間——明清之際保標行跡考 [Through troubled waters: Tracing the armed escort services during the Ming-Qing transition]. *Xin Shixue* 新史學 [New history] 29 (2): 165–214.

Chen Hua 陳樺, and Liu Zongzhi 劉宗志. 2005. *Jiouzai yu jipin: Zhongguo fengjian shidai de shehui jiouzhu huodong (1750–1911)* 救災與濟貧——中國封建時代的社會救助活動 [Disaster relief and economic support: Social assistance in imperial China, 1750–1911]. Beijing: China Renmin University Press.

Chen Jo-shui 陳弱水. 2005. *Gonggong yishi yu Zhongguo wenhua* 公共意識與中國文化 [Public consciousness and Chinese culture]. Taipei: Linking Publishing.

Chen Xu 陳旭. 2010. *Qingguan: Yanjiu chuantong Zhongguo zhengzhi wenhua de yige dute shijiao* 清官：研究傳統中國政治文化的一個獨特視角 [Qing officials: A unique perspective to study traditional Chinese political culture]. Beijing: China Social Sciences Press.

Cheng, Chi Wai Louella 鄭志慧. 2007. "Between History and Fiction: Making Sense of *Lao Can You Ji* as a Text in Ruins." PhD diss., University of Hong Kong.

Cheng Kat Hung Dennis 鄭吉雄. 2013. "Shilun Zisi yishuo" 試論子思遺說 [Reexamining the philosophy of Zisi]. *Wen Shi Zhe* 文史哲 [Journal of literature, history and philosophy], no. 2: 63–79.

Cheng Zhaozhi 成肇智. 2017. *Study on Warm Disease*. Translated by Chen Jiaxu. Beijing: Renmin weisheng chubanshe.

Chu Wan-Li 屈萬里. 1984. *Shuyong lunxueji* 書傭論學集 [A collection of Chu Wan-Li's articles]. Taipei: Linking Publishing.

Chung Joscha 鍾欣志. 2012. "Zouxiang xiandai: WanQing Zhongguo juchang xinbian" 走向現代：晚清中國劇場新變 [Toward modernity: Innovations in the Chinese theater of the late-Qing dynasty]. PhD diss., Taipei National University of the Arts.

Cronon, William. 1992. "A Place for Stories: Nature, History, and Narrative." *Journal of American History* 78 (4): 1347–76.

Cullen, Frank, Florence Hackman, and Donald McNeilly, eds. 2007. *Vaudeville Old and New: An Encyclopedia of Variety Performers in America*. New York: Routledge.

Dai Mingshi 戴名世. 1986. *Dai Mingshi ji* 戴名世集 [Collection of Dai Mingshi]. Beijing: Zhonghua shuju.

Ding Fubao 丁福保, ed. 2012. *Foxue da cidian* 佛學大辭典 [Dictionary of Buddhist studies]. Taipei: Hwa Dzan Amitabha Buddhist Society.

Dodgen, Randall A. 2001. *Controlling the Dragon: Confucian Engineers and the Yellow River in Late Imperial China*. Honolulu: University of Hawai'i Press.

Dong Zhongshu 董仲舒. 2016. *Luxuriant Gems of the Spring and Autumn*. Edited and translated by Sarah A. Queen and John S. Major. New York: Columbia University Press.

Duara, Prasenjit. 1988. *Culture, Power, and the State: Rural North China, 1900–1942*. Stanford: Stanford University Press.

Edgerton-Tarpley, Kathryn. 2008. *Tears from Iron: Cultural Responses to Famine in Nineteenth-Century China*. Berkeley: University of California Press.

Editors of Encyclopedia Britannica. 2021. "Huang He Floods." *Encyclopedia Britannica*. Accessed April 10, 2023. https://www.britannica.com/event/Huang-He-floods.

Elvin, Mark. 1993. "Three Thousand Years of Unsustainable Growth: China's Environment from Archaic Times to the Present." *East Asian History*, no. 6: 7–46.

Elvin, Mark. 2004. *The Retreat of the Elephants: An Environmental History of China*. New Haven, CT: Yale University Press.

Elvin, Mark, and Ts'ui-jung Liu, eds. 1998. *Sediments of Time: Environment and Society in Chinese History*. Cambridge: Cambridge University Press.

Epstein, Maram. 2001. *Competing Discourses: Orthodoxy, Authenticity and Engendered Meanings in Late Imperial Chinese Fiction*. Cambridge, MA: Harvard University Asia Center.

Esherick, Joseph W. 1987. *The Origins of the Boxer Uprising*. Berkeley: University of California Press.

Fang Baochuan 方寶川, ed. 1997. *Taigu xuepai yishu (di yi ji)* 太谷學派遺書（第一輯）[Written legacy of the Taigu School (first collection)], vol. 4. Yangzhou: Jiangsu guangling chubanshe.

Fang Xiaoru 方孝儒. 1967. *Xunzhi zhai ji* 遜志齋集 [Collection of Fang Xiaoru]. Taipei: Taiwan Commercial Press.

Feng, Xiangjun. 2023. "*The Travels of Lao Can* as a Book of Prophecy." *Journal of the Royal Asiatic Society*, Series 3, no. 33: 203–28.

Ge Hong 葛洪. 1990. *Baopuzi* 抱朴子 [The master who embraces simplicity]. Shanghai: Shanghai guji chubanshe.

Ge Zhao-guang 葛兆光. 1998. "Cong wu zhu ben, li yi qie fa—Wuxu qianhou zhishi ren de foxue xingqu" 從無住本，立一切法──戊戌前後知識人的佛學興趣 [Buddhism as a focal point of interest for intellectuals in 1898]. *Ershiyi Shiji* 二十一世紀 [Twenty-first century], no. 45: 39–46.

Guan Kean-Fung 顏健富. 2014. *Cong shenti dao shijie: Wanqing xiaoshuo de xin gai'nian ditu* 從「身體」到「世界」：晚清小說的新概念地圖 [From "body" to "world": The new conceptual map of late Qing fiction]. Taipei: National Taiwan University Press.

Han Rongjun 韓榮鈞. 2017. *Huang Baonian yu Taigu xuepai yanjiu* 黃葆年與太谷學派研究 [Study on Huang Baonian and the Taigu School]. Beijing: Social Sciences Academic Press (China).

He, Jianjun. 2021. Spring and Autumn Annals *of Wu and Yue: An Annotated Translation of Wu Yue Chunqiu*. Ithaca, NY: Cornell University Press.

Henry, Eric. 1987. "The Motif of Recognition in Early China." *Harvard Journal of Asiatic Studies* 47 (1): 5–30.

Ho, Peng-Yoke. 2003. *Chinese Mathematical Astrology: Reaching Out to the Stars*. Needham Research Institute Series. London: Routledge.

Ho, Peng-Yoke. 2005. "Chinese Number Mysticism." In *Mathematics and the Divine: A Historical Study*, edited by Teun Koetsier and Luc Bergmans, 45–60. Amsterdam: Elsevier.

Holoch, David. 1980. "*The Travels of Laocan*: Allegorical Narrative." In *The Chinese Novel at the Turn of the Century*, edited by Milena Doleželová-Velingerová, 129–49. Toronto: University of Toronto Press.

Hsia, Chih-tsing. 2004. "The Travels of Lao Ts'an: An Exploration of Its Art and Meaning." In *C. T. Hsia on Chinese Literature*, 247–68. New York: Columbia University Press.

Hsu Hui-Lin 許暉林. 2015. "Jing yu qianzhi: Shi lun Zhongguo xushi wenlei zhong xiandai shijiao jingyan de qiyuan" 鏡與前知：試論中國敘事文類中現代視覺經驗的起源 [Mirrors and foresight: The origin of modern visual experiences in Chinese narrative literature]. *Taida zhongwen xuebao* 臺大中文學報 [Bulletin of the Department of Chinese Literature NTU], no. 48: 121–60.

Hu Shih 胡適. 1986. *Baihua wenxue shi* 白話文學史 [History of vernacular literature]. Changsha: Yuelu shushe.

Hu Shih 胡適. 2013. *Hu Shi gudian wenxue yanjiu lunji* 胡適古典文學研究論集 [Collection of Hu Shi's studies on classical literature]. 2 vols. Shanghai: Shanghai guji chubanshe.

Hu Wei-Lun 胡薇倫. 2007. "Taiwan gaozhong guowen xuanwen dianfan zhi dishan xianxiang tanjiu" 臺灣高中國文選文典範之遞嬗現象探究 [The research of Taiwan senior high school Chinese subject paradigms]. MA thesis, National Chung Hsing University.

Huang Ko-wu 黃克武. 2014. "Lingxue yu jindai Zhongguo de zhishi zhuanxing—minchu zhishi fenzi dui kexue, zongjiao yu mixin de zai sikao" 靈學與近代中國的知識轉型——民初知識分子對科學、宗教與迷信的再思考 [Pneumatology and knowledge transfer in modern China: Early Republican intellectuals' reconsideration on science, religion, and superstition]. In *Sixiang shi 2* 思想史2 [Intellectual history 2], edited by Yang Cheng-Hsien et al. 楊正顯等. Taipei: Linking Publishing.

Huang, Martin W. 1994. "Author(ity) and Reader in Traditional Chinese Xiaoshuo Commentary." *Chinese Literature: Essays, Articles, Reviews (CLEAR)* 16: 41–67.

Hurvitz, Leon, trans. 2009. *Scripture of the Lotus Blossom of the Fine Dharma (the Lotus Sūtra)*. New York: Columbia University Press.

Huters, Theodore. 2005. *Bringing the World Home: Appropriating the West in Late Qing and Early Republican China*. Honolulu: University of Hawai'i Press.

Institute of Modern History of the Chinese Academy of Social Sciences 中國社會科學院近代史研究所. 1982. *Yihe tuan shiliao* 義和團史料 [Historical materials on the Boxer Uprising]. Edited by the Editorial Committee of Modern Historical Sources 《近代史資料》編輯組. Beijing: China Social Sciences Press.

Ji Ming 冀命. 1903. "Shuo Hangzhou Gaoziheng daomai Yan Qu Wen Chu sifu kuangshan de Qingshing" 說杭州高子蘅盜賣嚴衢溫處四府礦山的情形 [On Gao Ziheng from Hangzhao illegally selling mines of the four *fu* of Yan, Qu, Wen, and Chu]. *Shaoxing Baihuabao* 紹興白話報 [Shaoxing vernacular newspaper], 1903, 1.

Jia Guojing 賈國靜. 2019. *Huanghe Tongwaxiang juekou gaidao yu wanQing zhengju* 黃河銅瓦廂決口改道與晚清政局 [The Yellow River's changing course at Tongwaxiang and the political situation in the late Qing dynasty]. Beijing: Social Sciences Academic Press (China).

Jiang Haowei 蔣浩偉. 2018. "Cong 'chenwei' dao 'kexue'—lun Lao Can Youji zai Qingmo minchu de piping yu jieshou" 從「讖緯」到「科學」——論《老殘遊記》在清末民初的批評與接受 [From apocryphal writing to science: On *Lao Can Youji*'s criticism and reception in late Qing and early Republican period]. *Ming Qing xiaoshuo yanjiu* 明清小說研究 [Journal of Ming Qing fiction studies], no. 4: 47–62.

Keulemans, Paize. 2014. *Sound Rising from the Paper: Nineteenth-Century Martial Arts Fiction and the Chinese Acoustic Imagination*. Cambridge, MA: Harvard University Asia Center.

Kory, Stephan N. 2019. "Omen Watching, Mantic Observation, Aeromancy, and Learning to 'See': The Rise and Messy Multiplicity of Zhanhou 占候 in Late Han and Medieval China." *East Asian Science, Technology, and Medicine*, no. 50: 67–132.

Kwong, Luke. 2001. "Self and Society in Modern China: Liu E (1857–1909) and *Laocan Youji*." *T'oung Pao* 87 (4): 360–92.

Lean, Eugenia. 2007. *Public Passions: The Trial of Shi Jianqiao and the Rise of Popular Sympathy in Republican China*. Berkeley: University of California Press.

Lee, Haiyan. 2007. *Revolution of the Heart: A Genealogy of Love in China, 1900–1950*. Stanford: Stanford University Press.

Lee Ming-huei 李明輝. 2012. *Siduan yu qiqing: Guanyu daode qinggan de bijiao zhexue tantao* 四端與七情：關於道德情感的比較哲學探討 [Four buddings and seven feelings: A comparative philosophical investigation of moral feelings]. Taipei: National Taiwan University Press.

Lee Ou-fan Leo 李歐梵. 2010. *Diguo mori de shanshuihua: Lao Can Youji* 帝國末日的山水畫：老殘遊記 [The travels of Lao Ts'an]. Taipei: Locus Publishing.

Li Bin 李斌. 2016. *Minguo shiqi zhongxue guowen jiaokeshu yanjiu* 民國時期中學國文教科書研究 [Study on middle school Chinese textbooks in the Republican period]. Beijing: Peking University Press.

Li Boyuan 李伯元. 1998. *Zhongguo xianzaiji* 中國現在記 [Present-day China]. Edited by Liu Ke 劉柯. Changsha: Yuelu shushe.

Li Boyuan 李伯元. 2006. *Xiuxiang Xiaoshuo* 繡像小說 [Illustrated diction]. Beijing: National Library of China Press.

Li Fang et al. 李昉等, eds. 1961. *Taiping guangji* 太平廣記 [Extensive records assembled in the Taiping era, 976–984], vol. 5. Beijing: Zhonghua shuju.

Li Min 李旻. 2019. "Xin er you zheng: Zhongguo kaoguxue sixiangshi shang de Xu Xusheng" 信而有徵：中國考古學思想史上的徐旭生 [Borne out by the evidence: Xu Xusheng in the history of archaeological thoughts of China]. *Kaogu* 考古 [Archaeology], no. 6: 105–20.

Li Zhi 李贄. 1975. *Fenshu, Xu fenshu* 焚書·續焚書 [A book to burn, another book to burn]. Beijing: Zhonghua shuju.

Liang Qichao 梁啟超. 1998. *Xin min shuo: Shaonian zhhongguo de guominxing gaizao fang'an* 新民說：少年中國的國民性改造方案 [On new citizen: Young China's national character reinvention project]. Zhengzhou: Zhongzhou guji chubanshe.

Liang Yuyu 梁玉瑜, and Tao Baolian 陶保廉. 1994. *Yixue dawen* 醫學答問 [Answers to questions on medicine]. Beijing: Zhongguo Zhongyiyao chubanshe.

Lin Tien-Jen 林天人. 2006. "Qingchu hefang zhengce yu hegong yanjiu: Yi Jin Fu de zhihe wei kaocha zhongxin" 清初河防政策與河工研究：以靳輔的治河為考察重心 [A research of river engineering plans and hydraulic engineers from the Ch'ing dynasty: Focus of the theories and technology of hydraulic engineering of Chin-fu's (1633–1692)]. *Dili Yanjiu* 地理研究 [Journal of geographical research] 45: 93–121.

Linz, Juan J. 1993. "State Building and Nation Building." *European Review* 1 (4): 355–69.

Liu, An. 2010. *The Huainanzi: A Guide to the Theory and Practice of Government in Early Han China*. Translated by John S. Major et al. New York: Columbia University Press.

Liu Chi-Hui 劉紀蕙. 2011. *Xin zhi tuopu: 1895 shijian hou de lunli chonggou* 心之拓璞：1895 事件後的倫理重構 [The topology of psyche: The post-1895 reconstruction of ethics]. Taipei: Flaneur Culture Lab.

Liu Dashen 劉大紳. 1985. "Guanyu Lao Can Youji" 關於《老殘遊記》 [About *Lao Can Youji*]. In *Liu E ji Lao Can Youji ziliao* 劉鶚及老殘遊記資料 [Information on Liu E and *Lao Can Youji*], edited by Liu Delong et al. 劉德隆等, 390–421. Chengdu: Sichuan renmin chubanshe.

Liu Delong 劉德隆. 1993. "Yi feng Huang Baonian gei Liu E de xin" 一封黃葆年給劉鶚的信 [A letter from Huang Baonian to Liu E]. *Wenxian* 文獻 [The documentation], no. 1: 286–87.

Liu Delong 劉德隆, and Liu Yu 劉瑀. 2019. *Liu E nianpu chanbian* 劉鶚年譜長編 [The extended chronicle of Liu E]. Shanghai: Shanghai Jiao Tong University Press.

Liu Delong 劉德隆, Zhu Xi 朱禧, and Liu Deping 劉德平. 1987. *Liu E xiaozhuan* 劉鶚小傳 [Biography of Liu E]. Tianjin: Tianjin renmin chubanshe.

Liu E 劉鶚. 1907. "Lao Can Youji Erbian" 《老殘遊記》二編 [*Lao Can Youji* second collection]. *Riri xinwen* 日日新聞 [Tianjin daily news], 1907. Collection of newspaper clippings held in Kyoto University Institute for Research in Humanities Library.

Liu E 劉鶚. 1936. 《老殘遊記》二集 [Sequel to *Laot'san Yuchi*]. Translated by Lin Yutang 林語堂. In *A Nun of Taishan (A Novelette) and Other Translations*, translated by Lin Yutang, 1–112. Shanghai: Commercial Press.

Liu E 劉鶚. 1989. "劉鶚：老殘遊記二集" The Sequel to *Lao Can Youji*: Chapters 7–9. Translated by Timothy C. Wong. *Renditions* 32: 20–45.

Liu E 劉鶚. 1990. *The Travels of Lao Ts'an*. Translated by Harold Shadick. New York: Columbia University Press.

Liu E 劉鶚. 2007. *Liu E ji* 劉鶚集 [Collection of Liu E]. Edited by Liu Delong 劉德隆. 2 vols. Changchun: Jilin wenshi chubanshe.

Liu E 劉鶚. 2013. *Lao Can Youji xinzhu* 老殘遊記新注 [Newly annotated *Lao Can Youji*]. Annotated by Hsu Shaochi 徐少知. Taipei: Liren shuju.

Liu Houzi 劉厚滋. 1931. "Zhang Shiqin yu Taigu xuepai" 張石琴與太谷學派 [Zhang Shiqin and the Taigu School]. *Fu Ren xuezhi* 輔仁學誌 [Fu Jen studies] 9 (1): 81–124.

Liu I-ch'ing 劉義慶. 1976. *A New Account of Tales of the World*. Translated by Richard B. Mather. Minneapolis: University of Minnesota Press.

Liu Ji 劉基. 1987. *Yuli zi pingzhu* 郁離子評注 [Annotated collection of Liu Ji]. Annotated by Fu Zhenggu 傅正谷. Tianjin: Tianjin guji chubanshe.

Liu, Lydia H. 1995. *Translingual Practice: Literature, National Culture, and Translated Modernity—China, 1900–1937*. Stanford: Stanford University Press.

Liu Mengyang 劉孟揚. 2008. *Tianjin quanfei bianluan jishi* 天津拳匪變亂紀事 [Records of the Boxer Rebellion in Tianjin]. Vol. 118 of *Huizu diancang quanshu* 回族典藏全書 [The complete collection of the Hui], edited by 吳海鷹 Wu Haiying. Lanzhou: Gansu wenhua chubanshe.

Liu Sufen 劉素芬. 2018a. "Liu E lihuo yuanyin zaitan" 劉鶚罹禍原因再探 [A reinterpretation of the case of Liu E's Exile]. *Yangzhou daxue xuebao (renwen shehui kexue ban)* 揚州大學學報（人文社會科學版）[Journal of Yangzhou University (humanities and social sciences edition)] 22 (5): 80–92.

Liu Sufen 劉素芬. 2018b. "Wanqing tiaoyue tizhi xia de yanwu jiaoshe yu Zhong Han maoyi" 晚清條約體制下的鹽務交涉與中韓貿易 [Salt business and Sino-Korean trade under the treaty system in late Qing dynasty]. *Diyu Wenhua Yanjiu* 地域文化研究 [Regional culture study], no. 2: 20–38, 154.

Liu Yuxi 劉禹錫. 1990. *Liu Yuxi ji* 劉禹錫集 [Collection of Liu Yuxi]. Edited by Bian Xiaoxuan 卞孝萱 and the Research Committee of Liu Yuxi ji 《劉禹錫集》整理組. Beijing: Zhonghua shuju.

Loewe, Michael. 1994. *Divination, Mythology and Monarchy in Han China*. Cambridge: Cambridge University Press.

Lu, Li. 2020. *Translation and Nation: Negotiating China in the Translations of Lin Shu, Yan Fu and Liang Qichao*. London: Canut.

Lu Xun 魯迅. 2011. *Zhongguo xiaoshuo shilue* 中國小說史略 [A brief history of Chinese fiction]. Shanghai: Shanghai guji chubanshe.

Luo Lun 羅倫. 1987. *Jingan shijixu* 敬菴詩集序 [Preface to poetry collection of Jing'an]. Vol. 3 of *Ming wenhai* 明文海 [Ming word sea], edited by Huang Zongxi 黃宗羲. Shanghai: Shanghai guji chubanshe.

Lupke, Christopher. 2007. "Liu E." In *Chinese Fiction Writers, 1900–1949*, edited by Thomas Moran, 104–15. Detroit: Thomson Gale.

Ma Qi et al. 馬齊等, eds. 1985. *Qing shilu* 清實錄 [Qing veritable records], vol. 239. Beijing: Zhonghua shuju.

May, Edwin C., and Sonali Bhatt Marwaha, eds. 2015. *Extrasensory Perception: Support, Skepticism, and Science*. Santa Barbara: Praeger.

McMahon, Keith. 2002. *The Fall of the God of Money: Opium Smoking in Nineteenth-Century China*. Lanham, MD: Rowman & Littlefield.

Miao, Huaiming 苗懷明. 2017. *Xiangfeng yiku wei cangsheng* 相逢一哭為蒼生 [A tearful encounter for the sake of the people]. Jiangsu: Jiangsu renmin chubanshe.

Miller, Elizabeth Carolyn. 2021. *Extraction Ecologies and the Literature of the Long Exhaustion*. Princeton, NJ: Princeton University Press.

Mostern, Ruth. 2021. *The Yellow River: A Natural and Unnatural History*. New Haven, CT: Yale University Press.

Nash, Linda. 2013. "Furthering the Environmental Turn." *Journal of American History* 100 (1): 131–35.

Needham, Joseph, Ling Wang, and Gwei-Djen Lu. 1971. *Physics and Physical Technology: Civil Engineering and Nautics*. In *Science and Civilisation in China*, by Joseph Needham, vol. 4, pt. 3. Cambridge: Cambridge University Press.

Perry, Elizabeth J. 1980. *Rebels and Revolutionaries in North China, 1845–1945*. Stanford: Stanford University Press.

Pi Kuo-Li 皮國立. 2019. *Jindai Zhongxiyi de boyi: Zhongyi kangjun shi* 近代中西醫的博弈：中醫抗菌史 [The contest between modern Chinese and Western medicine: An antibacterial history in China]. Beijing: Zhonghua shuju.

Pietz, David A. 2015. *The Yellow River: The Problem of Water in Modern China*. Cambridge, MA: Harvard University Press.

Pietz, David A., and Mark Giordano. 2009. "Managing the Yellow River: Continuity and Change." In *River Basin Trajectories: Societies, Environments and Development*, edited by François Molle and Philippus Weste, 99–122. Wallingford, UK: CABI.

Pomeranz, Kenneth. 1993. *The Making of a Hinterland: State, Society, and Economy in Inland North China, 1853–1937*. Berkeley: University of California Press.

Qian Xuantong 錢玄同. 2010. *Qian Xuantong wenxuan* 錢玄同文選 [Anthology of Qian Xuantong]. Chengdu: Sichuan wenyi chubanshe.

Raine, Anne. 2014. "Ecocriticism and Modernism." In *The Oxford Handbook of Ecocriticism*, edited by Greg Garrard, 98–117. New York: Oxford University Press.

Rankin, Mary Backus. 1986. *Elite Activism and Political Transformation in China: Zhejiang Province, 1865–1911*. Stanford: Stanford University Press.

Raphals, Lisa. 2002. "A 'Chinese Eratosthenes' Reconsidered: Chinese and Greek Calculations and Categories." *East Asian Science, Technology, and Medicine*, no. 19: 10–60.

Ren Guang-yu 任光宇. 2018. "Wang-Liu lianhe faxian shuo han jiagu wen faxian yanjiu xinlun" 王劉聯合發現說和甲骨文發現研究新論 [New argumentations on oracle and research with Wang-Liu co-discovery proposition]. *Guangxi shifan daxue xuebao: zhexue shehui kexue ban* 廣西師範大學學報：哲學社會科學版 [Journal of Guangxi Normal University: Philosophy and social sciences edition] 54 (6): 394–408.

Roddy, Stephen. 2019. "The Nakedness of Hope: Solastalgia and Soliphilia in the Writings of Yu Yue, Zhang Binglin, and Liang Shuming." In *Chinese Environmental Humanities*, edited by Chia-ju Chang, 59–79. Cham: Springer.

Rogaski, Ruth. 2004. *Hygienic Modernity: Meanings of Health and Disease in Treaty-Port China*. Berkeley: University of California Press.

Rojas, Carlos. 2015. *Homesickness: Culture, Contagion, and National Transformation in Modern China*. Cambridge, MA: Harvard University Press.

Ruan Yuan 阮元. 1980. *Shisan jing zhushu* 十三經注疏 [The Thirteen Classics with commentaries and appended collation notes], vol. 2. Beijing: Zhonghua shuju.

Schinz, Alfred. 1996. *The Magic Square: History of Chinese City Planning*. Stuttgart: Axel Menges.

Schonebaum, Andrew D. 2004. "Fictional Medicine: Diseases, Doctors and the Curative Properties of Chinese Fiction." PhD diss., Columbia University.

Schwartz, Benjamin I. 1985. *The World of Thought in Ancient China*. Cambridge, MA: Harvard University Press.

Sen Kim-Soon 辛金順. 2015. *Zhongguo xiandai xiaoshuo de guozu shuxie: Yi shenti yinyu wei guancha hexin* 中國現代小說的國族書寫：以身體隱喻為觀察核心 [Nationhood writing in the modern Chinese fictions: Focused observation on body metaphors]. Taipei: Showwe Information.

Seow, Victor. 2022. *Carbon Technocracy: Energy Regimes in Modern East Asia*. Chicago: University of Chicago Press.

Shang Wei 商偉. 2016. "Bizhen de huanxiang: xiyangjing, toushi fa yu daguan yuan de menghuan meiying (zhong)" 逼真的幻象：西洋鏡、透視法與大觀園的夢幻魅影（中） [A lively illusion: Occidental lens, linear perspective, and the phantom of the Grand Prospect Garden (II)]. *Cao Xueqin yanjiu* 曹雪芹研究 [Studies of Cao Xueqin], no. 2: 103–23.

Shen Bao 申報. 1876. "Lun Aumen qisi" 論澳門緝私 [On anti-smuggling in Macau], January 21, 1876.

Shen Bao 申報. 1885. "Chushi xuzhi ba" 出使須知跋 [Postscript to the information for ambassadors going abroad], November 12, 1885.

Shen Bao 申報. 1887. "Lun yangwu shou zai deren" 論洋務首在得人 [The priority of foreign affairs is putting the right person in charge], April 10, 1887.

Shen Bao 申報. 1888. "Lun Zhongguo dang zhuyi yu E" 論中國當注意於俄 [China should be aware of Russia], August 26, 1888.

Shen Bao 申報. 1891. "Lun Yingguo gong zhizao yi zhifu, jinri duo fang Huazhi, yi yu Zhongguo zhengli, e Hua minsheng ye jian wei" 論英國工製造以致富，近日多仿華製，以與中國爭利，而華民生業漸微 [The British manufacturing industry is getting rich, and recently they have been imitating Chinese products in order to compete with China for profits, while the Chinese people's livelihood is diminishing], December 13, 1891.

Shen Bao 申報. 1892. "Lun yi linxuan shicai yi zhong shi shi" 論宜遴選使才以重使事 [On the appropriateness of selecting talents for focusing on diplomatic missions], July 10, 1892.

Shen Bao 申報. 1904. "Meiru Li Jiabai ziansheng jiangyi" 美儒李佳白先生講義 [Lecture notes of Mr. Li Jiabai, the American Confucian scholar], May 3, 1904.

Shen Bao 申報. 1908. "Lun Xijiang yu quanguo zhi guanxi (Youyang)" 論西江與全國之關繫（酉陽）[On the relationship between the Xijiang River and the whole country (Youyang)], January 6, 1908.

Shen, Sung-chiao. 2006. "Discourse on Guomin ('the Citizen') in Late Qing China, 1895–1911." Translated by Hsiao Wen Chien. *Inter-Asia Cultural Studies* 7 (1): 2–23.

Sheng Cheng 盛成. 1983. "Guanyu Lao Can Youji" 關於《老殘遊記》[About *Lao Can Youji*]. *Qing Mo Xiaoshuo Yanjiu* 清末小說研究 [Journal of late Qing fiction studies], no. 7: 10–19.

Shih, Chang-Qing. 2004. *The Two Truths in Chinese Buddhism*. Delhi: Motilal Banarsidass.

Sima Qian 司馬遷. 1982. *Shiji* 史記 [Records of the grand scribe], vol. 1. Beijing: Zhonghua shuju.

Slingerland, Edward G., trans. 2003. *Confucius Analects: With Selections from Traditional Commentaries*. Indianapolis: Hackett.

Steinmeyer, Jim. 2006. *The Glorious Deception: The Double Life of William Robinson, aka Chung Ling Soo, the Marvelous Chinese Conjurer*. Cambridge, MA: Da Capo.

Su Ya-Li 蘇雅莉. 2004. "Gaozhong guowen kecheng biaozhun yu guowen keben xuanwen bianqian zhi yanjiu (1952–2004)" 高中國文課程標準與國文課本選文變遷之研究（1952–2004）[A study of the changes in high school curriculum standards for Chinese language and the selection of texts in Chinese language textbooks (1952–2004)]. MA thesis, National Chengchi University.

Tan Sitong 譚嗣同. 1981. *Tan Sitong quanji (zengding ben)* 譚嗣同全集（增訂本）[Collection of Tan Sitong (expanded edition)], edited by Cai Shangsi 蔡尚思 and Fang Xing 方行. Beijing: Zhonghua shuju.

Tang Geng 唐庚. 1995. *Tang Zixi wen lu* 唐子西文錄 [Tang Zixi's comments on poetry and literary works]. Shanghai: Shanghai guji chubanshe.

Tao Zongyi 陶宗儀. 1988. *Shuofu* 說郛 [Florilegium of minor literature]. Shanghai: Shanghai guji chubanshe.

Tarumoto Teruo 樽本照雄. 1983. *Shin-matsu shousetsu kandan* 清末小說閑談 [Idle talk on late Qing novels]. Kyoto: Horitsu bunka sha.

Tsai Tai-bin 蔡泰彬. 1998. *Wanming Huanghe shuihuan yu Pan Jixun zhi zhihe* 晚明黃河水患與潘季馴之治河 [The Yellow River floods in late Ming and Pan Jixun's river regulation]. Taipei: Lexis Book.

Tsu, Jing. 2005. *Nationalism, and Literature: The Making of Modern Chinese Identity, 1895–1937*. Stanford: Stanford University Press.

Wang, Chong. 1962. *Lun-Hêng: Miscellaneous Essays of Wang Chong*. Translated by Alfred Forke. New York: Paragon Book Gallery.

Wang, David Der-wei. 1997. *Fin-de-Siècle Splendor: Repressed Modernities of Late Qing Fiction, 1849–1911*. Stanford: Stanford University Press.

Wang, David Der-wei. 2000. "Crime or Punishment? On the Forensic Discourse of Modern Chinese Literature." In *Becoming Chinese: Passages to Modernity and Beyond*, edited by Wen-Hsin Yeh, 260–97. Berkeley: University of California Press.

Wang, David Der-wei. 2004. *The Monster That Is History: History, Violence, and Fictional Writing in Twentieth-Century China*. Berkeley: University of California Press.

Wang, David Der-wei 王德威. 2007. *Ruhe xiandai, zenyang wenxue? Shijiu, ershi shiji Zhongwen xiaoshuo xinlun* 如何現代，怎樣文學？十九、二十世紀中文小說新論 [The making of the modern, the making of a literature: New perspectives on nineteenth- and twentieth-century Chinese fiction]. Taipei: Rye Field.

Wang Daw-hwan 王道還. 2013. "'Tian yan lun' yuanzhu wenben de laili ji xiangguan wenti"《天演論》原著文本的來歷及相關問題. In *Wenhua fanyi yu wenben mailuo: WanMing yi jiang de Zhongguo, Riben yu Xifang* 文化翻譯與文本脈絡：晚明以降的中國、日本與西方 [Cultural translation and textual context: China, Japan, and the West since the late Ming], edited by Peng Hsiao-yen 彭小妍, 337–66. Taipei: Institute of Chinese Literature and Philosophy, Academia Sinica.

Wang Fan-sen 王汎森. 1985. *Zhang Taiyan de sixiang (1868–1919) ji qi dui ruxue chuantong de chongji* 章太炎的思想 (1868–1919) 及其對儒學傳統的衝擊 [Zhang Taiyan's thoughts (1868–1919) and their impacts on the Confucian tradition]. Taipei: China Times Publishing.

Wang Fan-sen 王汎森. 2003. *Zhongguo jindai sixiang yu xueshu de xipu* 中國近代思想與學術的系譜 [A genealogy of modern Chinese thoughts and scholarship]. Taipei: Linking Publishing.

Wang Huizu 汪輝祖. 1939. *Xuezhi xushuo* 學志續說 [Sequel of subjective views on learning governance]. Changsha: Commercial Press.

Wang Jinfeng 王勁峰. 1995. *Zhongguo ziran zaihai quhua: Zaihai quhua, yingxiang pingjia, jianzai duice* 中國自然災害區劃：災害區劃、影響評價、減災對策 [Regionalization of hazards in China: Regionalization, assessment, and strategies]. Beijing: China Science and Technology Press.

Wang Xiangjin 王象晉. 2001. *Qunfang pu* 群芳譜 [Manual of aromatic plants]. Jinan: Qilu shushe.

Wang Xuejun 王學鈞. 1990. "'Er si chuan dao' kaobian—Liu E yu Taigu xuepai guanxi lun kao zhi yi"「二巳傳道」考辨──劉鶚與太谷學派關係論考之一 ["Er si chuan dao"—On the relationship between Liu E and the Taigu School]. *Ming Qing xiaoshuo yanjiu* 明清小說研究 [Journal of Ming Qing fiction studies], no. Z1: 304–18.

Wang Xuejun 王學鈞. 1992. "Liu E de zibian zhuang—Lao Can youji" 劉鶚的自辯狀──《老殘遊記》[Liu E's self-defense: *Lao Can Youji*]. *Nanjing ligong daxue xuebao (shehui kexue ban)* 南京理工大學學報（社會科學版）[Journal of Nanjing University of Science and Technology (social sciences edition)] 8 (3–4): 394–408.

Wang Xuejun 王學鈞. 1993a. "Lao Can Youji de Taigu xuepai guan" 《老殘遊記》的太谷學派觀 [The Taigu School's views in *Lao Can Youji*]. *Jiangsu Shehui Kexue* 江蘇社會科學 [Jiangsu social sciences], no. 4: 98–102.

Wang Xuejun 王學鈞. 1993b. "Taohuashan chuandao shilun" 桃花山傳道釋論 [Analysis of the sermon in the Peach Blossom Mountain]. *Shinmatsu Shōsetsu Kara* 清末小說から（通訊）[Newsletter of late Qing fiction] no. 16: 103–4.

Wang Xuejun 王學鈞. 2000. "Liu E yu Huang Baonian: 'Er si chuan dao' xukao" 劉鶚與黃葆年：「二巳傳道」續考 [Further studies on Liu E and Huang Baonian: 'Er si chuan dao']. *Shinmatsu Shōsetsu Kara* 清末小說から（通訊）[Newsletter of late Qing fiction], no. 23: 120–34.

Wang Xuejun 王學鈞. 2003. "Sanjiao guiyi tianxia weigong—Liu E yu Taigu xuepai sixiang lunpian" 三教歸一天下為公——劉鶚與太谷學派思想論片 [Syncretism of Confucianism, Buddhism, Taoism and the public-oriented spirit: On the ideologies of Liu E and Taigu School]. *Nanjing ligong daxue xuebao (shehui kexue ban)* 南京理工大學學報（社會科學版）[Journal of Nanjing University of Science and Technology (social sciences edition)] 16 (1): 81–87.

Wang Zhaosan 王昭三. 1914. "Qiannianyan zhi kexue jieshi" 千年眼之科學解釋 [A scientific explanation of clairvoyance]. *Dongfang zazhi* 東方雜誌 [The Eastern miscellany] 11 (4): 11–12.

Wang Zhaosan 王昭三. 1915. "Qiannianyan zhi rushou fangfa" 千年眼之入手方法 [Method of using clairvoyance]. *Dongfang zazhi* 東方雜誌 [The Eastern miscellany] 12 (5): 11–12.

Watson, Burton. 1971. *Chinese Lyricism: Shih Poetry from the Second to the Twelfth Century, with Translations*. New York: Columbia University Press.

Wei, Yan. 2020. *Detecting Chinese Modernities: Rupture and Continuity in Modern Chinese Detective Fiction (1896–1949)*. Leiden: Brill.

Wei Yuan 魏源. 1976. *Wei Yuan ji* 魏源集 [Collection of Wei Yuan]. Beijing: Zhonghua shuju.

Will, Pierre-Etienne. 1985. "State Intervention in the Administration of a Hydraulic Infrastructure: The Example of Hubei Province in Late Imperial Times." In *The Scope of State Power in China*, edited by Stuart R. Schram, 295–348. Hong Kong: School of Oriental and African Studies and Chinese University of Hong Kong Press.

Wong, Kwok-Yiu. 2017. "Reform Spirit and Regional Theaters: Yu Zhi's (1809–1874) Shuji Tang Jinyue and the Xiqu Reform Movement." *Monumenta Serica* 65 (2): 363–400.

Wong, Timothy C. 1983. "Notes on the Textual History of the Lao Ts'an Yu-Chi." *T'oung Pao* 69 (1): 23–32.

Wong, Timothy C. 1989. "The Name 'Lao Ts'an' in Liu E's Fiction." *Journal of the American Oriental Society* 109 (1): 103–6.

World Health Organization. 2022. *WHO International Standard Terminologies on Traditional Chinese Medicine*. Geneva: World Health Organization.

Worster, Donald. 1990. "Transformations of the Earth: Toward an Agroecological Perspective in History." *Journal of American History* 76 (4): 1087–106.

Wright, Tim. 1984. *Coal Mining in China's Economy and Society, 1895–1937*. Cambridge: Cambridge University Press.

Wu Jutong 吳鞠通. 1995. *Wenbing Tiaobian* 溫病條辨 [Detailed analysis of epidemic warm diseases]. Vol. 1004 of *Xuxiu Siku Quanshu* 續修四庫全書 [Sequel to the *Siku Quanshu*], edited by the Editorial Committee of Xuxiu Siku Quanshu 《續修四庫全書》編纂委員會. Shanghai: Shanghai guji chubanshe.

Wu, Shellen Xiao. 2015. *Empires of Coal: Fueling China's Entry into the Modern World Order, 1860–1920*. Stanford: Stanford University Press.

Wu, Zeyuan. 2020. "Becoming Sages: Qin Song and Self-Cultivation in Late Imperial China." PhD diss., The Ohio State University.

Xiaohengxiangshi zhuren 小橫香室主人. 1971. *Qing chao ye shi da guan* 清朝野史大觀 [A comprehensive view of unofficial histories of the Qing dynasty]. Taipei: Taiwan Zhonghua shu ju.

Xu Jian 徐堅. 2014. "Faxian jiagu: Kaoguxue shi de shijiao he xiefa" 發現甲骨：考古學史的視角和寫法 [Discovering oracle bones: Perspectives and historiography in the history of archaeology]. *Huaxia kaogu* 華夏考古 [Huaxia archaeology], no. 4: 143–50.

Yan Weiqing 嚴薇青. 1985. "Liu E he Taigu xuepai" 劉鶚和太谷學派 [Liu E and Taigu School]. In *Liu E ji Lao Can Youji ziliao* 劉鶚及老殘遊記資料 [Information on Liu E and *Lao Can Youji*], edited by Liu Delong et al. 劉德隆等, 631–42. Chengdu: Sichuan renmin chubanshe.

Yang, Chung-Wei. 2022. "Pictorials and the Transformation of Chinese Fiction in the Era of Photolithography (1900–1910)." PhD diss., Columbia University.

Yang Ji-kai 楊際開. 2004a. "WanQing bianfa sixiang zhong de hanxue yu foxue (shang)" 晚清變法思想中的漢學與佛學（上）[Sinology and Buddhism in the late Qing modernization thought I]. *Ershiyi Shiji (Wangluo Ban)* 二十一世紀（網絡版）[Twenty-first century online], no. 32.

Yang Ji-kai 楊際開. 2004b. "WanQing bianfa sixiang zhong de hanxue yu foxue (xia)" 晚清變法思想中的漢學與佛學（下）[Sinology and Buddhism in the late Qing modernization thought II]. *Ershiyi Shiji (Wangluo Ban)* 二十一世紀（網絡版）[Twenty-first century online], no. 33.

Yang Jui-sung 楊瑞松. 2016. *Bingfu, huanghuo yu shuishi: "Xi fang" shiye de Zhongguo xingxiang yu jindai Zhongguo guozu lunshu xiangxiang* 病夫、黃禍與睡獅：「西方」視野的中國形象與近代中國國族論述想像 [Sick man, yellow peril, and sleeping lion: Chinese images from "Western" perspective and the discourses of modern Chinese national identity]. Taipei: National Chengchi University Press.

Yang Ting 楊頲. 2017. "Gu Jinan Cheng shuixi yu kongjian xingtai guanxi yanjiu" 古濟南城水系與空間形態關係研究 [A study on the relationship between urban water systems and spatial forms in the ancient Jinan city]. PhD diss., South China University of Technology.

Yao Lufeng 姚魯烽. 1991. "Quanxin Shi yilao Yongding He hongshui de fasheng guilu" 全新世以來永定河洪水的發生規律 [The regularity of the flood of the Yongding River during the Holocene]. *Dili Yanjiu* 地理研究 [Journal of geographical research] 10 (3): 59–67.

Ye Chengzong 葉承宗, and Ye Chengtiao 葉承祧. 1640. *Chongjen Licheng xianzhi* 崇禎歷城縣志 [Gazetteer of Licheng County], vol. 13.

Yinshun 印順. 1984. *Jingtu yu chan* 淨土與禪 [Pure land and Zen]. Taipei: Zhengwen Publishing House.

Yuan Jiao 袁郊. 1985. *Ganze yao* 甘澤謠 [Tales of sweet enrichment]. Beijing: Zhonghua shuju.

Yuan Ke 袁珂. 2006. *Zhongguo gudai shenhua* 中國古代神話 [Ancient Chinese mythology]. Beijing: Huaxia Publishing House.

Yunzhi et al. 允祉等, eds. (1723) 1987. *Yuzhi shuli jingyun* 御製數理精蘊 [Imperially composed essence of numbers and their principles]. Shanghai: Shanghai guji chubanshe.

Zhang Hao 張灝. 1988. *Lieshi jingshen yu pipan yishi—Tan Sitong sixiang de fenxi* 烈士精神與批判意識——譚嗣同思想的分析 [The spirit of martyrdom and critical consciousness: An analysis of the Tan Sitong's thoughts]. Taipei: Linking Publishing.

Zhang, Jiayan. 2014. *Coping with Calamity: Environmental Change and Peasant Response in Central China, 1736–1949*. Contemporary Chinese Studies. Vancouver: University of British Columbia Press.

Zhang Lei 張耒. 1990. *Zhang Lei ji* 張耒集 [Collection of Zhang Lei]. Edited by Li Yian 李逸安, Sun Tonghai 孫通海, and Fu Xin 傅信. Beijing: Zhonghua shuju.

Zhang Xiaoqin 張曉琴. 2010. "Zhongxue yuwen jiaocai zhong gudai xiaoshuo xuanwen yanjiu" 中學語文教材中古代小說選文研究 [Research on ancient fictions of Chinese textbooks in middle school]. MA thesis, Shanghai Normal University.

Zhang Yi'nan 張軼男, and Chen Jinhua 陳金華. 2019. "Lun Chanfo Shuiyue Yu 'liyi Fenshu'" 論禪佛水月與「理一分殊」 [On the Chan Buddhist metaphor of "water-moon" and Zhu Xi's theory of one principle in multiple manifestations]. *Hualin Guoji Foxue Xuekan* 華林國際佛學學刊 [Hualin international journal of Buddhist studies] 2 (2): 208–43.

Zhao Erxun 趙爾巽 et al. 1977. *Qing shigao* 清史稿 [Draft history of the Qing dynasty], vol. 4. Beijing: Zhonghua shuju.

Zhao Fujie 趙馥潔. 1988. "Hetu Luoshu" 河圖洛書 [The Yellow River Chart and the inscription of the River Luo]. In *Zhongguo ruxue cidian* 中國儒學辭典 [Dictionary of Chinese Confucianism], edited by Zhao Jihui 趙吉惠 and Guo Hou'an 郭厚安, 755. Shenyang: Liaoning renmin chubanshe.

Zhao, Gang. 2006. "Reinventing China: Imperial Qing Ideology and the Rise of Modern Chinese National Identity in the Early Twentieth Century." *Modern China* 32 (1): 3–30.

Zhao, Qinguang. 1989. "Chinese Mythology in the Context of Hydraulic Society." *Asian Folklore Studies* 48 (2): 231–46.

Zhejiang chao 浙江潮 [Tide of Zhejiang]. 1903a. "Liu Tieyun yumai Zhejiang quansheng lukuang hu" 劉鐵雲欲賣浙江全省路礦乎 [Is Liu Tieyun selling railroads and mines of the entire province?], June 1903, 1–2.

Zhejiang chao 浙江潮 [Tide of Zhejiang]. 1903b. "Mai Zhejiang quansheng kuanlu zhe fei Liu Tieyun yiren ye bieyou ren ye" 賣浙江全省礦路者非劉鐵雲一人也別有人也 [Not just Liu Tieyun but somebody else is also selling Zhejiang mines and railroads], July 1903, 159–61.

Zheng Guanying 鄭觀應. 2013. *Shengshi Weiyan* 盛世危言 [Words of warning to a prosperous age]. Vol. 1 of *Zheng Guanying Ji* 鄭觀應集 [Collection of Zheng Guanying]. Beijing: Zhonghua shuju.

Zhou Guidian 周桂鈿. 1997. "Hetu Luoshu" 河圖洛書 [The Yellow River chart and the inscription of the River Luo]. In *Zhongguo ruxue* 中國儒學 [Chinese Confucianism], edited by Pang Pu 龐樸, 50. Shanghai: Dongfang chuban zhongxin.

Zhou Xinguo 周新國. 2010. "Paihuai yu xuepai yu jiaopai zhijian de huo huashi—Taigu xuepai fazhan guiji tantao" 徘徊於學派與教派之間的活化石——太谷學派發展軌跡探討 [Taigu School: A fossil-like subject for research]. *Yangzhou Daxue Xuebao (Renwen Shehui Kexue Ban)* 揚州大學學報（人文社會科學版）[Journal of Yangzhou University (humanities and social sciences edition)], no. 3: 81–86.

Zhou Xinguo 周新國. 2014. *Taigu xuepai shi gao* 太谷學派史稿 [History of the Taigu School]. Beijing: Shehui kexue wenxian chubanshe.

Zhu Hu 朱滸. 2018. "WanQing chouzhen yiyan de xingqi ji qi yiyi" 晚清籌賑義演的興起及其意義 [The rise of charity performance for relief collection in the late Qing dynasty and its significance]. *Shixue Yuekan* 史學月刊 [Journal of historical science], no. 8: 45–51.

Zhu Xi 朱熹. 1994. *Zhuzi yulei* 朱子語類 [Classified sayings of Master Zhu]. Beijing: Zhonghua shuju.

Zhu Xi 朱熹. 2019. *The Original Meaning of the "Yijing": Commentary on the Scripture of Change*. Translated by Joseph Alan Adler. New York: Columbia University Press.

Zhuangzi 莊子. 2013. *The Complete Works of Zhuangzi*. Translated by Burton Watson. New York: Columbia University Press.

Index

Analects, 74, 131, 134
Andes mountains, 143
apocrypha (*chenwei*), 118, 130–35, 139

Bakhtin, Mikhail, 20n21
banditry, 56–58, 60, 136n27
Bao Shichen, 53
Bao Zheng, 47
biaoju (armed escorts), 60
Bluntschli, Johann Kaspar, 26
Bo Hai Sea, 3 fig. 0.1, 6–7
body-state, 27
Book of Changes (*Yijing*), 33, 131, 134, 137, 138n31
Book of Odes (*Shijing*), 70, 73–75, 103
Book of Rites (*Liji jingjie*), 74
Boxer Uprising (1899–1901), 7, 20, 33–38, 45; medical analogy to, 37–38; supporters of, 48; Yellow River floods and, 136n27
bribery, 47–48, 62. *See also* corruption
Buddhism, 60, 74, 114–15; Consciousness Only sect of, 77; Flower Garland sect of, 109; Neo-Confucianism and, 105–6; Pure Land sect of, 109–10; Westernizing faction and, 105. *See also* Taigu school

calendric calculations, 130–34
camellia flowers, 78
Cao Xueqin, 70–73
Carey, Mark, 143–44

Cheng-Zhu school of Neo-Confucianism, 114–15, 118
Chinese medicine, 17–19, 27–28; hydraulic engineering and, 28–32, 43, 45, 46, 66
Chinese Relief Society, 83
Ching Ling Foo, 86
citizenship, 5, 26–27, 83. *See also* nation-building
civil engineering, 17n16
Cixi, Empress Dowager, 48n1, 122, 125
coal mining, 9–10, 16, 32; environmental damage from, 142n1; foreign investment in, 52–53; scandals with, 50–51; Western Affairs Movement and, 143–44
Confucianism, 5, 60–62, 67, 74–77; apocrypha of, 131; Chinese medicine and, 28; Wang Chong on, 104n19. *See also* Neo-Confucianism; Taigu school
Consciousness Only sect (Weishi), 77
corruption, 47–49; definition of, 59; with government-private funds, 59, 63. *See also* incorruptible officials
Cronon, William, 143n2

Da Yu (mythical hero), 6, 15, 45, 140; as doctor, 28–29; *hetu* and, 132; mathematics and, 137; river control method of, 128–29, 133
Dai Mingshi, 96n6
Daoism, 60, 114–15; *qin* and, 123. *See also* Taigu school; Three Teachings

dike systems, 7, 11–14, 138–39; civil engineering of, 17n16; of Da Yu, 128–29, 133; "government," 12, 55; of Grand Canal, 21n21; medical analogies to, 29–33; oblique, 12–14, 13 fig. 0.2, 17n16, 54, 58; "peoples," 12, 55, 80–81; sabotage of, 34, 64–65
disaster relief, 82–87
divination, 11, 16–17, 131. *See also* prophecy
Doctrine of the Mean, 103
Documents of Antiquity, 29, 128, 131–33
Dong Zhongshu, 74–75
Doyle, Arthur Conan, 41, 42
Duara, Prasenjit, 2n1

ecocritical studies, 141–43
Edgerton-Tarpley, Kathryn, 4
embankment system, 12–14, 13 fig. 0.2; civil engineering and, 17n16; of Grand Canal, 21n21. *See also* dike systems
environmentalism, 2–3, 6–7, 16–17, 141–44
Epstein, Maram, 28
extrasensory perception, 103–4

Fang Ruo, 85, 112
Feng Menglong, 119
Flowers in the Mirror, 95–96
Force Supreme, 138–39
Four Books, 103
Furun (Shandong governor), 8–9

Gang Bi, 48n1
Gang Yi, 9, 48, 50, 51
Gao Deming, 81
Gao Weizhi, 81
Giordano, Mark, 2–3
gong (government) versus *si* (private) affairs, 55–64, 66–67
"government dikes," 12, 55. *See also* dike systems
Grand Canal, 3 fig. 0.1, 7, 8n7, 21n21
"Guangling Melody," 122–27
Guangxu Emperor, 134

Hai Rui, 47
Han dynasty (202 BCE–220 CE), 11n9, 71n4, 74, 104n19, 131
Han Gao, 124n15
heavenly principle (*tianli*), 59
hetu, 131–34, 137
Hong Liangji, 135
Hongze Lake, 3 fig. 0.1, 20n21, 82
Hsia, C. T., 23, 61, 91, 129
Hu Shih, 23, 89–91, 102, 111
Huang Baonian, 117–20, 122, 125–27
Huanghe. *See* Yellow River
human nature (*xing*), 76n11
Huxley, T. H., 50
hydraulic engineering, 65–66, 82, 128–30, 138; Chinese medicine and, 28–32, 43, 45, 46, 66; civil engineering and, 17n16; nation-building and, 2, 5–6, 140–44; Pan Jixun on, 11
hydraulics, 22–23, 50–56, 64–68, 74–82
hygiene, 18, 26

incorruptible officials (*qingguan*), 47–50, 57–64, 67–68. *See also* corruption
industrialization, 9, 16, 50–51, 142
Inner Cannon of the Yellow Emperor, 29, 46
insurance policies, 86

Ji Kang, 124
Jiang Wentian, 118
Jiayan Zhang, 12n11
Jin dynasty, 107n24
Jin Fu, 20n21, 128
Journey to the West, 36

Kangxi, Emperor, 48
Keulemans, Paize, 42

land mortgage strategy, 53
landscape descriptions, 89–96, 110–11, 141; national sentimentality in, 100–103; of Yellow River, 96–100
Latour, Bruno, 143n2
Lee, Haiyan, 21–22
Lee Ou-fan Leo, 76, 93

Li Boyuan, 34, 90, 112–14
Li Guangxin, 115–18, 129
Li Hongzhang, 60n8
Li Suxin, 129
Li Taijie, 120
Li Yuanying, 44n26
Liang Qichao, 19, 26–27, 45, 89–90, 141
Liu Chengzhon, 8
Liu E, 1–6; conversion experience of, 116–17; engineering career of, 8–11, 14–16, 50, 65, 110; family of, 4, 7–8, 18n18; on "Guangling Melody," 122–27; landscape descriptions of, 89–92, 110–11, 141; as mathematician, 137nn28–29; pen name of, 1, 90; scandals of, 9–10, 50, 64; smuggling charges against, 10; surveying by, 96–100, 108n25; Taiguist opponents of, 117–18; Western Affairs Movement and, 11; on Yu Xian, 49
Liu E, works of: *Chart of the Course of the Yellow River*, 8, 15; "Clarification on Mining Affairs," 32; *Five Essays on River Management*, 54n6, 76n11; *Maps and Studies of Changes*, 15–16; *Tortoise Shells in the Collection of Tieyun*, 16. See also *Travels of Lao Can*
Liu Fenggao, 93
local government officials, 4n2, 140; incorruptible, 47–49, 58–64, 67–68; river regulation by, 55–58
Lu Shufan, 83
Luo Lun, 75
luoshu, 131n24, 137

māndārava flower, 77, 78
mandate of heaven (*tianming*), 39, 131
Mao Qingfan, 116n6, 120
Mathematical Classic of the Zhou Gnomon, 137
measurement units, 98
medical discourse, 17–19. See also Chinese medicine
"Melody of Sea Waters and Heavenly Winds," 122–23, 125, 139

Mencius, 76n11
Ming dynasty (1368–1644), 4, 62, 73
moral cultivation, 103–4, 109
music, 119–27

Nash, Linda, 143n2
nation-building, 1–4, 16–25, 82–88, 140–44; citizenship and, 5, 26–27, 83; disaster relief and, 82–87; hydraulic engineering and, 2, 5–6, 140–44
national sentimentality, 100–103
Neo-Confucianism, 60–62, 67, 105–6; Cheng-Zhu school of, 114–15, 118; *wei* and, 131
Nian Uprising, 7n5, 116n5
Nüwa (Daoist deity), 70–72, 129, 142

oblique dikes, 12–14, 13 fig. 0.2, 17n16, 54, 58. See also dike systems
opium use, 26, 39–41
Opium Wars (1839–1842 & 1856–1860), 6, 53
oracle bone scripts, 11, 16–17

Pan Jixun, 11–12, 20n21, 128
Peking Syndicate Limited, 9–10, 16, 50
"people's dikes," 12, 55, 80–81. See also dike systems
Peru, 143
Pietz, David, 2–3
precognition, 103–4
prophecy, 11, 16, 113, 130–39
public health, 18, 26

qi, 19n19, 30
Qian Xuantong, 90
Qiao Shu'nan, 116n6, 125
qin music, 122
Qu Yuan, 70

railway construction, 9–10, 32, 50–53, 143–44
Restoration Society, 32n12
Rojas, Carlos, 58
Russo-Japanese War (1904–1905), 53

Sayings of the Insiders, 124, 132
science fiction literature, 141–42
self-cultivation, 60n9, 77n12, 114
Self-Strengthening Movement, 6
sentimentality, national, 100–103
Shadick, Harold, 8–9, 31n10, 116–17
Sheng Xuanhuai, 9n8
Shi Nai'an, 95
Shi Shilun, 47
si (private) versus *gong* (government) affairs, 59–60, 62–64, 66–67
Sima Zhao, 124
Smith, Adam, 50
Song dynasty (960–1279), 47, 59, 61–62, 93
Song Jing, 133n26
Songs of the South (*Chuci*), 73
spirit possession, 36–37
Spring and Autumn Annals of Wu and Yue, 133

Taigu school, 24–25, 44, 77n12, 112–21; music of, 122–27, 139; syncretic beliefs of, 4–5, 104, 105; Yellow Cliff massacre of, 116, 124–25; Yellow Dragon's prophecies of, 130–39; Yellow River governance and, 128–30
Taiping Uprising, 116n5
Tales of Sweet Enrichment (*Ganze yao*), 72
Tan Sitong, 138n31
Tang dynasty (618–907), 93n3, 106n23
Tang Yin, 95
Tao Qian, 123–24
Three Heroes and Five Gallants, 20
Three Teachings, 60, 61, 77, 114
Tieyun. *See* Liu E
Tongwaxiang, 3 fig. 0.1, 6–7
translation practices, 2, 31n10
Travels of Lao Can (Liu E), 8, 29–38, 112–13, 140–44; Chinese medicine in, 27–28; emotional trauma in, 74–82, 87, 140; flood control in, 74–82; literary precedents of, 70–74; murder investigation in, 41–45, 62–64, 67; music in, 122–27, 139; underworld scene in, 33–35, 64–66

United League (Tongmenghui), 32n12

vassal states strategy, 53

Wang Chong, 104n19, 108
Wang, David Der-wei, 20–21, 42–43, 44
Wang Daxie, 116n6
Wang Huizu, 48
Wang Jing, 128
Wang Wei, 78
Wang Xuejun, 118
Wang Zhengyi, 60n8
"warm diseases," 27, 29–31
Water Margin, The, 95–96
Wei, Yan, 44n25
Wei Yuan, 39n21
Weng Tonghe, 63n11
Western Affairs Movement, 6, 10–11, 14, 32; Buddhism and, 105; industrialization and, 143–44; opponents of, 51
Will, Pierre-Etienne, 4n2
Worster, Donald, 143n2
Wu Dacheng, 8, 15, 134
Wu Jianren, 90
Wu Jutong, 29–30
Wu Woyao, 141–42

Xia dynasty (2205–1766 BCE), 6, 16, 29
Xie Lingyun, 102–3
Xu Tong, 61n10
Xu Xusheng, 51–52

Yama, underworld lord, 33–35, 64–66
Yan Fu, 50
Ye Tianshi, 27n3
Yellow Cliff massacre (1866), 116, 125
Yellow River, 6, 128–30, 135–39; apocrypha and, 118, 130–35, 139; course change in 1855 of, 3 fig. 0.1, 3–4, 6–7, 56; course change in 1887 of, 7n5; freezing of, 76; Grand Canal and,

8n7, 21n21; ice jam on, 73, 97–99;
landscape descriptions of, 96–100
Yellow River Chart, 39, 131
Yellow River Conservancy, 8, 134
Yellow River floods, 10; of 1889, 57, 69, 76,
80–81; Boxer Uprising and, 136n27;
disaster relief, 82–87; economic
impacts of, 7; embankment system for,
12–14, 13 fig. 0.2; emotional trauma
after, 74–82, 87, 140; fatalities from, 8;
literature on, 70–74; local governance
of, 4n2, 55–58; medical analogy to,
29–33; opium analogy to, 39–41; revolutionaries and, 33–35; storytelling
and, 38–41. *See also* dike systems
Yihequan. *See* Boxer Uprising
yin (overflow of water), 74
yin-yang concept, 18–19, 30n5, 33, 137–38
Yongding River flood (1907), 84–86

Zeng Jize, 27n1
Zhang Binglin, 142n1
Zhang Jizhong, 115–16
Zhang Ruishan, 122n13
Zhang Yao, 8, 76n11, 80
Zhang Zhidong, 9n8, 19
Zhao Boju, 93–94
Zheng Guanying, 83n17
zhiyin, 119
Zhou dynasty (1152–1056 BCE), 16, 39, 73
Zhou Taigu, 114, 115
Zhu Naifang, 120n11
Zhu Xi, 59, 61, 106
Zhuangzi, 29, 37–38

www.ingramcontent.com/pod-product-compliance
Ingram Content Group UK Ltd.
Pitfield, Milton Keynes, MK11 3LW, UK
UKHW060204160426
5217IPUK00007BA/137